BETWEEN HOLLYWOOD AND MOSCOW

D1523716

AMERICAN ENCOUNTERS/GLOBAL INTERACTIONS

A series edited by Gilbert M. Joseph and Emily S. Rosenberg

BETWEEN

HOLLYWOOD

AND MOSCOW

THE ITALIAN COMMUNISTS

AND THE CHALLENGE OF MASS

CULTURE, 1943-1991

Stephen Gundle

Duke University Press   Durham and London   2000

Amazon   1019169

AMERICAN ENCOUNTERS/GLOBAL INTERACTIONS

A series edited by Gilbert M. Joseph and Emily S. Rosenberg

This series aims to stimulate critical perspectives and fresh interpretive frameworks for scholarship on the history of the imposing global presence of the United States. Its primary concerns include the deployment and contestation of power, the construction and deconstruction of cultural and political borders, the fluid meanings of intercultural encounters, and the complex interplay between the global and the local. American Encounters seeks to strengthen dialogue and collaboration between historians of U.S. international relations and area studies specialists.

The series encourages scholarship based on multiarchival historical research. At the same time, it supports a recognition of the representational character of all stories about the past and promotes critical inquiry into issues of subjectivity and narrative. In the process, American Encounters strives to understand the context in which meanings related to nations, cultures, and political economy are continually produced, challenged, and reshaped.

© 2000 Duke University Press

All rights reserved   Printed in the United States of America on acid-free paper ⊗   Designed by C. H. Westmoreland Typeset in Times Roman with Antique Olive display by Keystone Typesetting, Inc.

Library of Congress Cataloging-in-Publication Data appear on the last printed page of this book.

Originally published as *I comunisti italiani tra Hollywood e Mosca: la sfida della cultura di massa, 1943–1991* by Giunti Gruppo Editoriale 1995.

Frontis art: Communist beauty queen, Milan 1956. (From the archives of the Istituto milanese per la storia della Resistenza e del movimento operaio).

To the memory

of Pier Paolo D'Attorre

Contents

Acknowledgments

Many people have helped me during the preparation of this book. In particular, I owe a debt of gratitude to Paul Ginsborg, under whose guidance the project began. He has been both an example to me and an unfailing source of advice and constructive criticism over the years. I also wish to thank David Ellwood, Franco Minganti, Maurizio Vaudagna, Judith Adler Hellman, Stephen Hellman, David Forgacs, Graham McCann, Martin Conway, and Darrow Schecter, all of whom were good enough to comment in detail on earlier drafts of part or all of the manuscript. It is not possible to mention by name all those who were kind enough to share their opinions or experiences with me, but I should like to put on record my gratitude to the following: Luigi Arbizzani, Saveria Bologna, Ugo Casiraghi, Ennio Correnti, the late Pier Paolo D'Attorre, Piero De Sabatta, Fidia Gambetti, the late Michele Pellicani, Catia Mazzeri, Patrick McCarthy, Marisa Musu, Alfio Neri, Patrizia Tabossi, the late Antonello Trombadori, and Albertina Vittoria. Katia Pizzi was an invaluable source of help and encouragement while I was researching this book. I owe much of my knowledge of Italian popular culture to her. Thanks must also be expressed to the staff of the Gramsci Institutes of Bologna and Rome, where much of the documentary research was undertaken. My mother, Doreen Gundle, was generous with material support in the early stages of my research and, with my sister Alison, has been patient in waiting to see the results. The Social Science Research Council (now Economic and Social Research Council), the Fondazione Einaudi, and the British School at Rome provided financial assistance, as did Churchill College, Cambridge, which awarded me a junior research fellowship that was instrumental in granting me the opportunity to develop the work.

Introduction

One evening in September 1987 I visited the provincial *L'Unità* festival in Modena, a prosperous city in Emilia-Romagna, the region of Italy with the strongest left-wing traditions and the highest density of Communist Party membership in Western Europe. The annual fund-raising festival of the local federation of the Italian Communist Party (Partito Comunista Italiano — PCI) was in full swing. As usual, the event was organized on a grand scale. In a prefabricated open-air exhibition area on the edge of town numerous eating places, stalls, and displays had been set up, and there was a full program of debates and entertainments. Families, young people, couples, and the elderly mingled in large numbers among bars, commercial stands, booths of domestic and international pressure groups, bookshops, and raffle and game stalls. The laughter and chatter, and the relaxed good humor of those dining on the rich Emilian cuisine or in the Hungarian and Russian restaurants, indicated that the festival was an occasion of some importance in community life. The only reminders of its political character were the numerous red flags fluttering in the breeze and repeated loudspeaker announcements of the day's program of attractions.

By any standard the festival was impressive. Few if any other political forces in the world could have recruited sufficient volunteer labor or have performed the organizational feat of staging an event on this scale in a provincial city. Yet as I wandered amid the crowds several things caught my attention. First, I came across a small conference area annexed to the *Rinascita* bookshop, where approximately fifteen people, mostly in their late twenties or thirties, had gathered. They were awaiting the beginning of a roundtable discussion on the curious theme of "Neo-individualism, culture of the body, and social climbing." However, half an hour after the advertised starting time, none of the speakers had arrived. As an official paced about morosely, the audience began to drift away.

Outside, in a large green area bordered by cake stalls, ice-cream parlors, and a fun fair, a senior member of the national PCI directorate was about to address a rally of several hundred people, the majority of whom seemed to be aged fifty or over. Beginning punctually, the speaker offered his audience a familiar, if stylishly delivered, denunciation of the government and its policies. During his speech he went out of his way to reject a prevailing conception of modernity that equated progress with constant expansion in the consumption of material goods. "Italy may be a bit richer, and there may be a few more consumer goods around, but this does not mean that the nation has progressed or become more civilized," he declared. In the next breath, and apparently unaware of the contradiction, he went on to defend the PCI against those who claimed it was not modern by referring to the enormous material progress that had been achieved under forty years of Communist local government in Modena. After touching on various themes, the official observed that, despite the lamentable tendency of young people to entrust the government parties (in particular the Christian Democrats and the Socialists) with their votes, nothing was being done about youth unemployment. Instead, he thundered, referring to the recent tour and televised concert of a visiting American pop star, the authorities offered them Madonna. At this remark much of the silver-haired crowd burst into sustained and enthusiastic applause.

Leaving the rally, I ventured into the area behind the speaker's platform to encounter a set of huge painted boards marking the entrance to "Strelax," the cabaret-bar-café-discotheque of the Young Communist Federation. Here large numbers of teenagers dressed casually in jeans and T-shirts sat talking and drinking in the shadow of billboards featuring satirical portraits of Oliver North and Pope John Paul II. In one corner a tall black-and-yellow-striped tower announced: "bienvenu, benvenido, benvenuto, welcome, wilkommen." A large panel to one side read "Foundation of Friends of the State of Strelax." Beneath this heading was a semi-serious list of idols and hero figures including Vladimir Majakowski, the mutineers of the Bounty, Brigitte Bardot, Winnie and Nelson Mandela, Sandro Pertini, Sacco and Vanzetti, Che, Mary Poppins, Sitting Bull, the Three Stooges, the cartoon adventurer Corto

Maltese, Charlie Chaplin, Rosa Luxemburg, and the 1960s footballer Gigi Riva.

In the mid-1980s the PCI was still by any standard a large party. It had a membership of some 1.5 million, and, even after the serious setback suffered in the general election of June 1987, it held 26.6 percent of the popular vote. Every year it organized dozens of festivals similar to the one described above. They bore witness to the popular appeal and organizational capacity of the PCI, to the scale and diversity of its subculture, and to its ability to draw in people of all ages and act as a part of community life. Right up until its dissolution in February 1991, the PCI was an important force not only in terms of its electoral standing and its membership but also socially and culturally. Yet the above scenes also offer telltale signs of the crisis the party experienced in the final period of its existence as it made awkward attempts to come to terms with new themes alien to the Communist political culture, struggled to make sense of the waning appeal of an orthodox political language to younger people, and faced signs of generational segmentation within the party. For the first time evidence emerged of dysfunctions in a once impressively smooth-running organization. Moreover, the PCI was no longer sure of its capacity to project itself as modern; a certain defensiveness transpired that derived from the awareness that the party could no longer confidently sustain a cultural project geared to the whole of society. In its responses to crisis it displayed an eclecticism that suggested an uncertain identity.

In the four decades following the end of the Second World War a tremendous transformation took place in Italian society. In the 1940s Italy was a devastated country that had for nearly two years been a major theater of the war in Europe. It was also a country that had experienced most of the changes of the industrial era in a narrow and limited way. The only area that matched the social composition, level of urbanization, and standard of living of the more advanced countries of Northern Europe was the industrial triangle of the Northwest. In the 1940s some 42 percent of the active population worked on the land, between 15 and 20 percent was wholly illiterate, and for a good many more the Italian language was an unfamiliar tongue. Despite the expanding presence of the state, the existence of a national network of mass communications, and the attempts at social and cultural integration undertaken under Fascism, whole areas of the country and parts of even the most advanced regions lived in a manner that had remained basically unchanged for centuries. To exacerbate matters the country had little experience of genuine democratic government, and, with the exception of the Catholic Church and recently formed mass political parties, its institutions were weak.

Already by the end of the 1950s much had changed. Italy had not merely recovered from the disruption of the war but was undergoing a far-reaching process of development that would broaden its industrial base, witness a great expansion of the cities, see a shift of the population from the South to the North, and permit improved standards of living for virtually all sectors of the population in the medium term. Taken over the whole period from the postwar years to the 1980s, this transformation was a dramatic one of historic proportions. The country became a leading industrial power, and, indeed, by the late 1970s the expansion of the tertiary sector meant that it was taking on many of the features of a postindustrial society. Although economic development was uneven and in many respects chaotic, it heralded a huge improvement in educational and literacy levels and a significant process of cultural and linguistic integration. It would not be correct to say that the Italians of the 1980s had nothing in common with those of the 1940s, for, apart from any other consideration, certain old defects and disequilibria persisted, albeit in a modified form. Nevertheless, development turned Italy into a mass, predominantly urbanized, and secularized society in which democratic political procedures commanded virtually unanimous support.

Throughout this process of change, the PCI remained a powerful force and, in electoral terms, the second-largest political party. Whereas most communist parties in Western Europe declined dramatically in the late 1940s and social democratic parties lost support in the 1950s, the PCI not only conserved a substantial membership but actually saw its electoral standing rise slowly yet continuously up until 1977. This unusual fortune may be attributed to three things: objective factors arising from the nature of Italian industrialization, peculiar structural features of the country's political system, and the astuteness and intelligence of the party leadership.

The objective factors are numerous and can only be hinted at here. Above all, the shift from a long-standing system of rule that involved the repression of the lower classes in the cities and the mass of the population on the land to a system of consensual government based on liberal

Between Hollywood and Moscow

democracy and consumer capitalism was highly disruptive. Most importantly, urbanization and the development of a mass consumer culture uprooted tradition, stimulated aspirations, and undercut the influence of the Church. This did not favor the left at all levels or in the longer term, but it undermined traditional authority and contributed to the electoral growth of the PCI. So, too, did the contradictory character of Italian modernization, which held out a promise of prosperity and tolerance that prior to the late 1960s was denied by low wages, violations of trade union rights, and institutional practices that remained authoritarian.

The Communists benefited generally from these tensions because they were the only real force of opposition. The liberal center was much weaker than in other countries, and in any case the parties associated with it were subordinate allies of the dominant Christian Democratic Party (DC). For its part, the Socialist Party lost its electoral primacy on the left in 1948, and, following a long period of subalternity to the PCI, it was sucked into the DC system of power in the mid-1960s. Thus it lacked autonomy and was poorly placed to respond adequately to the pressures and demands arising in society. In this context the PCI became the home, or at least the reference point, not merely of those who sought to create a new economic and social order but of those who desired economic justice, political reform, and wider citizenship.

There were limits as to how far the PCI could effectively give voice to these aspirations. As a communist party with historical and political links to the Soviet Union, it was never considered a fully legitimate potential party of government. It possessed an ideology and an organizational structure that were geared to a total form of politics whose aim was to reorganize society completely, not merely improve it or correct its malfunctions. Yet the party managed to retain credibility, despite its long-term oppositional role, owing to the skill with which its leaders and representatives cultivated the PCI's role as a mass, national force. From the end of the war the party won a huge following among the workers and peasants of the North and Center, but it also sought to reach out to the petite bourgeoisie and to the middle classes. In contrast to a party like the French Communist Party (PCF), which was always reluctant to risk diluting its purity by mixing too freely in the waters of the mainstream of society, the Italian Communists sought, while remaining faithful to their basic purposes, to penetrate Italian society and become a force in every sphere of national life. In short, they tried to think out and put into practice a vision of the transition to socialism cast largely in national terms.

For the PCI cultural struggle always had a special significance. This sphere was not treated as a secondary, good only for reinforcing loyalties and forging useful alliances, although tactical considerations of this sort were always important. Culture was a sphere in which the party could assert a fuller influence than it could in the political arena, given the barrier against its participation in government. By winning support for their ideas among artists and writers, and intellectuals of all types, leading Communists thought they could determine the ideas and values that were dominant in the nation. In this way the party could shape events and policies from the vantage point of civil society. A product of Italian social and political theory, this conception of the active role of culture in the struggle for socialism was not adopted by any other political party in Europe. However, although the attention the PCI accorded to ideological and cultural struggle lent it a special fascination for outsiders, it is as well to be aware of the ambiguous status of these activities for the left. Perry Anderson, Martin Jay, and others have shown that cultural struggle first took shape in the West in response to the defeats and setbacks of the 1920s and 1930s.[1] It was not a sphere in which progress could be achieved but rather a place of refuge to which intellectuals fled when political advance seemed impossible. Cultural policy was not an expression of a fuller, more radical variety of politics but rather a symptom of the extreme difficulties revolutionaries faced and, to some extent, of their impotence. Although the PCI's greatest theorist, Antonio Gramsci, anchored cultural struggle to a political project by conceptualizing its role in preparing and improving the conditions for political advance and conquest of the state, it would be disingenuous to imagine that the PCI was exempt from problems of this nature. Nevertheless, because it was unique in its ambition and range of application, the PCI's attempt to harness the energies of intellectuals, and use them to construct a counterhegemony to that of the political, economic, and religious forces that dominated postwar society, deserves investigation.

To compensate for its loss of power in 1947–48, the party also gave rise to a subculture. Alongside workplace cells, it founded territorial sections that offered opportunities for recreation and socialization in addition to political activity. Affiliated organizations were also created for women, young people, peasants, former partisans, and so on; all of

Between Hollywood and Moscow

these had their own symbols, publications, and calendar of events that added new layers to Communist identity and rounded out the concept of party membership. In working-class areas of some northern cities and in the central regions where the party was strongest, the subculture formed a significant pole of community life.

Left-wing subcultures had existed previously in a variety of contexts. Socialist parties in Germany and Austria had consciously sought to organize the social and cultural life of workers in the last two decades of the nineteenth century, and, in the prefascist period in Italy, the Socialist Party had also given rise to a plethora of recreational associations. However, the PCI's subculture was different because it was created considerably later than others, well after the heyday of subcultures of this type, which may be located between the beginning of the century and 1914. After the Second World War neither the German nor the Austrian socialist parties even attempted to reestablish cultural networks, and the other subcultures that did exist, such as that of the Dutch and Belgian socialist parties or the PCF, tended to be belated protractions of more robust prewar experiences. For this reason the Italian Communists can be considered to have created the last great left-wing subculture in Western Europe.

Because they were created relatively late, the institutions of this subculture had to cope from the beginning with the sorts of challenges that undermined and fragmented other subcultures, such as those posed by mass communications, commercial cultural industries, and state- and company-organized leisure activities. In several ways, they responded creatively and flexibly to these challenges, with the result that some features of the PCI's subculture — its festivals and certain recreational activities and publications, for example — proved remarkably long lasting. But continual difficulties arose that derived from the impact of consumerism, the trend toward the privatization of leisure, and the relative normalization of political life. Whatever leading Communists might have assumed or expected, no one in the postwar period could live in a world entirely or even largely shaped by left-wing rituals and institutions. Moreover, the PCI's tenacious attachment to a certain type of intellectual politics, although it brought the party kudos, locked it into an outdated view of the way social and political consensus was constructed and maintained.

Before the late 1980s, the greatest challenges the PCI faced were in the economic boom of the late 1950s and 1960s. During this period virtually all of Western Europe's great social democratic parties experienced decline and responded by undertaking the programmatic and organizational deradicalization symbolized by the 1959 Bad Godesburg conference of the German Social Democratic Party (SPD). Although workers extended their social rights and many parties entered government in the 1960s, the cultural achievements of the labor movement, including newspapers and publishing enterprises, educational circuits, and sports clubs, lost autonomy and ceased to be a factor in the collective composition of the class. In *Late Capitalism* Ernest Mandel acknowledged that "the reabsorption of cultural needs achieved by the proletariat into the capitalist process of commodity production and circulation leads to a far-reaching reprivatization of the recreational sphere of the working class." This, he said, represented "a sharp break with the tendency of [earlier] epochs . . . towards a constant extension of the spheres of collective action and solidarity of the proletariat."[2]

For many socialists who identified the progress of their movement with the consolidation and extension of the forms of class organization typical of the golden age of classical social democracy before 1914, this development was equivalent to a tragedy. As right-wing social democrats reacted by discarding many conventional presumptions and reference points, seeking instead to further the interests of the working class purely through public policy, left-wing socialists and communists conducted a desperate rearguard battle to shore up fading institutions and rituals. Even in Britain, where no articulated socialist culture had ever existed, intellectuals like Richard Hoggart expressed dismay at the new "candy floss world" and the corrupting effects it was having on a once proud and independent class.[3]

As economic development and consumerism undercut conventional hierarchies and values, social democratic parties gradually turned into what Otto Kirchheimer in 1966 called "catch-all" peoples' parties.[4] In part of their own volition, in part against their will, they accepted more of the principles of Western capitalism. Unable or unwilling to adapt, communist parties declined further almost everywhere.

At this time the PCI found that its own vision of modernity was undermined by a real process of modernization that brought prosperity and undermined the collective dimension of life. Its organization and subculture were also significantly weakened. But there was no wholesale liquidation of a collective grassroots culture that conserved considerable vitality. In part because of the Gramscian heritage, the PCI was able to adapt and survive. It did not cease to be a cultural force, despite the competition of the mass media and commercial culture. Rather, it found ways to respond and recast its cultural activities in order to conserve their influence and purpose.

This capacity for adaptation and survival makes the PCI's subculture a particularly interesting case. Most previous studies of the cultural activities of left-wing parties, such as Guenther Roth and Roberta Ascarelli's analyses of the SPD and Kurt Shell and Helmut Gruber's studies of Austrian socialism,[5] have concentrated on either the period before the 1930s or particular cities, or both.[6] Here the case will be investigated of a party that, in a context of full parliamentary democracy, was forced to contend not only with the cinema and the commercial press but also with television, pop music, youth counterculture, and the star system as well as mass mobility and unprecedented prosperity. Moreover, these were not separate challenges; they were elements and consequences of the adoption of an American-inspired strategy for economic growth and social integration.

The PCI did not find it easy to keep alive its struggle for hegemony in the face of these challenges. The party often failed to understand change and was disoriented by it. Moreover, it never really grasped the appeal of either mass culture or the consumer society. In the chapters that follow particular attention will be paid to the difficulties the party faced, to its problems and inadequacies. Its saving grace was not that it possessed some secret recipe for success, even though the party was widely seen abroad in the 1970s as a paradigm for socialists who believed that the social and cultural consequences of economic growth represented a challenge and not a motive for surrender. Rather, although certain biases, such as those against commercial entertainment and individualism, were rooted in Marxist-Leninism, the PCI demonstrated a great deal of flexibility in practical matters. A gradual attenuation of hostile judgments allowed for a reasonably swift move to more considered assessments of novelties. This meant that the party could maintain its struggle for hegemony and, in a context such as that of the 1970s, which was marked by economic crisis in the West and the defeat of the United States in Vietnam, advance and extend it with considerable success. However, the growing gap between the model of social and cultural relations promoted by the party and the reality of everyday life could not forever be masked.

The aspiration to establish the cultural hegemony of the working class diminished in plausibility and eventually dissolved. By the mid-1980s it was clear that the American model of modernization had won out. The festivals, the press, and other features of the culture of the left did not disappear, but they were no longer bearers of alternative values; rather, they were consumed in much the same way as their commercial equivalents.

This book is concerned with the PCI over the whole of its postwar existence, from 1943 until the final division and dissolution of the party in 1991. It differs from all other studies of the party in two ways. First, it is primarily concerned with the cultural dimension of the PCI's strategy and activities at both the elite level and the popular level. Conventionally separated from its political dimension or ignored altogether, the PCI's cultural policies and cultural activities are here treated as full and integral parts of its being as a political force. Second, the focus is outward, not inward, looking: the overall purpose is to examine the transformations in Italian economic, cultural, and social life from the point of view of the PCI. The treatment is diachronic because in this way cultural activity can most effectively be examined in relation to political conflict. The PCI was not, in its self-perception, a ghetto party, and its institutions were not static; rather, they evolved and changed in response to the challenges of each phase of the postwar era.

The English edition of this book differs in several ways from the Italian edition, which was published in 1995 by Giunti under the title *I comunisti italiani tra Hollywood e Mosca: la sfida della cultura di massa, 1943–91*. This earlier version was substantially longer and contained extended treatments of Italian politics, popular culture, sexual mores, and consumption. For reasons of brevity and owing to the appearance of several volumes in English that provide detailed analyses of Communist politics and postwar Italian politics and society in general,[7] it has been decided to concentrate here on the cultural activities and policies of the PCI.

1

The Pen and the Sword

Politics, Culture, and Society after the Fall of Fascism

Far more than at any time in the years that followed, the framework of Italian political life was subject to change and redefinition between 1943 and 1947. The years of the struggle for Liberation and postwar reconstruction saw the interplay of many possible visions of national development, by no means all of which were compatible with the restoration of a moderate set of arrangements in the country. One of the most powerful visions was articulated by the Communist Party, which during this period of transition came to occupy a position of unprecedented prominence. The earliest organizer of an armed resistance, the PCI was also the first party to signal its willingness to participate in a government of national unity in 1944 and the force that most easily won a mass following among the workers and some sections of the peasants. That it was able to insert itself so decisively into the life of the country after an absence of almost twenty years bore witness to how the party successfully interpreted widespread hopes and aspirations. Naturally, it was most closely associated with class conflict and uncompromising confrontation with employers and with the Fascists and their supporters. But it was also practical in the way it took up and aimed to resolve problems. It tried to be flexible, adapting its politics and organizational forms to social groups not usually incorporated into left-wing activities. Most importantly, the party leader, Palmiro Togliatti, struggled to impose a new, more national image on the party. The aim, he repeatedly declared, was not to make the revolution or create a Soviet-style regime, but to build a new society in which the bases of a pluralist and representative order would be so firmly established as to rule out any future resurgence of Fascism.

In tandem with this view went an unprecedented emphasis on intellectuals and culture. To an extent not previously witnessed, Togliatti's PCI valorized the role of the intellectual in legitimating social and economic relations. Because the collapse of Fascism was held to have signaled the demise of monopoly capitalism and the historic defeat of the old ruling class, little attention was paid to specific government policies. Instead, every effort was devoted to the struggle to weld together a new, progressive ruling bloc and consolidate its hegemony in society. This involved an unusual involvement with culture.

Before I look at this area in detail, it may first be useful to consider why it was that the PCI, and Togliatti in particular, attached so much importance to action in an area that, by any usual standard, was rather remote from the pressing tasks at hand. Although the cultural policy of the party in the immediate postwar years, and in particular its relationship with the intellectuals, has been the subject of much debate in Italy, it is rarely appreciated that a well-directed strategy aimed at achieving a hegemonic position within national thought and culture was virtually without precedent in the history of the European working-class movement.[1] To be sure, the party's intervention resembled the stance adopted by the French Communists during the Popular Front, with Togliatti on occasion employing the same language as Maurice Thorez did eight years previously, but in its aims and articulation the policy of the PCI was infinitely more ambitious.[2]

The PCI leader, like much of the Italian intelligentsia, viewed the realm of culture as a vital sphere in the construction and maintenance of a social order. Intellectuals were, as Togliatti would repeat on more than one occasion, the "connecting tissue" of the nation. Thus on the eve of the collapse of Fascism and in the period of transition that followed, their attitude became central. From July 1943 Togliatti appealed to them directly in radio broadcasts from Moscow. If they placed themselves at the service of the fatherland and spread word of the coming liberation in schools, offices, factories, the army, the universities, and families, he declared, they would win recognition before the nation and perform their natural leadership function.[3] The vital importance of their role was again stressed in April 1945 when Togliatti drew attention to the considerations on this theme contained in Gramsci's prison notes. "The intellectuals," he explained, "can orient the development of this state in one way or in another depending on whether they serve the reactionary, egotistical, nationalistic, and imperialistic castes, which can do nothing but carry

Between Hollywood and Moscow

Italy along the road to ruin, or whether rather, by modifying their orientation, they offer support to a solid alliance with the working class, with the working masses of the cities and the countryside and collaborate with these in the construction of a new society."[4]

During this chapter I suggest that, although the emphasis on cultural and ideological struggle perfectly suited some of the objectives of the PCI leadership, it did not adequately express the demands for structural renewal that were widespread in the country. The problem was not simply that the collaboration of the working class in the reconstruction was by no means as indispensable as was widely thought, but that the means by which the party proposed to forge its hegemony were at least partially outdated. The role of the traditional intellectual in legitimating social arrangements had not been superseded in Italy, but it had already begun to be undermined by the extended functions taken on by the state in the interwar years and the emergence of strategies of integration typical of mass society that would rapidly become the norm in successive years. The PCI's failure to take account of these developments weakened its action in crucial ways.

Togliatti and the Strategy of the PCI

When Palmiro Togliatti set foot on Italian soil for the first time in eighteen years on 27 March 1944, the positions of the main contenders for power in the peninsula were already well defined. Following the Allied landing in Sicily in July 1943 and the tumultuous workers' protests in the North the previous spring, Mussolini had been deposed, and his position as prime minister had been taken by the military veteran Marshal Badoglio, whose task it was to confine pressures for change within the contours of a flexible, but nevertheless relatively strict, continuity. Badoglio abolished the Fascist Party and began secret negotiations with the Allies, which eventually resulted in the proclamation of the armistice on 8 September 1943. In response to the betrayal of their former ally, the Germans occupied the North and Center of the country, recuperating Mussolini in the process and installing him at the head of a puppet administration, the Italian Social Republic, based in Salò. Italy thus found itself divided in two. In the liberated zones of the South, Badoglio and the king, having fled the capital on the eve of the armistice, basked in the protection of the

Allies and offered at least the semblance of continuity in constitutional authority while the democratic parties began to regroup and prepare for a process of political transition. In the North, the German occupiers and their Fascist collaborators imposed a vicious regime of control, challenged by a nascent Resistance movement that expanded rapidly in 1944 and would ultimately help liberate the towns and cities of the Po valley in spring 1945.

Togliatti had been delayed somewhat in his efforts to return to Italy, and by the time he reached Naples the PCI had already begun to re-form. Nevertheless, following a meeting of the party's national council on 30–31 March, he was able to overturn the line of conduct followed by the Communists up to that point and recast the party's approach to the whole question of Italian political development after Fascism. In a shift of policy that would become known as the *svolta di Salerno,* Togliatti stressed the need for absolute priority to be accorded to a united war effort against the Germans and the Fascists. The resolution of all other matters, including the question of the monarchy, could be postponed until the end of the war.

The sensitivity to intermediate goals and alliances was a constant feature of Togliatti's politics. In response to the consolidation of Nazi power in Germany he had elaborated the moderate platform adopted in striking contrast with the previous uncompromising line at the seventh Comintern congress in 1935 and that found a natural extension in the subsequent formation of the European Popular Fronts.[5] Even before this, in the second half of the 1920s, he had embraced the view that the middle classes needed to be won to democracy before there could be any hope of advancing to socialism. The tragic experience of Fascism taught him before many of his colleagues in the international Communist movement that a democratic bourgeois state was infinitely preferable to an authoritarian one and that disunity on the left could only lead to defeat.

The *svolta* and the related insistence on the avoidance of revolutionary confrontation were justified by reference to Antonio Gramsci, a former leader of the party whose death shortly after his release from prison on health grounds had provoked an international outcry in 1937. In 1943–44 few people in Italy had any recollection of who Gramsci was. Many of the several thousand mostly young militants who belonged to the PCI's clandestine network were unfamiliar with his name, and no one beyond Togliatti's immediate circle knew of the existence of the notebooks Gramsci had written between the late 1920s and the early 1930s. There thus existed an enormous margin of discretion as to how Gramsci and his ideas were presented.[6] That the party leader should have chosen to address the question in a way that conformed to his own political outlook is not surprising. But the very careful manner in which a highly partial and in some respects distorted image of the figure of Gramsci was employed should nonetheless be mentioned. The motivation for this was as much internal as external, since at no point did Togliatti totally dominate the PCI in the way, for example, that Thorez controlled the PCF. In marked contrast with most other European Communist parties, the PCI had escaped full Stalinization in the 1930s, and the party chief was obliged to mediate between the various components of a strikingly heterogeneous leadership in order to win support for his line.[7] This meant that a sound and absolutely unimpeachable justification was required for the new policies that were advanced from March 1944.

This was all the more important because the party itself constituted the first terrain of change. From almost the very start, the need to refound the PCI as a "new party" on different bases from those on which it had originally been founded in 1921 was stressed.[8] In Togliatti's design, experienced cadres schooled in a harder, less compromising variety of Communism than that on offer in the mid-1940s still had a role to play, but it was not to such men that he looked to turn the idea of the new party into a living reality. Shortly after he resumed full powers of leadership, Giorgio Amendola, Mauro Scoccimarro, Celeste Negarville, Girolamo Li Causi, and others who had determined policy in his absence were dispatched to the regions in order to supervise activities on the ground in the closing months of the war.[9] In their place Togliatti installed a number of handpicked young men of an educated middle-class background in strategic positions in the PCI apparatus. The Neapolitans Italo De Feo and Massimo Caprara were brought into his private office, the latter becoming his personal secretary. Following the liberation of Rome in June 1944, Pietro Ingrao, Mario Alicata, Paolo Bufalini, Fabrizio Onofri, Antonello Trombadori, and Carlo Salinari, to name but the most prominent, were appointed to departments of the party organization, the staff of the Communist press, the leadership of the Roman federation of the PCI, and the central committee.[10] Although some had already participated in acts of armed resistance, the most important quality they possessed was that they were unaffected by the previous history of Italian Communism and uncontaminated by contact with the more Bolshevik sections of the party.

The role of these young men, all of whom had come into contact with communism in the late 1930s or during the war years, has to be seen in relation to the overriding need to redesign the party profile at the very highest level and thus make it much more difficult for those who opposed the moderate political line to suggest radical alternatives. As almost the only member of the PCI old guard to feel completely at ease with ideological and cultural issues, Togliatti had little difficulty in establishing his preeminence in this field. Combined with his privileged access to Gramsci's legacy of ideas, this expertise ensured that the cultural policy of the PCI in the postwar years was, much more even than its politics, Togliatti's personal fief. It was the field in which his domination was least vulnerable, the control center from which he sought to orient the party as a whole.[11]

At first Gramsci was presented simply as a martyr in order to highlight the price the party had paid in its long opposition to Fascism. "The best of all of us, Antonio Gramsci, died in prison, tortured and driven to an untimely end by Fascist beasts on the express orders of Mussolini," Togliatti declared in his first public speech following his return.[12] In the months that followed, however, a more precise image was furnished. In a speech delivered in Naples toward the end of April 1945 that was of fundamental importance in framing the image of the postwar PCI, Togliatti referred to Gramsci as the founder and head of the party.[13] In this way he provided a version of its history that canceled the decisive role of Amedeo Bordiga, the sympathizer of Trotsky who materially founded the party in 1921 and led it until he was removed at the behest of the International in 1924. To stress further the connection between his own leadership and the man who in practice led the PCI for just two brief years between 1924 and 1926, Togliatti also implied that Gramsci had continued to inspire the party even after his imprisonment. "In the face of grave difficulties," he said, party cadres struggled to keep in touch with their spiritual leader in the 1930s, receiving from him "words that were a cry, that illuminated our path before us." In general terms this was hardly true, but Togliatti also made a specific claim that was of particular importance as far as his own policies were concerned. Just a few days before his death, Togliatti said, Gramsci "communicated to us . . . that the struggle of the working classes and of our vanguard party should, in the

Between Hollywood and Moscow

period of Fascism's final demise and even after, be a national struggle if we wanted the working classes and the people to fulfill the function demanded of them in the history of our country and of humanity."[14] Whatever the importance attached to the national point of departure in the prison notebooks, and it was by any measure considerable, the particular suggestion that advice was issued to the PCI in March or April 1937 concerning its future conduct was entirely false. As Giuseppe Fiori's biography of Gramsci revealed over two decades later, there was no attempt to contact the party in the last few days of his life or any attempt by the party to make contact with him.[15]

This is not to say that the connection between Gramsci and Togliatti was not a strong one or that the latter was not influenced by the prison notebooks. The point, rather, is that a manipulation of the party's past took place in order to underwrite a new line that was potentially far from popular with party militants. Although Togliatti possessed sufficient authority to convince members of the PCI's national council of the need to pledge support for the Badoglio government, resistances to the policy persisted at all levels.[16] This made it difficult for him to carry through effectively the reform of the party itself that was the direct corollary of the assumption of national responsibilities. Every argument that could be deployed in its support was therefore grasped, and, where these were lacking, reasons were improvised or invented.[17]

Because of their intellectual qualifications and experience of cultural opposition to Fascism, Alicata, Salinari, and the others were well able to assist Togliatti both in the task of diffusing a new culture in the party and in that of rendering it more recognizably national in its broader identity. But although action on the cultural plane was certainly necessary to the legitimation of the party itself, there must be some doubt as to whether the mode in which the PCI leader sought to apply his strategy to culture actually served the task of welding together a new bloc of progressive forces in the country.

The Premises of Hegemony

From the start, Togliatti was committed to change within the existing framework of institutional power. This was not only a strategic option but the reflection of an intimate conviction concerning the nature of politics that never seems to have been shaken despite the opposition it aroused within his party. In place of the strategy of direct democracy, which was most forcefully theorized by Eugenio Curiel, leader of the Resistance's Youth Front,[18] Togliatti argued for a close alliance with the Christian Democrats, a newly formed party of Catholics that aspired to take over the old rural base of Don Sturzo's Popular Party. In the period leading up to and well beyond the Liberation, this was the linchpin of his policy. Yet Togliatti's aim of winning a central place for his party in a new Italy never depended just on the achievement of a political alliance. Considerable attention was also paid to the opportunity that the collapse of Fascism furnished for the construction of a new pattern of hegemony in society. Very shortly after his return to Italy, Togliatti made preparations for the publication of a monthly magazine, *La Rinascita,* that from its first issue in June 1944 would be the special standard-bearer of his whole politico-cultural project. The "rebirth" of the title referred to the need to reintroduce Marxism into Italy. If the working-class movement was to succeed in promoting the social and political regeneration of the country, the PCI leader argued in an opening programmatic statement, it had to raise its sights above the practical political realm and "make an effort to embrace fields of inquiry, polemics, and work where our influence was not felt in the past." Such a task, Togliatti wrote, obliged the party "to gather together to help us in this new activity, different forces, not regularly enrolled in our movement, but convinced like us of the need to break with a past first of decline then of collapse and beat the path to a radical renewal of both our political life and our culture."[19]

Given these premises, it was inevitable that Togliatti should choose to open the battle on the cultural front by attacking Benedetto Croce, the neo-Hegelian philosopher and historian who had dominated Italian culture in the first two decades of the century and whose influence was still very considerable at the end of the war. It was Croce, more than any other single individual, who had justified and propagated an idea of the intellectuals as disinterested servants of the spirit detached from politics. Although no supporter of Mussolini, he had remained in Italy, maintaining a position of critical independence that made him a reference point for many young intellectuals who found in his doctrine of the autonomy of culture a sort of protection from the totalizing pretensions of the regime. In the new context it was necessary to demolish such notions and harness the energies required to create the cultural conditions for the formation of a new progressive bloc of forces in society. Marxism, which Croce, with typical conceit, had proclaimed dead in 1908, the year of his own critical detachment from it, was to be the instrument of this battle. Marxists did not erect artificial or hypocritical barriers between the various fields of activity of a nation, Togliatti claimed. The strength of their doctrine lay precisely in its "unitary and realistic conception of the world."[20]

The attack on Croce centered on a very specific issue. In a short review of Croce's *For the History of Communism as a Political Reality,* a small volume published in 1943, Togliatti suggested that it was no accident that Mussolini had tolerated the philosopher, for far from opposing Fascism, Croce had served its purposes by acting as "champion of the struggle against Marxism." "He held the Chair in this discipline," the PCI leader went on, "instituting between himself and Fascism an open collaboration that was the price of the faculty granted to him to venture a timid little gibe against the regime from time to time."[21] This was a disgracefully cowardly role to perform at a time when Marxists were unable to defend themselves or answer back. It was, Togliatti concluded, "a stain of a moral order that we cannot forgive him and which he will not succeed in canceling."

These barbed comments produced a swift reaction from Croce, who was so outraged that he even raised the matter in the Council of Ministers, to which he, as a Liberal representative, belonged, as did the PCI leader. Togliatti's subsequent apology and withdrawal, although they did not signal the end of a process of belittlement that would continue in successive months and years, indicated that the PCI had no intention of engaging in an all-out assault on Crocean Idealism. Indeed, it would soon become apparent that the Communists' determined attempt to dent Croce's reputation as a siren of freedom was linked to an aspiration to inherit his cultural mantle rather than demolish it. The reintroduction of Marxism into the national culture was not presented as a divisive or disruptive process involving a long-awaited settling of accounts, but a necessary and almost natural development that would be of general benefit.

The figure of Gramsci served a dual symbolic purpose here by giving the party an organic cultural reference point and by deflecting attention away from Marxist-Leninism and the cultural models of the Soviet Union under Stalin. In 1944–45 there was little or no trace in Italy of either the substance or the style of the philosophy of the arts formally adopted following the Soviet Writers' Congress of 1934, at which Gorky and Zhdanov had unveiled the aesthetic doctrine of socialist realism and defined the role of the artist as one of service to the people, to the party, and to the cause of socialism. Following Togliatti's return and proclamation of the need to make the PCI a mass party, anyone who shared its general aims, regardless of their own philosophical or religious convictions, was invited to join. Naturally, this greatly enhanced the party's appeal to those young intellectuals whose assistance was required if the working class was to succeed in forging a new framework of cultural hegemony in the nation. Such persons were not expected immediately to exchange their beliefs for a Marxist philosophy that had yet to be integrated into Italian thought and letters, but rather were encouraged to rethink the cultural traditions of the nation from the perspective of the working-class movement and reorient their work accordingly. No traumatic crises of conscience were therefore necessary for the intellectual Communist, whose role was essentially unredefined by his new political allegiance and whose ideas were subject to evolution as opposed to transformation as a result of enrollment in the party. The PCI was supremely successful in winning a wide range of intellectuals to its side. Their consciences shaken by the experience of war and foreign occupation, and their faith in the ruling elite shattered, many educated people turned to the party. Most of them were young, but many renowned men of culture, including the philosophers Galvano Della Volpe, Antonio Banfi, and Cesare Luporini; the critic Natalino Sapegno; the historian Delio Cantimori and the archaeologist Ranuccio Bianchi Bandinelli; not to mention the painters Renato Guttuso and Mario Mafai and poets of the caliber of Umberto Saba and Salvatore Quasimodo, aligned themselves with the party. So, too, did some intellectuals like Massimo Bontempelli and Curzio Malaparte who had once been notorious Fascists. Many had their own personal reasons for so doing. The PCI's invitation to collaborate enabled members of the cultural elite to purify themselves, put the black period of the regime behind them and find a new justification for their existence in relation to a social project. But the terms in which Togliatti cast the tasks of cultural renewal were also appealing. In the South, and among the intellectuals of Rome and Naples above all, where the influence of Croceanism was strongest and the intellectual continued to be unambiguously identified with the figure of the humanist and man of letters, the emphasis placed on the national past and its reinterpretation was most effective. Some aspects of this approach had even been prefigured in the early 1940s by the Roman magazine *La ruota,* to which many future Communists contributed.[22] To the connection established there with the nineteenth-century politician and literary critic Francesco De Sanctis, who was held up as an example of an intellectual who had contributed to the development of a more democratic and politically aware tradition of cultural activity in Italy, Togliatti had merely to add the names of Antonio Labriola, the first Italian Marxist, and Gramsci to establish a bridge with the contemporary struggles of his party.

By any standard, the intellectuals who gravitated toward the PCI did indeed perform several important functions. Their presence identified the party with high culture, won it prestige, gave it a high profile, and assisted the conquest of a substantial measure of influence among intellectuals and in the arts. The front of ideas was important because it enabled the PCI to tie its political project to the experiences and culture of the Italian people. This in turn enabled it to seek the respect of sectors of the population normally diffident toward socialism and communism. By proving themselves to be cultivated and respectful of national traditions, Communist leaders aimed to confound the bourgeois impression that their party comprised uncultivated barbarians and hotheads. Togliatti himself particularly reveled in this role. With his calm, cultured oratory, he caught many by surprise. Many knew he had been Stalin's collaborator and a senior official of the Comintern. By revealing that he was also a man of considerable erudition, with a profound knowledge of the Italian classics, he brought to light a side of his character that was the least expected and one that in some small way enhanced his party's claim to be a national rather than a foreign-inspired force.[23] Yet it may be questioned whether Togliatti's mode of posing the issue of working-class hegemony was a valid one in the context of Italian society as it emerged from the war. "If hegemony is ethico-political," Gramsci had written, "it must be economic; it must necessarily be based on the decisive function exercised by the leading group in the decisive nucleus of economic activity."[24] Togliatti's party seemed to overlook this. Because it believed that capitalism was moribund and that the pattern of social relations associated with it was destined to inevitable decline, it engaged in a struggle for hegemony that bypassed crucial structural issues of reconstruction even as workers mobilized to seize control of factories and businesses of all types.

The Pen and the Sword   **21**

In at least one other way, the PCI's cultural action seemed to owe more to a conventional sense of the intellectual and culture than to a Gramscian one. In the prison notebooks Gramsci extended the concept of the intellectual in important ways, analyzing the broad position of the educated in society and their increasing subordination to patterns of organization and objective processes in modern capitalism. The sort of intellectual courted by Togliatti was, by contrast, of a narrowly traditional type: the "man of letters," the artist, the philosopher, the writer; in other words, not at all the sort of figure whose role was emerging as central in the organization of consensus in capitalist society (the technical expert, the scientist, the industrial manager) but rather a category whose status and social function had been defined in an earlier phase of social development and whose values were frequently extraneous to modern experiences. By translating the question of the politics of culture into a battle to influence the rarified and somewhat closed environment of university professors, literary magazines, scholarly debates, and institutionalized artistic activity, albeit shaken up by the changed order in society, Togliatti betrayed an archaic conception of culture separate from the real socioeconomic context and therefore extraneous to the life of the mass of the people, their customs and preferences.

The enormous significance that was attributed to activities in the cultural field offers proof that the PCI leader's vision of hegemony rested on an idea of the state similar to that held by the theorists of Liberal Italy: weak, noninterventionist, and in any event much less important in forging the texture of social order than the ideas and values circulating in civil society. In the first quarter of the century this had been a true picture, and it was to a certain extent understandable that it should also have seemed valid in 1944–45, when the country was in disorder, few institutions of the state functioned normally, and people were thrown on to their own resources. But it was by no means a complete picture.

Fascism had undoubtedly been a parasitic and deeply regressive phenomenon, a block in many ways to national development, but it was wrong to imagine, as the left sometimes did, that everything had stood still for twenty years. The regime saw a phase of capitalist reorganization in Italy that lay the basis for the assumption of new interventionist functions in the economy and in society on the part of the state. Its formal framework may have changed little under Mussolini, but new institutions were created that controlled a state voluntary sector, administered

Between Hollywood and Moscow

welfare, organized recreation, and produced and diffused news and entertainment by electronic means. In consequence, the balance of hegemony shifted toward the state and away from conventional methods of consensus formation. For this reason, by addressing itself to traditional intellectuals, the PCI may be said to have underlined the function of a figure that was becoming less relevant in social terms. Indeed, by offering such persons a platform and prestige, the party accorded them a position more prestigious even than bourgeois society itself. To be sure, the preindustrial nature of large sectors of Italian society and particularly the cultural sphere facilitated this, but it did not represent an adequate reflection of the needs of the moment. Moreover, although intellectuals were attracted by the gestures of the PCI, which induced in them a new sense of pride and self-esteem after a period in which they had been relatively marginalized, in the long run their link with the party would prove to be tortuous, often extremely difficult, and ultimately unsatisfactory for many of those concerned.

Resistance, Liberation, and the Battle for a "New Culture"

In the recent history of Italy, the Resistance occupies a special, if not undisputed, place. Accorded a position of unrivaled importance in the left's version of the foundation of the Republic, its military role has often been exaggerated.[25] Yet there can be little doubt that its contribution to the redefinition of the idea of the nation as something popular and democratic was considerable. Under the direction of the Communist-led Garibaldi brigades, which alone accounted for almost half the total number of partisans active in the field, ordinary people — workers, peasants, students, and shopkeepers — were drawn en masse into events whose outcome was crucial to the destiny of the nation.

It was against this background that a massive increase in PCI membership occurred. In mid-1943 the PCI had a membership of approximately 5,000. During 1944 it expanded to 502,000. By the fifth congress of the party in December 1945 this figure reached 1,771,000.[26] The party was made up mainly of lower-class people; in 1946, 53 percent of its members were industrial workers and a further 23 percent were agricultural laborers or sharecroppers.[27] Mostly the PCI was concentrated in those areas of the country where the hardest struggle had been fought against the Germans. Emilia-Romagna and Tuscany contributed over one-third of the total membership, for example, whereas the organization remained weak in the South and many other central regions. The important influence of prefascist traditions of collective solidarity in certain areas should not be underestimated as a factor in explaining the boom in Communist membership, but neither should the specific role of the Resistance be overlooked. The PCI emerged as the force people identified as most clearly representing their interests in areas in which the partisan brigades, led by Communists, had succeeded in tying the armed struggle to the conditions of life of the population.[28]

The resonance of the great hopes and aspirations of the Liberation was strongly felt on the cultural plane. Among intellectuals, writers, and educated persons in general the prospect of a complete regeneration in national life was highly attractive. The proclamations and debates published at the end of the war in the left-wing and radically oriented magazines, including *Il Ponte, Società,* and *Il Politecnico,* indicated that reconstruction was seen as a global project investing the whole organization of social life. It represented a qualitative shift with respect to the past, a new beginning, which was characterized on the political plane by the leadership of "the most advanced and popular forces." Yet reconstruction was also unitary and consensual, and no more so than in the values of humanity, solidarity, and progress that it was seen to express.

These hopes fueled the passions of a generation of intellectuals. But in the North of Italy intellectuals were inspired by more specifically left-wing ideas than was often the case in Rome and the South. It was the expectation of change and not any vaguely defined appeal to national traditions that stood at the basis of the PCI's appeal. In the pages of *Il Politecnico,* the weekly publication that presented itself as the expression of the Cultural Fronts, the concern with the social dimension of intellectual and artistic activity was paramount. Indeed, in the view of the writer Elio Vittorini, who edited the magazine from its inception, those currents that had been contaminated by contact with Fascism could no longer be considered culture at all. Less influenced than their southern counterparts by Idealism, which they in any case identified more with the Fascist Giovanni Gentile than Croce, northern intellectuals were tendentially more European and cosmopolitan in outlook. Far from being a figure of importance the PCI had to measure up to, Croce, for Vittorini, was "an example not only of cultural tradition that translates itself into political meaning, but also of culture that has declined into pseudo-culture." "Cultural pomp," he wrote in 1947, "is not at all the same thing as culture."[29]

Views of this sort betrayed important differences with the PCI leader's approach. If the recuperation of national roots and the formation of a progressive national culture were the guiding principles of the PCI's action to stimulate artists and writers to address themselves to the new situation in the country, for many of these the search for new sources of inspiration had already taken a different route. Although the PCI strove to insert itself in national life, and stressed the continuity of its activity with the progressive traditions of Italian culture, a considerable number of the intellectuals who joined the party at the close of the war dreamed of redefining culture and setting it on a new basis by breaking with the suffocating cultural nationalism that they had come to know and loathe under the Fascist regime.

In the interwar years men like Cesare Pavese, Mario Soldati, and Giaime Pintor, as well as Vittorini, had found in the down-to-earth realism of the new American novel a source of inspiration; others were fascinated by the French cinema of Jean Renoir and Marcel Carné, or even by jazz. After the war *Il Politecnico* adopted a program of renewal that aimed to introduce these and other such influences into the mainstream of Italian culture. The project did not encounter the wholehearted support even of Banfi, but the magazine nonetheless constituted one of the most lively and original reference points in the immediate postwar years. Articles were published on cultural phenomena such as psychoanalysis and existentialism, which had not been allowed to circulate under Fascism, as well as surveys of working-class and peasant life in Spain, Japan, France, and the USSR.

From a very early stage the manner in which many northern intellectuals became politically engaged aroused the disapproval of some of those who had adhered to the party on the basis of Togliatti's program. For the Christian Left the idea that culture became "progressive" through contact with the popular masses, as the Cultural Fronts thought, was politically sectarian and ideologically divisive.[30] The PCI leader, however, was careful not to endorse such criticism. In private letters to Vittorini and Mafai he confirmed the ideological openness of the party. It was not its job, he said, to tell artists what they should write or how they should paint. Yet there was always a substratum of distaste for contemporary European and American culture in Togliatti's outlook. As Rossana Rossanda would comment in 1965, this derived first and foremost from his own formative intellectual experiences.[31] Influenced, like Gramsci, by Crocean Idealism in the years of its ascendancy, the PCI leader nurtured a hatred for the old currents of positivism and scientism that this had replaced.[32] There was thus no attempt to incorporate the Marxist variants of positivism and rationalism, which enjoyed a certain following in the North, into the formal patrimony of the party. But Togliatti was wise enough to know that outright rejection of this or that view was not necessary or desirable in 1944–45. The party scarcely needed to take any stand at all in a context in which interest in its ideas was great and a new social orientation blossomed in the arts.

Toward the end of the war a spontaneous trend in realistic representation took place in the cinema, in literature, in the theater, and in painting as the nation's artists, or a significant segment of them, sought to transfer the pain, misery, sacrifice, and heroism of the time directly into their chosen art form. Stories taken from life, autobiographical experiences, and a sort of oral history all filled the first books, plays, and short stories to appear after the Liberation. In more recent years the neorealist literature and film of the 1940s has been closely scrutinized and its limits exposed.[33] In the context in which they first appeared, however, the works of Eduardo De Filippo, Vittorini, Beppe Fenoglio, Vasco Pratolini, Roberto Rossellini, and Vittorio De Sica exercised an important cultural function and appeared to represent something completely new with respect to the dominant artistic codes of the time. For those engaged in it, neorealism indicated the discovery of the nation not as something grandiose and pompous but as popular experience, common solidarity, endurance, and hope.

It was the cinema that acted as the site of the most ambitious and aesthetically successful attempt to translate the new principles of social awareness into the reality of a given cultural form. Films such as *Roma città aperta* (Rome open city), *Paisà* (Paisan), and *Sciuscià* (Shoeshine) introduced a new style of filmmaking that would have a lasting influence on Italian and world cinema. Their rejection of many of the outward signs of a confectioned product in favor of simple, almost documentary-style dramas shot with the participation of nonprofessional actors in the streets and fields where the real conflicts and struggles of the Italian people were unfolding gave them a unique feel that captured the passions of the moment. Cinematic neorealism represented something more than a stylistic innovation, however, even if this was to be its most enduring quality. It entailed not just a conception of filmmaking that rested on more realistic and issue-oriented forms of expression inside the cinema but also, and by no means secondarily, a battle to turn the cinema itself into an instrument for the regeneration of the social order.[34] This extremely ambitious project rested on the assumption that a new order of relationships in society was about to be created and that a totally new culture would replace discredited forms typical of the Fascist period. At the very least it required that the parties in government embark seriously on a radical program of national regeneration. What it reckoned without was the more cautiously conservative approach of the cultural policy of the PCI, but also, and much more seriously, the broad failure of the left to assert itself at the heart of the state.

Political Alliances and Cultural Policy

The PCI leadership expected that elections would shortly reveal the high level of support the left commanded in the country and force a shift in the priorities of the coalition government. As Togliatti put it in an interview published in *L'Unità* on 11 December 1945, "After the elections . . . when we and the Socialists will without doubt find ourselves at the head of the largest electoral coalition, political agreement with the DC will become the axis of governmental stability in a republican regime." "Ever since the liberation of Rome," he said, "we have been working with this perspective in mind."[35] In fact, nothing of the sort occurred. The elections were repeatedly postponed, and when the Italian people were finally called to elect the Constituent Assembly in June 1946, it was the DC that emerged as the largest party, with 35.2 percent of the poll. To make matters worse the Socialist Party, which politically had been under the PCI's shadow ever since 1944, won 20.7 percent to the latter's 18.9 percent and topped the polls in Milan and Turin. Even the referendum on the future institutional shape of the new regime, which was held at the same time, produced only the narrowest of majorities for the republic. Despite the early advances following Liberation, the left as a whole was revealed to be particularly weak in the South, where there was a net majority for the monarchy and neither Socialists nor Communists averaged more than 10 percent. Following this setback, Togliatti was compelled to cede ground to Pietro Secchia and other hard-line members of the leadership. However, the strategic supremacy of his national view was never in danger as long as it remained the cultural axis of the party. The reinforcement of the national emphasis hinging on Gramsci that took place in 1946–47 thus guaranteed that the high ground of policy remained firmly in the party leader's hands.

Nevertheless a clampdown on diversity occurred as the rational approach was accompanied by a stronger sense of party discipline. Both Banfi's journal *Studi filosofici* and *Società* were subject to sanctions. However, it is the dispute over *Il Politecnico*, and in particular the celebrated exchange between Togliatti and Vittorini, that are most frequently referred to in discussions of changes in the relationship between the PCI and the intellectuals who flocked to it in 1944–45, not only because the issues at stake emerged with great clarity but also because Vittorini's journal was the only one that addressed itself to a potentially mass readership.

The first attack by one of Togliatti's closest collaborators, Mario Alicata, concentrated on the cultural reference points of *Il Politecnico*. In an article in the May–June 1946 issue of *La Rinascita*, he suggested that it was entirely inappropriate that a writer such as Hemingway should be held up as the standard-bearer of the "new" culture the left wished to forge. A novel like *For Whom the Bell Tolls* (which happened to contain an unflattering portrait of the French Communist André Marty) was neither revolutionary nor useful, he argued. Rather, it provided "extreme proof of Hemingway's incapacity to understand and judge (that is, in the end, to *narrate*) something that goes beyond the self-centered sensations of his own elementary and immediate experience." It was not enough merely to be "human," Alicata went on, or to contribute to "an enrichment of taste, ridding it of certain provincial perspectives, giving it a more lively and modern sense of art and of expression." What was required was art that exposed the truth and motivated men in "a consequent struggle for justice and freedom."[36]

In response Vittorini widened the dispute to include more fundamental issues of politics and culture. But when Togliatti intervened personally a few months later, his basic argument differed little from that of Alicata. *Il Politecnico* had been welcomed, he said, as a contribution to the renewal of culture, but the initial promise of mediation between the lay and

Catholic currents that had gravitated toward the PCI had not been maintained: "The approach announced at the outset was not followed coherently; on the contrary, it was substituted, little by little, by something different, by a strange tendency toward a sort of encyclopedic 'culture' in which an abstract search for the new, the different, and the surprising took the place of coherent choice and meaningful inquiry, and news and information . . . suffocated thought." The preference for the superficial and the ephemeral that allegedly marked the publication led not only to confusion, Togliatti insisted. It also opened it to the danger of "engaging in or giving credit to fundamental errors of ideological approach."[37]

The conflict, in short, was not just one between the modernist and the cosmopolitan tastes of Vittorini and the more traditional and national ones of Togliatti. Ultimately, it raised the question of whether the new party proclaimed by Togliatti was genuinely pluralist or whether the "open door" policy had been a tactic tempered in the final analysis by the formal observance the PCI maintained of the cultural policy of the Soviet Communist Party. For Vittorini the fact that the party had welcomed all showed that it accepted ideological pluralism and that it was "concerned . . . to reopen itself to every sort of stimulus to its own ideology and reopen it to every sort of contact," evolving it and enriching it with new experiences.[38] But, as another of Togliatti's collaborators, the *Ordine Nuovo* veteran Felice Platone, pointed out, the party's real aim had been to build as wide an alliance as possible on the political plane against Fascism, and its openings on the cultural terrain had not therefore had the reform of the party as their goal but the unity of all who opposed the reactionary ideology of Fascism and wished to defend the possibility of progress in culture. "It is obvious," Platone wrote, "that by opening its doors to other ideologies the party had not meant to renounce its own or to express disinterest in the ideological and cultural orientations of its members."[39]

Vittorini's view of cultural activism demanded a measure of autonomy from politics. He insisted that "the line that divides progress from reaction in the field of culture is not exactly identifiable with the line that divides them in politics."[40] In his view, politicized culture policed by small-minded watchdogs could never properly enrich a progressive project, whereas writers such as Sartre or Kafka had, regardless of their politics, contributed enormously in his view to the development of a critique of man's contemporary condition.

It would be wrong to suggest that the "new culture" of the North or specifically *Il Politecnico* constituted a feasible alternative to the broad lines of cultural renewal sketched by Togliatti. As a general proposal it was eclectic and often incoherent, as even a cursory perusal of the magazine reveals. Moreover, it corresponded to a hypothesis of political regeneration that proved to be very short-lived. Although it would be much criticized in later years, Togliatti's national approach was more consonant with the requirements of the country as well as those of the party, as even Pavese, a potential supporter of Vittorini, recognized.[41] By building on Idealism he aimed to appropriate the idea of the value and universality of an Italian cultural tradition stemming from the Renaissance and make the left the new custodian of the ethical heritage of the Risorgimento. The account with Croce was to be settled not by imposing new ideas but by drawing on the resources of Italian culture from Machiavelli to De Sanctis and, of course, Gramsci. But the exclusion of potentially fruitful inputs from other sources in such a peremptory and even contemptuous manner ultimately impoverished the whole perspective of cultural renewal. Although it was not Togliatti's intention, his attack on *Il Politecnico* ensured that a hypothesis of cultural regeneration was adopted that reinforced the very provincialism the PCI had claimed it wished to see overcome. It also dashed the hopes of all those who had hoped the party would promote a general opening-up process in Italian culture after the stifling closures of the Fascist period.[42] Sales of the magazine had started to increase by early 1946, but Togliatti's attack made it impossible for *Il Politecnico* to be distributed by PCI volunteers along with other Communist publications and ultimately led to its closure in December 1947. Vittorini himself, who was continually subjected to pressure in private from leading party officials, some of whom bore him considerable personal animosity, gradually moved away from the PCI and eventually declared himself an "ex-Communist" in 1951.[43]

The PCI's adherence to conventional and established models of culture served certain well-defined ends, but coupled with an approach to politics that placed all the emphasis on civil society to the neglect of the state and even economic action, it revealed a general perspective that was at odds with the emergent framework of Italian politics and society in the mid–twentieth century. In later years, as economic development provoked changes at all levels of Italian society, the party would find itself increasingly the prisoner of its own conservatism. But even in the mid-1940s when the party itself, no matter how ambiguously, represented the most novel element in national life, the tensions were by no means negligible. Perhaps nowhere more than in the field of popular culture was this apparent.

The Cultural Impact of America

The Liberation saw the rebirth in Italy of many of the autonomous forms of working-class culture that had been suppressed in the 1920s with the Fascist rise to power. The *Case del popolo,* or labor clubs, that from the end of the nineteenth century had represented the very kernel of proletarian organization and solidarity, were reappropriated or built anew with the aid of volunteer labor.[44] Alongside them, many of the cooperative and recreational initiatives of the past were also resumed. Naturally, Communist activists were intimately involved in such endeavors. In the drive to turn the PCI into a mass party, Togliatti stressed in 1944 that "the Communist sections in the districts of the towns and villages must become centers of popular life, centers where all comrades, sympathizers, and the nonaligned must go knowing that they will find there a party and an organization that is interested in their problems and that will offer them guidance. They must know that they will find there someone who can lead them, advise them, and if necessary offer them the possibility of entertainment."[45] In addition, activists were urged, sometimes against their will, to take part in the state recreational organization, the National Workers' Assistance Board (ENAL), formerly the Fascist National After-Work Institution (OND), and seek to orient it in a progressive direction.

This was a wise policy, for alongside the need for a material and political reconstruction of the country, there was also a great desire to live life to the full and forget the privations and pain of the recent conflict. People flocked to join the political parties that appeared on the scene, but they also eagerly took part in the cultural and recreational activities that blossomed on an unprecedented scale. The sports clubs were among the first to start up their activities again, with the first professional football matches being played within a month of the Liberation. Theaters also reopened for business, with the *riviste* (Italian-style musical revues) enjoying great popularity. Universally popular were the commercial dance halls and the dancing parties that were often organized by labor clubs and political organizations. In the traditional dances people recovered an almost forgotten pleasure,[46] and the wilder movements of the boogie woogie, introduced by American troops, somehow corresponded to a desire for a physical and spiritual liberation. In keeping with this mood, the radio broadcast much American or American-style music often played by Italian light orchestras such as the Lucio Milena sinfonia and the Pippo Barzizza orchestra, which translated the swing of the American big bands into an Italian idiom. In the big cities at least, it became quite common for young women to go out in the evening, albeit usually in approved male company. Although resources were scarce and for most people new clothes were but a dream, more daring fashions began to appear, with seamstresses adapting skirts and dresses in accordance with foreign novelties presented in magazines.

Many of the social and cultural innovations were intimately connected with the presence of Allied troops on Italian soil. From their first landing in Sicily in July 1943 the American forces in particular had a profound impact on a population that in many instances had no previous knowledge or experience of modern industrial civilization. The deployment of a vast and highly sophisticated war machine in the South represented a major rupture on a scale unprecedented since the Spanish and French invasions of the late fifteenth and early sixteenth centuries. As Giuseppe Galasso put it, "modern mechanical civilization cheerfully and noisily penetrated cities and towns . . . , the fabulous and far away America, country dear to the dreams and labors of the fathers, had come among us."[47]

American soldiers (much more than the British, who in fact dominated the occupation and were mainly responsible for Italy until 1946) were greeted not just as liberators but as the representatives of a more advanced and prosperous world that in its tangible aspects was immensely attractive. Thanks to the much needed medical and nutritional supplies they brought and their superior technological and organizational knowhow, the Americans aroused awe and admiration if not always deep affection.[48] Such items as DDT, chocolate, chewing gum, nylon stockings, dollar bills, and V-discs were symbols of a new way of life that fed popular fantasies and contributed to the changes in customs that marked life in urban areas and in the more developed regions.

The importance of cinema in the immediate postwar years cannot be overestimated.[49] On the eve of the war, there were approximately 5,000 cinemas in the country, mostly concentrated in the North and the larger urban centers. The number of tickets sold at the box office was 318 million per year. By 1946, the first year after 1938 for which figures are available, total ticket sales had risen to 417 million, and in 1947 this reached 532 million.[50] New cinemas also opened rapidly; no fewer than 6,551 were operating by 1948. Bound up with this expansion, which signaled the conversion of new social strata to modern industrial forms of leisure, was the return of Hollywood. With Allied control and the local industry all but inactive (Cinecittà having been turned into a refugee camp), Hollywood was able to dominate a large part of the market, off-loading an almost unlimited backlog of recent and not so recent products. In 1946 alone no fewer than 600 films were imported, and by 1948 the figure had risen to 668.[51] Undoubtedly, there were strongly imperialistic elements in the designs of Hollywood and its allies in the military and political establishment. But this can only be part of any explanation of the success of American films in postwar Italy. By furnishing a rich corpus of seductive attractions that were deployed in films that, generally speaking, were optimistic and upbeat and celebrated democracy, equality of opportunity, and urbanized prosperity, Hollywood did not only educate and amuse.[52] Through its transmission of ideas, fashions, and more modern, less cumbersome modes of interpersonal interaction, it paved the way for the future incorporation of ever wider strata into a pattern of consensus in which entertainment and material life were closely related aspects of a new model of society that had the consumption of goods as its primary rule of social conduct.

The deep resonance of the American impact on Italian popular culture was evident in the new products furnished by a publishing industry that clearly traded heavily on the enthusiasm for bright, visual forms of communication. Film magazines such as *Hollywood* enjoyed a wide following in urban areas; in June 1946 the first issue of *Grand Hôtel* appeared, an illustrated weekly that presented the classic themes of popular romantic literature in a graphic form. An enormously successful publication whose initial print run of 650,000 soon rose to over 1 million copies per week, *Grand Hôtel*'s cover always featured brightly colored illustrations of a starry-eyed young couple that not only made it stand out on any newsstand but also constituted an explicit invitation to enter an imaginary world of dreams and romance. As Angelo Ventrone has argued, the pedagogical function of *Grand Hôtel* was second only to the cinema and at the same time closely related to it.[53] Artists transposed the features of Hollywood stars onto the faces of their characters and copied their gestures and attitudes to give a more lively, modern sense of personal relations. In 1947 it was followed by two photoromance magazines, *Bolero Film* (Mondadori) and *Sogno* (Rizzoli), which relied exclusively on photographs.[54] By-products of the cinema age, these magazines acquired a mass, mostly female, readership among office and factory workers, seamstresses, shop assistants, and housewives. Crucially, they also reached some of the many peasant women for whom cinema was a very distant reality. Comics also experienced a boom. By 1950 average weekly comic sales had reached two million.[55] In this field the American trademark was so powerful that the publishers adapted to the formula and even presented their own perfectly indigenous products as though they too were American imports.[56]

Although much emphasis has been placed on the strength and charm of an articulated American cultural model and its impact on Italian culture, it would be quite wrong to imagine that everything was transformed. For large sections of the rural population, and those living outside the large urban centers of the North, little changed. The Americanisms of the immediate postwar years were a significant phenomenon, but they were circumscribed and often superficial in their effects. Conventional Italian passions continued to enjoy great popularity and would remain a focus of collective interest for many years to come. The sports of football and cycling, for example, neither of which was remotely American, probably constituted the most important unifying moments in popular culture (especially for men). Moreover, even in cinema there was a very notable degree of continuity with the past in the coordinates of popular taste. Many of the single films that did best at the box office were exactly the sort that had packed picture houses in the 1930s and early 1940s and included operatic and musical films, historical melodramas, comedy films starring comics from the revues such as Macario and Rascel, or swashbuckling adventures. On occasion these genres were renewed by the addition of an American touch or some references to recent political events, but in all major respects they reflected the autonomous character that Italian popular culture preserved even in the face of a powerful external model. Despite the great crisis in values and reference points when the Fascist regime fell, there was sufficient dynamism not only to rework novel inputs but also to give rise to radical alternatives to them.

The Popular Cultural Alternative

There was no sustained attempt on the part of the leadership to challenge or oppose the cultures and fashions of American origin that so markedly influenced tastes and customs in the mid-1940s. America, after all, was still viewed as an ally, and in any case there were many more important political and cultural tasks to worry about. But it is clear that the cultural model of the Communists was organized in a way quite different to the American model. It drew inspiration from local cultures, from traditions of community solidarity, and from the recent experiences of collective action and mobilization. It was not completely new either in the form it took or in content, but in a situation in which popular sympathy for the Soviet Union ran high and the movement of Liberation had contributed to the restoration of national dignity and independence, a range of new symbols and themes helped sustain and lend strength to the culture of the left. The martyrs and heroic survivors of the partisan struggle were seen as figures of legend, models of a new type of human behavior characterized by unselfish devotion to the common cause. The songs of the partisan bands became those of the left, and the Resistance fighter's red handkerchief knotted around his or her neck a sign of distinction. The commemoration of the dead and the marking of domestic and international anniversaries were integrated within a new pattern of collective rituals that gave left-wing culture a rhythm and a dynamic of its own.[57]

The PCI's attitude toward popular culture was complex. A benevolent view was taken of the spontaneous forms of identification with the left that marked grassroots initiatives. However, there was a strong sense within the party hierarchy that workers no longer belonged to a class that was isolated and denied legitimation. They were not merely a full part of society but its most prominent segment, that which most incarnated hopes for change and for a new order. Therefore there was a need for working people to have a culture that was equal to their new status, that drew on the very best elements of national and international culture and embodied the most advanced and democratic values. Stimulated by these considerations, the PCI sought to act as a vehicle for the promotion of the habit of study among its membership, with every party section encouraged to build up a library and organize reading and discussion groups. Pamphlet versions of Marxist-Leninist classics and recent essays by party leaders were made widely available by Edizioni di cultura sociale, Edizioni *Rinascita,* and Edizioni *L'Unità.*

To open the way for the formulation of a new universal culture in which the historic division between the culture of the elite and the common people would be overcome, radical and socially aware intellectuals committed themselves to finding new interlocutors among the proletariat. The underlying view was that there was a strong nexus between the acquisition of knowledge and the achievement of personal dignity. By means of study the lower classes could transcend the limited horizons of family, village, or quarter and gain a sense of belonging to a wider world. At the same time ignorance and superstition would be defeated and the resigned acceptance of exploitation, poverty, and backwardness overcome. Often, however, a good deal of self-delusion marked initiatives in this field. It was not only bourgeois intellectuals who were to blame but autodidacts like Negarville and Secchia, who cultivated an enormous respect for the books that had been the instruments of their own awakening and that they saw as the means to shake others out of their mental torpor.

One person who fell squarely into the latter group was Vittorini, himself a self-taught man who conserved a fond memory of the group of workers with whom he had exchanged books and opinions during his teenage years in the Sicilian town of Siracuse.[58] From the beginning *Il Politecnico* set itself the goal of bridging the gap "between the working masses and workers in the cultural field."[59] But almost immediately problems arose. Although ordinary people were encouraged to assist in the production of the magazine by sending in their own contributions, almost none of these was deemed to be of a sufficiently high standard to merit publication. Moreover, a strong dose of paternalism marked Vittorini's approach. This was evident both in the tone used in his responses to readers and in the decision to offer prizes to those whose preference for certain themes coincided with the tastes of the majority. Vittorini did at least try to engage in open debate with all, but shrank before suggestions that the language of his journal should be more simple and direct so as to be more widely accessible. To one reader who put it to him that there was a real detachment and a reciprocal incomprehension between workers and men of culture, he replied that "we do not entirely agree

Between Hollywood and Moscow

and [are of the view that] on the plane of common and concrete interests also of a cultural nature, to join together requires but a short step on both sides."[60]

Even though it was free of the snobbery that sometimes affected *La Rinascita* (which on occasion even published poems in French without translation), *Il Politecnico* never really resolved the general issue of how cultural distances might be bridged. Its contributors were aware of the need to avoid the pitfalls that the popular universities of the pre-1914 period fell into by trying to disseminate the official bourgeois culture in a simplified form, but failed to liberate themselves of the intellectual prejudices of their category in seeking a dialogue with the readership. In any event, the impact of their efforts was limited. Although Vittorini and his associates seemed to almost take it for granted that the dramatic alteration in the balance of class relations during the Liberation would win them a mass following, the magazine really only reached a student and lower-middle-class audience in significant numbers.[61] Well before the dispute with the PCI, sales failed to reach the desired level. In April 1946 *Il Politecnico* was selling just twenty-two thousand copies per week in contrast to the hundred thousand that were required to break even, with the result that it was compelled to turn itself into a monthly publication.[62]

In pursuing educational objectives at the expense of other types of cultural activity aimed at winning mass consensus, the left fell into a dangerous trap. As the following extract from an article by Giulio Trevisani, the editor of *Il Calendario del Popolo,* a magazine committed to popular education, testifies, the notion of culture was itself taken to be synonymous with educational achievement:

What is meant by "people" when we speak of popular culture? You begin with the base, i.e., from, alas, the very large number of illiterates. . . . These are followed by the semi-literate, the nonreader and the peasant, who represents the largest element of these categories, which appear in conditions directly related to popular culture. Above these stands the working class, whose most socially active part is represented by the autodidacts . . . but popular culture also touches vast strata of the petite bourgeoisie, possessors of modest qualifications. Popular culture passes through the high school and universities as integrator of the scholastic culture, and reaches even the minor intellectual furnished with higher qualifications who, when he can, likes to escape from his professional specialization and refresh himself. . . . All these are the people to whom reference must be made when you speak of popular culture.[63]

For Trevisani it was as if the great cultural changes of the 1930s and 1940s had never occurred. Yet as some others realized, workers were already part of a cultural sphere, albeit one that bore precious little relation to the patient and studious emphases of the left. The approach to this was complex. At one level educated left-wingers mostly welcomed the return of Hollywood, whose films they had adored before the embargo and which they preferred to the German films that had been the staple fare of cinemas in northern Italy in the last two years of the war. But there was growing concern that, taken together, the influx of comics, detective stories, and escapist diversions were a pernicious influence that appealed to the negative side of people's personalities and pandered to the lowest common denominator of taste. One of the first to raise the alarm was Lucio Lombardo Radice in *Vie Nuove,* the weekly magazine edited by Luigi Longo that sought to popularize the main themes of Communist policy and offer some degree of political and cultural guidance to a mass left-wing public. In an article on the reading habits of workers published in November 1946, he wrote:

> Poor quality, insignificant, and unintelligent literature is unfortunately very widespread among workers: American-style children's comics, with "strip cartoons" and the most hideous, idiotic, and monstrous adventures, the sports press of whatever standard and shoddy, cheap films. Women workers, in a certain sense, read more than men . . . but what dreadful reading matter! The most worthless and sickly love stories, and then a whole pseudobourgeois novelistic literature represented by dozens of publications such as *Grand Hôtel, Intimità,* and *Liala,* which are extremely widely read.[64]

Lombardo Radice was in no doubt as to why such literature was popular: "In my view the worker who reads the rubbishy biography of a soccer star, the typist in the tram who avidly devours a novel about a secretary who marries the boss, and the worker who is distracted by infantile stories of adventure or whodunits are motivated by the desire to escape for a moment from their own poverty and worries, to transfer onto 'heroes' and 'heroines' their own gnawing wish for a richer and more interesting life."[65]

There was no room for doubt either over what the effect of such influences was: "In this way their resistance is at least partially side-tracked and their capacity for struggle worn down. I firmly believe that literature of the 'popular novel' type (including 'strip cartoons,' who-dunits, love stories, and sporting myths) has a strongly conservative influence."[66]

A real point of contention arose here. It was thought that mass products produced by commercial enterprises or imported from the United States furnished a set of ideas and suggestions that favored individual, private solutions to life's problems in contrast to the faith in collective action and social solidarity that marked all strands of left-wing thinking as well as Catholic models in Italy. But at the same time there was a strong strain of cultural conservatism that revealed itself in a prejudicial hostility toward new and visual forms of communication that offered an immediate and predominantly emotional sensation of aesthetic pleasure. Devoid of artistic merit and inserted in a market organized according to the rules of profit, comics and the like were inimical to the representatives of a workers' movement whose cultural system rested on a very different set of presuppositions stressing the rational, cognitive aspect of cultural experience.

Convinced that in the long run its own, superior model of culture was destined to triumph over a frivolous and fundamentally alienating capi-talist culture, the left pursued a strategy designed to persuade workers of the merits of art, literature, and philosophy. As Giulio Preti argued, the goal of the working-class movement was "to substitute activity for passivity, spiritual commitment for superficial 'entertainment,' critical awareness for instinct, so that through it the proletariat gradually frees itself of that indirect form of exploitation that is offered by industri-alized sport, cinema etc. . . . and becomes the active creator of its own life."[67]

As part of this drive, both the Socialists and the Communists made every effort to promote their own press. In addition to the monthly *La Rinascita,* the PCI published four separate editions of its daily *L'Unità,* and from 1946 the weekly *Vie Nuove* was aimed at the magazine market. The party also encouraged the distribution of the women's magazine *Noi Donne* and sponsored a vast range of local and sectoral publications. Like all political papers, these enjoyed a notable success in the period following the Liberation. Interest in politics was high, and, after twenty years of government-censored information, people were eager to read about past and present events from different points of view. Yet the Communist press mirrored a common failing of the Italian press in pitching the level of its publications too high for an unsophisticated mass public. Furthermore, in formulating content, the requirements taken into account were less those of readers than of a political force seeking maximum support for its line. Despite certain concessions to what Trotsky, in his discussion of the left-wing press in the early 1920s, had called "natural as well as noble curiosity," the contents of the PCI's publications were marked by an unappealing tone mixing education and propaganda. Nothing, Trotsky had written, could be more guaranteed to isolate the party press from popular taste.[68] For these reasons even in more solidly "red" areas, from which the party could count on an army of volunteers to distribute its papers door to door, the PCI struggled to compete with commercial periodicals that functioned very effectively at a subpolitical level. Some perceptive members of the party leadership quickly realized this and urged the magazines to become more popular.[69]

To bring together traditionally separate sectors and create a genuine, unified culture "without adjectives" was the noble aim of Communist policymakers and intellectuals. But, as many were forced to recognize in the long run, there were structural difficulties in bridging the gap between high-level cultural action and the real level of comprehension of many of the party's followers. The narrow terrain on which Togliatti's cultural policy was applied did not readily lend itself to large-scale social initiatives. Intellectuals were recruited but not involved in practical work, and injunctions were issued to local party federations to involve militants in problems of culture, but little was done to provide clear guidelines as to how this might be achieved.[70] The result was frequently mutual incomprehension, as Lombardo Radice frankly admitted: "Men of culture in Italy, even if on the left and *even if Communists,* are unaware of the cultural needs of the workers: when made, their efforts to help workers along the road of culture have, in general, as a premise the exigencies and interests of the strata of high culture and the *techniques* of high culture. For this reason their efforts are in vain."[71]

The problem of communication, of the search for an appropriate language that would allow a real and fruitful exchange between intellectuals and workers, was one of pressing importance within the left. But, by underestimating the importance of the means of communication that found such successful deployment in the mid-1940s, the left's cultural spokesmen revealed the extent to which they were trapped in an old, pre-technical cultural model that belonged to the period prior to the 1920s. For to try and connect high and low by means of conventional forms of divulgation that bypassed new languages and media was ultimately a hopeless task in an age in which cinema and popular publishing were beginning to achieve just this integration of classes, tastes, and interests on a more advanced plane. The result was that many Communists, especially if they were intellectuals, were at best indifferent and at worst hostile to a major cultural transition that profoundly affected how consensus was formed and society integrated in postwar Italy. In political terms this was highly significant. It meant that a space was left free for other forces, principally the Catholics, to maintain an influence over the life of the popular classes through their appropriation of the instruments of the new culture. It also meant that at no point in the postwar period did the party exercise the sort of monopoly over the culture of its own members that many on the left assumed it should. This was no less true even after 1948, when left-wing popular culture in Italy once again took on some of the features of a closed culture, self-sufficient and proud, the expression of a section of the population that no longer commanded the legitimacy or authority of the Liberation period.

2

Bread, Love, and Political Strife

Cold War Communism and the Development

of Cultural Policy

Between 1947 and 1949 a shift of historic importance took place in Italian political life. The years that saw the exclusion of the Socialist and Communist Parties from government, the conquest of a parliamentary majority by the Christian Democrats in the divisive election of April 1948, as well as the breakup of trade union unity and integration of the country into the Western system of economic, political, and military alliances, marked the definitive end of national unity and most of the ideologies it had spawned. The new power bloc that Alcide De Gasperi sought to weld together with the aid of the Catholic Church and the support of the United States found its ideological cement not in any real or feigned continuity with the progressive framework of values that had commanded widespread support in the period immediately following the fall of Fascism, but in a robust anticommunism that mobilized a majority of the population in support of traditional, conservative norms.

From 1947 the PCI assumed an identity somewhat different from that which had made it so strikingly novel a force in the period following Togliatti's return to active politics. It took steps to reinforce the party organization and establish ideological conformity among its membership; it adopted a more confrontational approach on domestic issues and firmly opposed the country's ever more complete alignment with the West. Yet although this approach reflected the PCI's conformity to the new hard-line of the international Communist movement, it did not herald the complete cancellation of the strategic initiatives embraced in

1944. The party certainly became more sectarian, but it maintained a commitment to building alliances wherever possible that, in the often authoritarian and intolerant climate that marked DC rule, paid important dividends. In the eyes of many Communists of a certain generation, the years between 1948 and Stalin's death in 1953 would come to represent a sort of "golden age" in which the PCI was hard-pressed and political battles infused with unprecedented animosity, but in which faith in Communist values was unquestioned and belief in the ultimate triumph of good over evil total. Despite increased pressures for conformity, the nationally oriented cultural policy that the party developed, after 1951 in particular, also won lasting admiration even among the more critical components of the Communist intelligentsia.[1] In this phase the PCI was seen as having pursued a coherent and well-directed policy that enabled it to harness a wide variety of talents and offer a genuine alternative vision of national development that drew its main inspiration from the recently published edition of Gramsci's prison notebooks.

Yet culture was also the field in which socioeconomic change manifested itself most clearly. Although the PCI demonstrated a greater awareness of the role of the mass media than it did in the preceding phase, it failed to match the extraordinary efforts made at all levels by the Church and the DC to shape the reorganization of cultural production on modern, industrial lines and use commercially oriented entertainments to reinforce and even extend the hold they enjoyed in Italian society. Thus, even though it exercised a real measure of hegemony on the plane of high culture, the cold war years witnessed a substantial defeat of the PCI in the decisive field of popular culture. To be sure, the cultural world of the left attracted significant segments of the working class and the intelligentsia, and the PCI itself commanded a central place in community life. But in an age in which attractive new forms of information and entertainment would assume an ever more important social function, the PCI found itself reduced to a position of sometimes embarrassing subalternity in the very field in which it most often took its strength for granted.

Catholics, Culture, and Society

Within the anticommunism of the late 1940s and the 1950s various different elements coexisted. Under the DC the authoritarian nature of the state apparatus was confirmed and reinforced. In the interior ministry, in the police and the armed forces, in the judiciary and in the administrative class generally, the people and some of the methods of the Fascist period returned to the fore. The American presence in the economy, society, and culture in addition to its role in conditioning foreign policy options added an important new element of legitimation to these arrangements. Ultimately, however, the key element in the construction of a conservative order from which the left was excluded was the Church. For the Catholic hierarchy, the outcome of the election presented an unprecedented opportunity to complete the battle it had waged since 1946 against the influence of alien ideologies of revolution and emancipation that had circulated during and after the Liberation period, threatening to undermine the given structures of morality and power. Thus after 1948 a constant struggle was waged against alleged forces of subversion in politics, culture, and society that culminated in July 1949 when the Holy Office of the Vatican announced the formal excommunication of all Communist parties and supporters of such parties on account of their atheistic and materialist ideology.

In pursuing their campaign to exercise an extended influence over the social values and cultural models of the nation, Catholics did not make the mistake of bypassing the most powerful modern means of persuasion and entertainment. Indeed, the successful construction of a conservative framework of consensus that rested not merely on the state, the Church, and the economic power of the dominant elite but spread to cinema, radio, the press, and even to the expanding network of popular illustrated magazines derived largely from the skill and speed with which Catholics occupied positions of power inside state organisms, regulatory bodies, and the cultural industries themselves.[2] Here alliances were forged with conventionally minded functionaries, proprietors, and operatives to discredit the left and offer a new set of reference points for the heterogeneous social forces that had coalesced in support of the DC. These new values included not only respect for religion and support for the policies of De Gasperi but also recognition of the United States as the model society and source of comparison for future social and economic change.

Catholics boasted an involvement with cinema dating back to the 1920s, but, because they had a broad vision of cinema as a complex and powerful phenomenon capable of influencing society at various levels, shaping culture, morals, and aspirations, their own intervention emphasized organization. Despite the insistence on the need for films that educated and were morally uplifting for their audiences, only a handful of religious documentaries was ever produced. Instead, much recourse was made to the American films that continued to flood into the country. In 1949 they accounted for 73 percent of box office takings.[3] Optimistic and cheerfully escapist, such films contained no subversive impulses and functioned to blot out the memory of the recent past by restoring a model of pure fantasy equivalent to that which prevailed before the war. By contrast, much of the output of the domestic film industry was regarded with deep suspicion. Almost from the moment of the first appearance of the works of Roberto Rossellini and Vittorio De Sica, religious spokesmen and Christian Democratic parliamentarians attacked neorealism on account of its failure to show due respect for religious and temporal authority. The fact that it may have breathed a genuine Christian spirit, as some have argued, was irrelevant.[4] By portraying bandits and prostitutes, casting aspersions on national institutions and raising social problems, the films of this school stood in the way of the desire of the authorities for a return to the values and relations of a disciplined, orderly society. Thus neorealist works were branded as unsuitable for showing in the growing number of parish cinemas and subjected to repeated attack by Catholic Action in its campaigns in favor of public morality. Between 1947 and 1954 the sphere of cinema was marked by pitched battles over questions of interference, censorship, and artistic freedom.[5] Eager to defend a style of filmmaking that had won them international recognition and permitted contact with impulses toward change and renewal in society, directors sternly resisted the pressures for normalization. But with the progressive reintroduction of some of the privileges abolished at the insistence of the Allies in 1945, the government assumed a direct or indirect influence in virtually every sector of film production and distribution. The consequence was that, even though the local industry gradually increased its share of the domestic market from 10 percent in 1949 to 28 percent in 1953, as the American share dropped over the same period from 71 percent to 42 percent, less space than ever existed for social criticism.[6]

Although neorealism, encouraged by progressive critics who rarely looked beyond the single film, seemed willfully to ignore the industrial aspect of its own existence, Italian cinema was rapidly evolving into a major business concern. By the early 1950s over fifty-two thousand people depended on one aspect or another of the film industry for their livelihood, and between 1948 and 1952 Italy overtook France and Germany to become the leading European center of film production.[7] To this expansion corresponded a striking growth in the cinema audience. Just at the moment when filmgoing began to decline elsewhere it achieved a central place in Italian leisure.[8] Although the bulk of earnings remained concentrated in the large urban centers, where ticket prices were higher and auditoriums larger, new cinemas opening at a rapid rate, notably in small towns and in the South, accounted for much of the new audience. By 1956 some 10,500 cinemas were operating commercially in the peninsula.[9]

As the economic and productive aspects of cultural production underwent a marked industrialization, the DC acted as midwife at the birth of a new popular culture largely divorced from critical impulses and the conflicts of civil society. The return to the fore of the provincial stolidity and petit bourgeois pursuit of respectability that had characterized life under Fascism found a perfect correspondent in the lowbrow set of myths and pastimes imbued with the positive outlook and untroubled sense of optimism that only a restoration of order can bring.[10] As people began to look with hope to the future and put the worries of the recent past behind them, so the annual election of Miss Italia in Stresa, the San Remo song festival, spectator sports, and the new game of football pools, *Totocalcio,* all found eager followers. In the cinema, lighthearted comedies that were upbeat and cheerful unified audiences that had previously been divided by contrasting patterns of taste. But it would be wrong to see such films as Mario Castellani's *Due soldi di speranza* (Tuppence worth of hope) and Luigi Comencini's *Pane, amore e fantasia* (Bread, love, and dreams) purely in terms of political manipulation, even though they retained the earlier usage of popular and recognizable personality types and situations while replacing the concern with social contradictions by less controversial differences and rivalries, usually of a regional, generational, or sexual type. Rather, the phenomenon must be seen in the context of more general processes of change taking place in Italian politics, culture, and society. As Lino Miccichè puts it: "Where neorealism failed, its bastard form, which was the main and most apparent symptom of its failure, won out. Naturally the defeat of the old cinema, rather than a substitution (cultural) was a succession (industrial), and in this respect it was analogous to all that was occurring in civil society."[11]

The desire of the urban population and the middle class more generally for escapism and material improvement was also fed by the illustrated weekly magazines that doubled their circulation between 1947 and 1952, whereas that of the satirical and political press, which had been extremely popular in the immediate postwar years, dropped by half. In 1952 the total sales of the illustrated weekly press was 12.6 million, a figure that would rise to 15.75 million in 1962 and 21 million a decade later.[12] In a country in which, even as late as 1960, a mere 10 percent of the population read at least one book per year, and sales of daily newspapers were notoriously low, periodicals like *Oggi, Tempo, L'Europeo,* and *Epoca* reached a genuine mass audience.[13]

Oggi, the leader in the field, owed much of its success to the discovery of a widespread taste in republican Italy for stories about European royalty. More than any other magazine, it peddled modern-day fairy tales, mixing an aggressive conservatism in politics with ample coverage of the lives of foreign aristocrats, film stars, and prominent religious and political personalities, shown where possible in a private dimension. In February 1949, for example, much attention was devoted to the Rome wedding of Hollywood stars Tyrone Power and Linda Christian, the latter even appearing on the cover in the company of De Gasperi.[14] *Epoca* and other magazines, particularly film and women's publications, traded even more extensively on the enormous curiosity for all things American. They filled their pages with American news, tales of aid and generosity, new inventions, gossip about the stars, and images of material abundance. Advertisements for American products connected the dream specifically with the aspirations of readers.

With its potent mix of traditional and modern themes, the periodical press contributed vitally to the construction of a new pattern of consensus in the Italy of the DC. Beneath the surface of the major political events of the period, it functioned both to establish a rudimentary cultural network across the fragmented subnational texture of the life of popular Italy and to transmit a set of social values and ideological orientations wholly at variance with the left's perspective on collective action and cultural transformation.

The PCI and the "Battle of Ideas"

Defeated and, together with its Socialist allies, isolated from mainstream society, the PCI remained a force with a deep interest in culture. It was on this plane, after all, that Togliatti had concentrated much of his energy with the result that the party had asserted its novel presence with considerable success. But in the frontal clash of opposing blocs many of the subtleties and much of the originality of the new party's cultural vision ceased to be so evident. The cultural battles of the left became much more defensive and politically motivated as ideological rigor was demanded of all intellectuals who considered themselves Communists. For Togliatti this was a highly delicate moment. Caught between international pressures for conformity and the reversion to more conventional styles of political conflict at home, there was a danger that the national strategy would be canceled even as a hypothesis of cultural renewal.

If for the immediate postwar years it is possible to study the conduct of the party on the terrain of culture mainly in terms of the links it forged with an antifascist (or postfascist) intellectual elite, account must be taken in later years of the more concrete initiatives that were developed in an effort to institutionalize relations, broaden the basis of cultural action, and root it in the texture of the country. For at this time cultural policy inevitably took on a more assertive tone and embraced issues concerning cultural apparatuses as the threat to break the influence of progressives in areas as diverse as the cinema and the universities became real.

The first steps toward a greater degree of organization were taken in 1947. At the national organization conference in January, an intellectuals' section was set up as a subcommittee of the party's press and propaganda commission. Then at the sixth PCI congress in 1948 a full-fledged cultural commission was established under the direction of Emilio Sereni. These moves occurred because the dispute over *Il Politecnico* revealed that many of the intellectuals who had adhered to the PCI remained individualistic and aristocratic in their outlook, more preoccupied with abstract debates than party matters. For some leading Communists the lack of conformity was a direct result of Togliatti's unilateral decision to abandon all forms of cultural direction in the preceding period. "Writers, painters, sculptors, and scientists turned to us hopefully after the fall of Fascism expecting to receive words of clarification on their spiritual unease and of orientation for their practical activity," Luigi Longo declared in September 1948, in a veiled criticism of the party leader; "They have been abandoned to themselves by us. . . . In this way many have fallen back into the ideologies they wished or believed they could escape from, and today they remain without a guide, without a compass to orient them in their work."[15]

The appointment of Sereni represented a victory for the hard-liners. A Marxist-Leninist of unimpeachable orthodoxy, he had been closely involved with the northern party during the period of clandestine operations and was not among Togliatti's close collaborators. As one of the few Italians to embrace fully the cultural doctrines of the Soviet ideologist Zhdanov, he offered a guarantee that the development of cultural policy would conform to the demands for a restoration of orthodoxy emanating from the USSR.[16] After his substitution in 1951 it was said that his dogmatic devotion to Soviet priorities and especially to the peace campaign hindered the full development of the party's potential in the cultural field. This is unquestionably true in some respects, but if the PCI succeeded in shaping a cultural policy at this time that was articulated at various levels and well integrated with other dimensions of party activity, then much of the merit was his.

In the first few months of 1948 the PCI raised for the first time the question of cultural colonialism. In particular, Secchia, in his address to the sixth congress, warned that the PCI was faced with a reactionary offensive on various planes. "The great American trusts send us not only their riflemen, their spies, their agents, and organizers of sabotage and betrayal," he proclaimed, "but inundate our country with their books, their films, and their lowbrow ideological rubbish that should serve to weaken, disorient, and corrupt our people."[17] This theme was taken up by the Alliance of Culture, a coordinating committee in which Communists, Socialists, and independents joined forces to defend progressive cultural currents from attack. It was also echoed in the resolution ("For the preservation of Italian culture") that led to the constitution in July 1948, following the — mainly electoral — experience of the Alliance, of a cultural commission of the PCI. As the moving force behind both, Sereni stressed the importance of preserving a culture that was truly national in opposition to the cultural cosmopolitanism that was the typical product of American imperialism. The problem was not just that the ideology of monopoly capitalism posed a threat to the left, but that ever closer economic relations between Italy and the United States would result in "the suffocation and repression of national initiatives." Modern culture did not mean "an extravagant and artificial pursuit of the new and the original," but rather a struggle to deepen the roots of culture in the breast of the people, adapting it to their aspirations, tastes, and level of historical development.[18] On this basis the PCI appealed to all men of culture, regardless of ideological conviction, and took up the very corporate interests of culture that it had sought to undermine after the fall of Fascism.[19]

On the strength of this firm stance, the PCI attracted the interest and support of directors and screenwriters associated with neorealism, who signed a collective manifesto ("Difendiamo il nostro cinema!") published in *L'Unità* on 22 February 1948. Previously, little interest had been shown by the party in cinema, but from this moment on it became a major theme. An alliance was forged that would make the PCI into the party most identified with the interest of national filmmakers and in particular with those concerned to maintain and develop a creative link with the hopes and fears of the lower classes. For some ten years efforts were made at all levels to maintain a front in support of the best national film production, grouping together intellectuals, artists, trade unions, mass organizations, and the popular classes.[20] Although difficulties and incomprehensions were manifold, cinema was the only terrain on which a continuous campaign of this nature was sustained. For many it became the symbol of the cultural aspirations of the left, the clearest positive reference point for a political cause that otherwise faced defeat on all fronts.

Togliatti's position in the years after 1948 was an unusual one. The creation of formal structures for the formulation and enactment of cultural policy and the role of Sereni deprived him of direct control over a sphere that had previously been virtually his exclusive domain. Yet he remained the editor of *Rinascita* and continued to play a prominent part in relations with intellectuals. In this sphere, however, his interventions were of a very different type to the reassuring, open ones of 1944–46. If in the past he had been in the habit of correcting the intemperances of subordinates and engaging in private correspondence with recently recruited artists and writers, he now commented sharply on cultural developments, frequently reproving intellectuals and castigating former comrades in sarcastic notes published in *Rinascita* under the pseudonym of Roderigo Di Castiglia.[21] Although the PCI leader himself often qualified his remarks by saying that they were merely personal, Togliatti's interventions were really designed to ensure formal observance of the cultural canons of the international Communist movement. It was to his credit that no one was expected to toady to the gurus of Soviet culture as was the case in France (although this did not prevent some from doing so); but at the same time a stern defense was mounted of the party's right to intervene in the cultural sphere, and no open criticism whatsoever was brooked of Soviet positions.

Ultimately, the most decisive cultural event for which Togliatti was responsible in the period of Zhdanovism was the publication in six thematic volumes of Gramsci's prison writings. Preceded in 1947 by a volume of prison letters, which themselves had a major literary and humanitarian impact, the prison notebooks appeared in rapid succession between 1948 and 1951.[22] Edited under the supervision of the PCI leader and Felice Platone, they were published not by a party press but by the Turin publisher Einaudi, which served to maximize their influence on Italian letters generally and make the PCI seem more concerned with the cultural value of Gramsci's work than its political consequences.

To publish Gramsci at the height of the cold war, after the clampdown on national variants on socialist strategy, was a courageous act. It showed that Togliatti was determined to preserve at least the possibility of adapting communism to national conditions by reinforcing its links with an indigenous intellectual and cultural tradition. The presentation of the prison writings conformed to Togliatti's postwar maneuver. The prior publication of the letters served to underline Gramsci's 1944 image of martyr to the cause of democracy. Then the first volume of the notebooks, *Il materialismo storico e la filosofia di Benedetto Croce* (Historical materialism and the philosophy of Benedetto Croce), which brought together disparate notes written at different moments, highlighted his cultural concerns, which were only later supplemented with the appearance of his more political annotations.

The act of publication carried certain risks. As soon as the letters appeared, Croce announced, in polemic with the PCI, that "as a man of thought he was one of us."[23] Even though this idea was soon overcome, there was still a danger that some might seek to counterpose Gramsci to his party, to the political theory of the international Communist movement or to the Soviet Union. To preempt any such attempt and avoid a possible clash with the USSR or the party's staunch Marxist-Leninists, cuts were made to Gramsci's text eliminating embarrassing references to Trotsky, Amedeo Bordiga, and others. Togliatti also intervened to present his predecessor as a committed Leninist in politics whose original considerations were of strictly national relevance and were limited to particular themes like the role of intellectuals and the Italian South. By setting down certain authoritative lines of interpretation, Togliatti aimed to channel debate and provide a rigid framework for analysis of the contents of the notebooks.[24]

In a phase in which the PCI's alignment with the USSR was more or less total, the publication of Gramsci enabled Togliatti to keep his own strategy alive, to show that the national themes and methods he had advanced had not been completely eclipsed. In the medium term it granted him a base from which to proceed to a reestablishment first of the party's original cultural line and then of its political strategy as the Stalinist period drew to a close. The first step in this direction was taken at the seventh PCI congress in 1951, when Sereni was ousted and replaced at the head of the cultural commission by Carlo Salinari, a young literary critic personally loyal to Togliatti who was not even a professional party worker.[25] Then at a meeting of the cultural commission in April 1952 the party leader sanctioned a return to the emphasis on renewing culture by recuperating the progressive tradition of the past and promoting the wider diffusion of Marxism.[26]

For Asor Rosa, the years between 1951 and 1956 saw the most organic and complete elaboration of cultural policy of the postwar period.[27] Hard, schematic positions gave way to a more flexible, consensual approach based on persuasion and genuine collaboration. Both *Società,* under the officially approved editorship of Gastone Manacorda and Carlo Muscetta, and from March 1954 *Il Contemporaneo,* which Salinari himself edited in conjunction with Antonello Trombadori, cultivated intellectuals by subtle means, seeking to win cooperation through debate. But a considerable measure of ideological rigidity remained. The essential difference was that national reference points supplemented international ones, and Gramsci became the principal axis of a renewed battle in favor of realism.[28] However, the change of style did permit a more fruitful and easier relationship with intellectuals outside the party and, at the height of the PCI's delegitimation in the early 1950s, this was important. For it was precisely through debate and cultural activity that the PCI hoped to overcome the divisions of the political sphere and maintain contact with broad democratic sectors of public opinion.[29]

The impact of Gramsci's texts on the left intelligentsia was mixed. Although the prison writings would have a wide-ranging influence, the practical terrain on which they received most attention was that of philosophy and criticism. Political theory and historiography came a close second. However, in all fields it was in the interpretation of the past rather than the present that Gramsci won out. As far as the arts were concerned, the influence of the notebooks was extremely limited, in part because his idea of the "national-popular" was in any event more an analytical construct rather than a prescriptive aesthetic formula but also because the neorealist wave of the postwar years was ebbing fast by the time a Gramscian critical presence took shape. The result was a frustrating detachment of the real movement of artistic creation from the critical discourse of the party that would only be overcome with the abandonment of this discourse over a decade later.[30]

A further problem with the reception of Gramsci was the manner in which his writings fueled the position of those who embraced national cultural traditions at the expense of an engagement with the modern intellectual and philosophical currents of the bourgeois industrial world. Although Gramsci himself was anything but provincial, his work in this sense confirmed the provincial dimension of the dominant strand of left-wing culture in Italy. It also confirmed the view of those traditional intellectuals close to Togliatti who tended to see culture in an elitist way and treated the question of popular culture with some disdain.[31] It was not the apparatuses of cultural production and distribution as mechanisms of consensus that interested them but the alignment of intellectuals and the nature of the message their paintings, books, or films imparted.

This problem was common to virtually all Communist intellectuals and to Italian culture generally but was particularly pronounced among the Togliattian component of the party. Not by chance was it the Zhdanovist Sereni, whose greater sensitivity to the mass dimension of political activity made him the first real cultural organizer in the PCI, who sought to establish cultural policy on a much broader basis than before. This is not to say that he articulated a strategy that could be termed hegemonic in terms of the institutions. If pressure was put on the state to increase provisions or to support national cultural production, it was done so with the aim of winning the sympathies of operatives in those sectors and demonstrating the active interest of the party in such problems rather than actually outlining an alternative vision of public policy. The thrust of the party's approach in this sense remained rigorously extra- and anti-institutional. What Sereni added was a grasp of the need for systematic coordination at all levels including that of popular culture. Ignored in the reconstruction period (with the exception of *Il Calendario del Popolo* and related endeavors), the struggle for the creation of a genuine popular culture was fixed as one of the key objectives of the Alliance of Culture, and consequently of the PCI, in 1948. After Sereni's removal, the structures and institutions developed in this field at base level continued to be embraced within the resolutions on cultural policy that were approved by the cultural commission. But they were often referred to hastily and briefly, almost as a footnote.

Left-Wing Popular Culture between Folklore and Hollywood

The cultural activities of the PCI in the cold war years had various aims. Although they were principally a means to forge new social alliances with the intellectuals and consequently with the middle classes, they were also mechanisms for the involvement of youth and for the creation of a new culture of the masses. Already well established as a political organization with a mass base, the PCI intended, by widening the cultural dimension of its presence in the community, to promote its ideas among the people and ultimately realize the cultural unification of the popular classes. Unity was to be achieved by mobilizing support for a common front of cultural struggle around the themes announced by the party leadership and by the extension of a plethora of grassroots initiatives.

Two criticisms have been advanced of the PCI's popular cultural activities during this period. The first is that the party separated initiatives aimed at intellectuals from those destined for wider audiences, with the result that the former remained trapped in a pedagogical relationship with the workers, agricultural laborers, and housewives who formed the base of the PCI. The second criticism regards the reduction of cultural battles to mere appendages of political practice.[32] Both of these objections are broadly true, and, as will be seen, they had an impoverishing effect on Communist popular culture as a whole. However, if the question is viewed from below, then further critical observations may be made. No examination of the cultural activities of the labor movement can ignore the fact that workers already belonged to a cultural sphere that was shaped by both popular traditions and the mass entertainments that spread first through urban Italy in the 1930s and 1940s and then to the rural world in the 1950s. The strengths and weaknesses of the party-related culture therefore also need to be assessed in terms of its success in absorbing or displacing these influences. In seeking to do this, attention must be paid to the extent to which ideological purity was diluted in the pursuit of popular support.

The formal origin of the party's involvement with popular culture can be dated from August 1949, when the cultural commission published a resolution titled "Against Imperialist and Clerical Obscurantism," which mentioned as a priority the need to "develop a great movement for popular culture" that was democratic and national and therefore opposed to the logic of American imperialism.[33] In practice this meant that a new culture was to be created based on the popular classes and on the heritage of their experiences of work and struggle. From being disparate, occasional initiatives, libraries, cultural courses, film clubs, art exhibitions, amateur theatricals, musical and sporting competitions were to become aspects of the party's presence in society.

Given the scarcity of studies of this phenomenon it is difficult if not impossible to furnish a detailed overall picture of its dimensions.[34] Structures at local level varied enormously in quantity and quality depending on the size of party membership in a given town or region, the strength of preexisting customs of autonomous cultural organization, and the resources and the political orientation of the local party federation. Thus in Emilia-Romagna and Tuscany the network of Case del popolo and popular cultural activities existing since the Liberation furnished a ready foundation that Communists in the South completely lacked. In his diary of the period 1946–51 Giacomo Calandrone wrote about his impressions of the Sicilian delegates to the national organization conference of the party when they arrived in Florence in January 1947:

> The city was cold, but how much human warmth in the Florentine comrades! With what attention they surround the delegates of the southern regions and with how much cordiality they welcome us in the sections and Case del popolo! We have visited several of them: spacious buildings, libraries, game rooms, little theaters, billiards, bars. We think, with a touch of bitterness, of our sections, often nothing more than a simple room almost always on the ground floor. When shall we too manage to build sections and Case del popolo so welcoming, where anyone can feel at ease?[35]

Despite the great deployment of human resources in the South between 1949 and 1950 in the struggles for the land, the party would never succeed in implanting a sociopolitical subculture of the type associated with central Italy. Instead of forming the premise of a permanent innovation, the great moment of solidarity and collective identification of those battles was but a transient episode that would leave precious few traces on the patterns of civil and social life. Yet in the larger centers of the South at least intellectuals could often be drawn into party political or cultural forums with greater ease than seemed to be the case in the Center and North. Given that this was indicated as a key objective of cultural policy at local level, the party federations often went to considerable lengths to court the intellectuals and interest them in Communist-sponsored "houses of culture" or film clubs. But in the strongholds of Emilia-Romagna the number of students, teachers, technicians, and professional people enrolled in the PCI was often very low. In Bologna, for example, the total was just 970 in 1948, and this figure fell in the years that followed. In Modena the figure increased from 204 to 236 between 1950 and 1954.[36]

In terms of the general articulation of the party in society, this problem was not sufficiently grave to impede the development of a full range of cultural activities destined for the masses. Despite the fact that left-wing local administrations were barred from spending local revenues on libraries or intervening in support of local cultural institutions, the PCI was able, using its own resources, to sponsor or direct initiatives in a range of fields. The fact that the state-controlled workers' recreational organization continued to exist was evidently a handicap, as were the company-based social clubs, but it is difficult not to feel admiration for the extraordinary efforts that went into the creation of a new cultural network in and around the left in the early 1950s. Two facets of this experience merit analysis here. The first concerns the campaign in favor of the wider distribution of books, and the second, the short-lived experiment of the Mass Theater.

In September 1950 the popular book center was founded at the instigation of Sereni, the Socialist organizer Rodolfo Morandi, and a number of leftist intellectuals. Its aim was to strengthen and complement the activities of Il Calendario del Popolo by conducting a permanent campaign against the state of ignorance and illiteracy in which a large section of the population was held. In keeping with a tradition of left-wing thinking that dated from the involvement of progressive French intellectuals in popular education at the time of the Dreyfus affair, it was assumed that

Between Hollywood and Moscow

there was a nexus between the consolidation of democracy and the diffusion of modern, rational values. Books in this sense were not sources of individual enrichment or, still less, amusing pastimes, but political instruments in the purest sense. By promoting the habit of reading serious novels and texts of political and economic analysis among ordinary people, new ideas would circulate more easily and a wider potential basis for the general discourses of the left would emerge.

In this perspective there was more than a measure of intellectual self-deception. But the level of activity was relatively impressive, and the results reached were by no means negligible. In her study of the situation in Modena, Catia Mazzeri shows how the popular book center continued to organize special events such as the "Book Month," "The Children's Book Week," "The Labor Movement Book Week," and the "Exhibition of Democratic Books" throughout the 1950s. From 1954 the launch of the "Battle for the Book" added further impetus to the campaign. The methods used were various and on occasion highly inventive. Stands were erected outside factories and in working-class residential areas as well as inside the festivals of the PCI, where admission to certain entertainments could be gained by purchasing a volume. Door-to-door visits by volunteers also took place, and campaign caravans toured the poor and backward mountain districts, widening awareness of the left-wing press and distributing booklets.[37]

Many of the books promoted were cheap editions produced purely for consumption by the left-wing base. Only with the creation of the PCI's own publishing house Editori Riuniti in the mid-1950s would party texts begin to circulate in the normal channels of the book trade. Before that, the utilitarian paperbacks of Edizioni Sociali, the editions of *Rinascita* and *L'Unità,* and the Universale Economica of *Il Calendario del Popolo* constituted a submarket oriented toward mainly party political ends. These were supplemented by the considerable Italian-language output of Soviet presses. At a higher level, Gramsci and the Marxist classics were published by Einaudi, which, along with other mainstream publishers close to the left, collaborated actively in the effort in the hope of widening the potential circle of readers for their lists.[38] Party officials and prominent intellectuals lent direct support by holding public lectures on themes of cultural or historical interest. A recurrent theme of the book campaign concerned the obstacles that were repeatedly placed in the way of the establishment of municipal libraries. The activities of prefects in annulling or postponing the approval of the statutes of libraries funded by communes confirmed the left in its view that the authorities were determined to impede the cultural emancipation of the lower classes. In 1954 the intense pressure brought to bear on the issue resulted in victory.[39]

The Mass Theater was a quite different phenomenon. It was perhaps the only completely organic product of the grassroots culture of the PCI, even though some have tended to view it as a Soviet import. Little has been written about it, and it seems to have been forgotten by most, yet for a brief period it was viewed as the harbinger of a new collective popular culture made directly by ordinary people and immediately reflective of their experiences of economic and political struggle.[40] As such it deserves examination.

Although there were significant signs of renewal in the Italian theater after the war, for the most part it remained a bourgeois phenomenon, one of the art forms least sensitive to the impulse of change that swept through society. The same static qualities reigned in amateur theatricals in which the repertoires even of groups close to the left remained traditional. Against this background the Mass Theater represented a striking novelty. Born of the efforts of young amateur actors performing in cellars and cinemas to find a collective mode of writing and producing plays, it found precursors in the Russian revolutionary theater and in the France of the Popular Front. The aim was to conduct propaganda through theater, to raise awareness of the problems facing ordinary people with plays that represented the conflicts that stemmed from daily life.

After an initial period of activity in Rome during the 1948 election campaign, Mass Theater became a more coherent and compact movement from 1949 under the influence of the director Marcello Sartarelli. A theater of the people aimed at the people, it focused on specific events represented by those who had personally participated in them. It was no longer actors who held the stage but peasants, workers, and partisans who illustrated their lives, their experience of labor, and their militancy for a better future.[41] Mass theater found a fertile terrain in Bologna and Modena, where the rich heritage of the Resistance, peasant struggles, and political battles of the present and recent past formed a ready source of material for its endeavors. But the phenomenon also spread much more widely, and at the first national convention of Mass Theater held in Forlì in December 1951 companies were represented from all over

Italy.[42] In the Theater of the Stable, moreover, the movement extended its influence into the countryside.[43]

The first representation of Mass Theater under the direction of Sartarelli took place in Modena in October 1949, significantly in the municipal theater of the city. Titled *Un Popolo in lotta* (A people in struggle), the show consisted of events from the war of Liberation. The most notable representations that followed, however, took place out-of-doors, in Bologna's Margherita Gardens or the sports stadium in Modena, where enormous crowds were able to watch the shows that were staged during the annual festivals of the Communist press. The numbers participating also expanded on these occasions. Probably the largest and most ambitious representation was *Domani è gioventù* (Tomorrow is youth) held in Modena in September 1950. A company of no fewer than five thousand workers, peasants, artisans, and students recounted in a sequence of choreographed scenes the history and life of the labor force of the province before an estimated audience of twenty thousand people.[44] Clearly, in these forms Mass Theater lost some of its original dynamism and flexibility. Shows could not easily be assembled collectively and certainly could not be revised day by day. The actors mimed scenes to which a single speaker supplied either commentary or dialogue. Sometimes dances and choruses interspersed the scenes while in others classical music provided the chosen accompaniment.

The object of continuous discussion in the left press, Mass Theater also attracted the enthusiastic interest of the Socialist anthropologist Ernesto De Martino. It formed, in his view, an example of the shift that took place after 1945 away from traditional picturesque folklore toward what he termed "progressive folklore," which gathered the songs, slogans, and rituals of the Resistance and the Liberation, the land and factory occupations, and strikes.[45] A folklore of protest had always existed, De Martino claimed, but in the present context it was undergoing rapid development and winning new attention as an important cultural fact. The task of anthropology and folklore studies in this phase was to aid the rise of new forms like Mass Theater by assisting the absorption within it of given local progressive traditions and forces. This would enrich it and enhance within it those features of a new general culture of the masses that rendered it so promising.[46]

These considerations belonged to a broader reflection on the theme of popular tradition and popular culture developed by De Martino in the late 1940s and early 1950s. It is worth looking at this briefly because it constituted the only general challenge to the most basic premises of Communist cultural policy to be advanced during this period.

In a long essay published in *Società* in 1949, De Martino argued that the ascent of the masses and their contact with, and transformation of, the world of culture would not provoke a qualitative renewal of culture itself, as the PCI seemed to believe. At first at least, the "bursting of the subaltern popular world onto the stage of history" would, on the contrary, produce an inevitable "barbarization" of culture consequent on the universalization of the cultural habits of the popular classes. For this reason it was necessary to distinguish the archaic from the progressive elements of popular culture, so that it would be possible to discriminate between the former and the latter in practical political action. The organic basis for a new culture of this nature lay, De Martino argued, in a vital, nationally founded synthesis of the historicist tradition with the anthropological problematic. In this scheme the function of politically organized intellectual work would not have been education, but rather the mediation of a complex process of cultural transformation not unlike that alluded to by Gramsci.[47]

In the subsequent debate, De Martino's suggestive theses were vigorously attacked by several Communist intellectuals. In a contribution that was more Leninist than Gramscian in style, Cesare Luporini proclaimed not only that his talk of "barbarization" reflected a bourgeois point of view but that the forms of popular culture he referred to (folklore, magic, etc.) could never be progressive and were vestiges of the past that should be completely transcended.[48] Like many conventionally trained intellectuals, Luporini viewed folklore as a degraded reflection of the dominant culture, a world of backwardness, superstition, and prejudice that blocked the emancipation of the proletariat. What was needed instead, he argued, was a greater effort by popular education to diffuse modern ideas more widely and give the masses the necessary instruments to master culture and become thinking subjects. Broadly speaking, this reflected the general party position on those forms of folk and dialect culture that had been manipulated and exalted in an antimodernist key by Fascism. By appropriating such expressions the regime had aimed to accentuate regional differences and limit the influence of emancipatory ideologies on the rural population. Therefore, where the PCI took over

Between Hollywood and Moscow

and absorbed local traditions and dialects after the war, it did so in a defensive way to prevent their renewed instrumentalization by conservative forces. At no point did it consider them part of a new culture of the working classes.

This difference of perspective was reflected in the adoption of radically divergent attitudes toward Mass Theater. Although it found support from party federations in the zones in which it was strongest, leading officials and intellectuals soon came to find it rhetorical, celebratory, and aesthetically very unsatisfactory. There is some evidence to suggest that local approval was not total either. At the end of an article praising the efforts of those involved in the production of *Si sveglia il Tagliaboschi* (The woodcutter awakes) at the *festa dell'Unità* in 1952 published in the newspaper of the Modena PCI, Tiziano Tamignini admitted that "the audience was a bit cold."[49] Others writing in successive issues complained openly that the performance had been heavy, monotonous, slow moving, and repetitive. For these and other reasons, the experience was brought to an end and Mass Theater was liquidated as an aspect of cultural policy when the phase of Soviet domination ended.[50]

Although the PCI never showed any intention of making De Martino's line its own, the latter had the considerable merit of offering for the first time a vision of what a cultural policy might look like that was posed from the point of view of the common people. Yet the "subaltern popular world" he referred to mainly embraced the rural masses of his native South and the peasant classes of the central regions. Insofar as it seemed to exclude the urban population of the North of Italy, it did not amount to a complete reflection of the popular condition. In common with Luporini and others like him who viewed culture in a conventional elitist light, De Martino ignored the very mass pastimes that from their initial impact in the large cities were rapidly coming to characterize mass leisure. Yet it was precisely with the popularity of these that the PCI most had to reckon in its attempts to shape the culture of ordinary people.

The cinema presented by far the most important terrain of cultural action during this period. The party did everything possible to mobilize public opinion in support of the national film industry, encouraging people to choose films other than those offered by the omnipresent Hollywood. Far from being merely a campaign of intellectuals, the battle for the defense of neorealism was also conducted at base level. As Carlo Lizzani wrote at the outset of the campaign, the key lay in "*reawakening the critical spirit of the popular masses,* directing their tastes and preferences." There was a need to "deepen our effort of orientation and criticism," he wrote, "in order to subtract as much as possible the masses from the noxious influence of a cinema shot through with vulgarity, banality, and gangsterism."[51] To this end a major effort was made to ensure that the particular merits of neorealist films were brought to the attention of workers and their families. When Vittorio De Sica personally attended the relaunch of *Ladri di biciclette* (Bicycle thieves) in major cities after a first, disappointing release, the party helped mobilize audiences for the occasion. In this way it helped spread an awareness that film was about more than escapism and entertainment. It could also be a vehicle of enlightenment and solidarity.

Some on the left expected a much more practical form of intervention from the PCI. Left-wing filmmakers like Giuseppe De Santis and Elio Petri later lamented bitterly the lack of any nationally coordinated attempt to set up an alternative production and distribution network.[52] The result, they felt, was that directors were simply left at the mercy of private producers and entrepreneurs. The isolated initiatives undertaken in this area were similarly denied concrete backing. Following the production by the partisans' association ANPI of *Giorni di gloria* (Days of glory), a compilation of partisan film material, the Cooperative of Productive Cinema Spectators financed two films, *Achtung! Banditi!* and *Cronache di poveri amanti* (Chronicles of poor lovers), but the limited success of the latter ensured that a third project was never realized and that the cooperative died.[53] The only films that the PCI fully financed and promoted were the documentaries produced for showing in workplaces and party sections. These included the crude and gloomy *14 luglio* (14 July), on the assassination attempt on the party leader that took place on that date, and the moving *Togliatti è ritornato* (The return of Togliatti), on the popular festival held in Rome in September 1948 to mark his recovery. Among the other party documentaries were two films by Lizzani dedicated to Modena, the first *Modena, città dell'Emilia rossa* (Modena, city of red Emilia), presenting an account of the commune's achievements, the second *I fatti di Modena* (The events of Modena), concerning the tragic events of January 1950, when six workers were shot dead by the police. A further film *Nel Mezzogiorno qualcosa è cambiato* (In the Mezzogiorno something has changed) dealt with the mobilization of the southern population in the late 1940s.[54] All these films signaled an attempt to compete in some minimal way with the official cinema newsreels, and activists often looked on them with pride as proof that the Communists were also capable of producing their own documentary material.

Mass Audiences and Communist Morality

The lack of concrete support given to ambitious alternatives in the field of the cinema revealed a certain timidity in the PCI's policies but also a wariness of being trapped in a ghetto. This was entirely understandable in the highly difficult circumstances in which the party found itself. But by refusing to intervene directly it deprived many of the very support they most needed in their struggle to keep alive the flame of progressive culture. According to Lizzani, there were also additional reasons why no more Communist documentaries were made after 1948–50 until the 1960s. Whereas Gianearlo Pajetta, the first head of the PCI's press and propaganda office, was an enthusiastic believer in the use of film, his successors showed much less interest in this means. Also, the young filmmakers who shot the documentaries passed, almost immediately afterward, to fiction films. Those who might have followed in their footsteps were neither trusted nor taken seriously because they lacked the authority and influence of those who had taken part in the Resistance.[55]

For the PCI, the party press was by far the most important weapon at its disposal. The role of the daily *L'Unità* and other large circulation publications was to speak to a wide audience and address everyday issues in terms that people would find thought-provoking and comprehensible. It was thought to be essential for the party press to compete with the bourgeois press for a mass readership. This role was carried even further in the "flanking" newspapers, such as *Paese sera* in Rome, which the PCI's "press baron," Amerigo Terenzi, was instrumental in establishing. Precisely this conception was put in question at a meeting of the Cominform in December 1950 at which *L'Unità* was subjected to a "violent and unconditional" attack.[56] The PCI was sharply criticized for producing a paper in which insufficient space was accorded to working-class struggles, to the achievements of the USSR, to Marxist-Leninist theory, and to ideological battles.

Inside the directorate, Sereni, Secchia, Arturo Colombi, Ruggiero Grieco, and Rita Montagnana supported these criticisms and called for

L'Unità to be remodeled as an Italian version of *Pravda*. The paper's senior editor, Pietro Ingrao, who had discussed the matter beforehand with Togliatti, largely rejected the criticism; Platone and Onofri joined him in insisting that the party daily had to maintain its popular character.[57] Although some nods were made in the direction of rigor, a resolution of the directorate was published in which the status of *L'Unità* as "a popular and mass circulation newspaper" was confirmed.[58] This meant that the party organ could continue to act as a tool for shaping the views of a wide readership. Yet it should not be imagined, therefore, that relations were always easy between professional politicians and the party journalists who practically forged the PCI press. Even close collaborators of Togliatti, and the party leader himself, expressed dissatisfaction quite frequently with the insufficient political preparation of the mostly bourgeois men, sometimes former Fascists, who comprised the Communist press corps.[59] There were also objections to the amount of space given over to lightweight subjects, crime reports, and the serialization of the equivalent of penny dreadfuls ("Okay, they are awful but they are good for sales" was Platone's realistic comment).[60]

The question of sport was not an easy one for the left. Old prejudices against physical exercise mixed with a deep suspicion of both organized sporting activities and spectator sports in general. The rapid development of the latter under Fascism confirmed the judgment that they were principally a means to generate consensus by shifting attention away from pressing problems.[61] This led the left to neglect the issue in the immediate postwar years. *L'Unità*'s sports coverage was often attacked in the directorate as excessive. But with the continuing existence of the state organism the Italian National Olympic Committee (CONI), and the evident attraction of the sport facilities of the Catholic *oratori,* action eventually became necessary. Under the auspices of UISP, the Italian Union of Popular Sport, which became an autonomous association in 1948 following the dissolution of its parent body, the Fronte della Gioventù, two lines of action were developed. The first was one of sharp criticism of government policy on sport. This was seen as being elitist, overly concerned with the production of champions, and subordinate to the commercial interests of the big societies that dominated the most popular sports: cycling and football. The second was more practical in orientation. Although its membership was highly concentrated in Emilia-Romagna and Tuscany, UISP offered one of the few means whereby workers and peasants, both male and female, could practice such sports as track and field, swimming, and gymnastics. With few state or municipal structures available or exploited effectively, it filled an important gap that enhanced the presence of the left.[62]

In the PCI's drive to extend its influence as widely as possible among the lower classes, the festivals of the Communist press played an important role. From very humble beginnings the festivals gradually came to be a popular institution on a grand scale, the most long-lasting and deeply rooted manifestation of the PCI in popular culture. After the first successful experiments at Mariano Comense and Tradate Comasco in 1946, the *feste* multiplied, and September became the traditional month of the Communist press.[63] In cities large and small in which the PCI could count on a solid base of support, considerable efforts were made to associate the campaign to increase sales of party publications with relaxation and diversion. In the early years the political element remained paramount, but alongside the speeches, the propaganda material, and the papers, the party acknowledged the importance of sport competitions, popular music, dancing, and theater. Although some traditionalists were sharply critical of the widespread use of dances and games and of the weight that seemed to be accorded to purely money-making activities, there is no evidence of any attempts to suppress or limit these on the part of Pajetta, the principal inventor of the festivals, or other members of the leadership.[64] By 1949 some seven hundred festivals of varying sizes were taking place mostly in the countryside on the periphery of the large cities. They were important moments of solidarity, when the Communists and party sympathizers came together to learn, forge new bonds, and reaffirm their commitment despite the hostility of other sectors of the population and legal obstacles.

Communist leaders were themselves surprised by how the festivals seemed to attract the most varied manifestations of popular tradition. "The regions, the communes, and the quarters have brought to the *festa* their traditions, with an enthusiasm, a fantasy, and a passion that we ourselves did not suspect," Pietro Ingrao wrote in 1948. "Through the *feste dell'Unità* the party has established new links with the masses, it has better approached the sentiments and traditions of our country."[65] The most remarkable document of this development is the documentary *Togliatti è ritornato,* which offers a unique portrait of the PCI as a receptacle of the customs and folklore of the Italian regions. Beneath the closed shutters of the capital's immense grey buildings, the factory workers of the North, the agricultural laborers of the South, local bands and dancers, decorated allegorical floats, girls in regional costume, and squads of cyclists filed in a procession that stood as a tribute not only to Togliatti, who, according to Carlo Felice Casula, was consecrated as a "red Pope" in the film, but also to the party itself.[66]

Yet the impression generated by the film of this event and other accounts of the richness and variety of an ostensibly marginalized Communist subculture should not lead to the conclusion that the PCI constituted in any sense a closed world. Both Giuseppe Carlo Marino and Marc Lazar have perpetuated this long-held but erroneous view. Despite the isolation of the party in society and the inward-looking character of some of its rituals and procedures, members and sympathizers lived in the wider society, and their culture was by no means wholly determined by the PCI. Urban life as a whole in the 1940s and 1950s was shaped by mass commercial entertainments, and Communists and their families were in no sense insulated from them. The inquiries conducted by Lucio Lombardo Radice in the immediate postwar years (see chapter 1) revealed that this was widespread, and there is every indication that it continued to be so in successive years. In one detailed account of the reading matter of young people in a working-class quarter of Turin in which no fewer than 17 percent of all youth were enrolled in the Italian Communist Youth Federation (FGCI), the most popular publications by far were *Intrepido, Grand Hôtel, Annabella,* and *Calcio illustrato.* Compared to the two hundred copies of *Intrepido* bought each week, the FGCI publication *Avanguardia* sold sixty-six copies and *Noi Donne* twenty.[67]

Much the same situation applied to cinema. Although every effort was made to highlight the merits of progressive Italian and foreign films and illustrate the dangers of Hollywood, the films of the latter continued to exercise a great fascination for many who identified politically with the left. When, in 1954, Giuseppe Turroni went in pursuit of the filmgoing public for the magazine *Rassegna del film* he met a twenty-three-year-old student, enrolled in the PCI, who admitted preferring westerns and adventure films to Visconti's *La terra trema* (The earth trembles), which was "too intellectual and difficult." Another Communist also confessed to finding "complicated" films empty and sterile. Much preferred were American adventure films that "even if unlikely, do no harm."[68] For some, the love affair with Hollywood dated back to the prewar years; for others it was a more recent passion that the pressures of the cold war did almost nothing to extinguish.

Although such tastes and pursuits were to be deplored ideologically and indeed ran counter to official Communist morality, the PCI was compelled to recognize them practically if it was not to lose an opportunity to win mass sympathy. In this sense there was a marked contrast between the extreme severity with which Communist film directors who were perceived to flirt with the styles and techniques of American cinema were treated and the indulgence shown toward popular tastes. Even though his films were among the very few neorealist titles to win favor at the box office, the director of *Riso amaro* (Bitter rice), Giuseppe De Santis, was subjected to continual sniping from critics suspicious of the way he presented an image of popular culture that combined democratic, collective impulses with new fashions, sounds, and tastes associated with America and the mass media.[69] This was denounced as inaccurate and defeatist at a time when the purity and integrity of popular culture was an article of faith for the left.[70]

Yet in reality Communist grassroots culture was always highly permeable. In the postwar years one of the great attractions of the Case del popolo and party recreations was the Saturday evening dance. Inevitably, the music was not only traditional but included the new themes and rhythms of American origin that triumphed during the Liberation. At the local level the Communists also latched on very quickly to the taste for cinema, more quickly than to that for sport. From the end of the war it was customary for a *stellina dell'Unità* (*L'Unità* starlet) to be elected at festivals of the Communist press. Sometimes moral and political qualities were taken into account, but more frequently the winner was simply the girl who, in the words of the regulations submitted to the PCI directorate in June 1950, was judged to be "the most beautiful and the most suited to film work."[71] Throughout the 1950s the beauty contests organized by *Vie Nuove* constituted a striking example of how the rituals and aspirations engendered by Hollywood were absorbed by the Communist subculture. Although the annual competition never displaced the national Miss Italia pageant from its central position in popular culture, Miss *Vie Nuove* became a major event that aroused great interest and enthusiasm in Italian cities and provinces, not least because of the material prizes and the promise that the winner would receive a screen test. At the annual final in Rome, the girls appeared wearing not bathing costumes but evening gowns. They paraded before juries that included film directors such as Alessandro Blasetti, De Sica, Visconti, and Alberto Lattuada; the actors Yves Montand and Simone Signoret; and the writers Alberto Moravia and Elsa Morante.

For some, the competition served to attract young people to the party at a difficult time; for others it provided yet another way of involving the intellectuals. For yet others it was a means whereby the party could contribute to the formation of a national pool of actresses who would be different in attitude and looks from the American stars. "A healthy and robust girl of the people of typical Italian appearance" was to be chosen, not "an American-type cover girl," the film critic Ugo Casiraghi announced in a speech inaugurating the Milan heat of the first Miss *Vie Nuove* competition.[72] Yet it was extremely difficult to wage an aesthetic campaign of this sort. Even though the contestants virtually all came from Communist family backgrounds, their dreams had been influenced by cinema, and the organizers of the competition openly played on this. Moreover, on the page of the magazine devoted to news of local heats and festivals, an advertisement regularly appeared for a line of cosmetics named "Velluto di Hollywood" (Hollywood velvet).

The problem for the PCI was that it sought to construct a culture of its own at precisely the moment when the mass media developed under Fascism came to have a crucial role in the cultural life of the nation as a whole. Indeed, under the DC, the new texture of mass culture quickly came to fill the place of the long-absent national culture. In order not to be isolated completely the party was bound to compete with and react to this new cultural system. To do this effectively it had to partially absorb the values and orientations of a culture industry marked by a propensity for confirming either the specific social and political choices of the DC or Italy's close alliance with America.

To conclude, the case of *Vie Nuove* can be considered in light of these observations. Born as a "weekly of guidance and political struggle" in 1946, the magazine was compelled from a relatively early date to give ample coverage to leisure activities and sport to compete with commercial publications. By 1948 it had become less like *Rinascita* and more like the long-standing commercial weekly *La Domenica del Corriere*. Much space was dedicated to Hollywood cinema, which the magazine never rejected en bloc. Rather, it sought to distinguish between good and bad, recommending those stars and films that in some way seemed progressive or critical of the dominant ethic in American society. With its cover girls and garish advertisements it pursued what Concetto Marchesi, in his speech to the eighth PCI congress in 1956, called "la politica del sorriso" (a policy of cheerfulness).[73] Although Longo, the magazine's rather detached editor in chief, defended it from criticism within the leadership, there were many who grumbled about its heterodox approach. The minutes of the directorate meeting of 19 January 1949 record Togliatti's comments on *Vie Nuove* as follows: "First of all, widen the margins of the pages. As regards content: be more careful of the danger of producing a mishmash (*polpettone*) of indifferent quality. Sometimes there has been low-grade material, too much haste and confusion." Similar observations were made publicly by Antonello Trombadori. In 1949 he wrote to *Vie Nuove* complaining of the magazine'e excessive number of advertisements and its sympathetic presentation of American films. In his reply, the magazine's deputy editor Michele Pellicani argued that it was too simple to adopt the position of the "conscientious objector": "As Marxists we combat capitalist society but — as long as this is the society in which we live — we cannot ignore its laws and its customs and certain needs that flow from it. We cannot put ourselves outside reality. . . . Can we ignore the fact that workers drink *Zeta-Zeta* or that ninety out of every hundred films shown in Italy are American?"[74]

Further objections to the magazine's initiatives were registered in successive months, but these did not prevent its progressive evolution into an illustrated weekly very similar in style to *Epoca* or *L'Europeo*. With the adoption of full-color printing in April 1952, *Vie Nuove* dropped its original subtitle and became, like related publications, a "weekly of politics, current events, and culture." Party political content was reduced to a minimum while family and leisure interests were extended. In terms of sales these changes brought notable dividends. The print run stood at 258,000 in February 1952; but by autumn 1954 Longo was urging efforts to put it over the 400,000 mark.[75] The only real distinguishing feature was the attention the magazine continued to devote to the USSR and Eastern Europe.[76] Otherwise, it mainly presented a perfectly neutral mixture of attractively presented feature articles, human-interest stories, inquiries into social issues, sport, and news from the film world. The front cover occasionally featured Togliatti or other Communist leaders, but by the mid-1950s it was much more common to find film stars such as Gina Lollobrigida, Marisa Allasio, Totò, Amedeo Nazzari, or even Marilyn

Monroe. Inside, the advertisements for beauty products that had begun to appear in the late 1940s increased in number and regularity.

In this way the PCI won a proxy presence in the cultural model in formation. But at the same time the very model the party rejected and denigrated in cultural policy won recognition and institutionalization in a publication that was one of the most widely read by the party's rank-and-file supporters. This meant that it proved very difficult indeed for the party to resist the appeal of television and consumerism as they became dynamic elements in a broad process of social and cultural reorganization in the second half of the 1950s.

Volunteer labor is harnessed to build a sports field. (From the archives of the Istituto milanese per la storia della Resistenza e del movimento operaio.)

Donald Duck is enlisted in a fund-raising drive for the Communist press. (From the archives of the Istituto milanese per la storia della Resistenza e del movimento operaio.)

Traveling library sponsored by the PCI. (From the archives of the Istituto milanese per la storia della Resistenza e del movimento operaio.)

Intellectuals meet the people: artists draw the rice weeders. (From the archives of the Istituto milanese per la storia della Resistenza e del movimento operaio.)

Pro-Soviet floats at a Communist parade. (From the archives of the Istituto milanese per la storia della Resistenza e del movimento operaio.)

A contestant in the Miss *Vie Nuove* competition holds up a copy of the magazine. (From the archives of the Istituto milanese per la storia della Resistenza e del movimento operaio.)

The workers' proposal for a popular automobile. (From *Vie Nuove,* 4 May 1952, 20.)

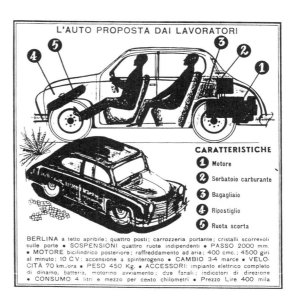

Mourners sign a book of condolences following Stalin's death. (From the archives of the Istituto milanese per la storia della Resistenza e del movimento operaio.)

3

What's Good for Fiat Is Good for Italy

Television, Consumerism, and Party Identity

in the 1950s

In different ways and in different spheres the developments of the period between 1954 and 1962 made a contribution to shaping the face of contemporary Italy equally important as the ten years that preceded it. If the political and cultural contours of the reconstruction were fixed in the postwar years, the successive decade witnessed a profound transformation in the pattern of economic and social life underlying it. From the poverty and simplicity in which the most common means of transport was the bicycle, and a decent pair of shoes a relative luxury, the country moved to a situation in which television and the motorcar were normal features of everyday life. Customs, attitudes, and a way of life expressing the distilled experience of deeply rooted traditions dissolved and made way for the triumph of new outlooks, aspirations, and totems. The scale and scope of change were such that many people who lived through it did not hesitate to describe the process in millenarian terms. The film director Vittorio De Seta, for example, likened it to a bomb. "Certainly something tremendous happened," he said. "We are all afraid of the atomic bomb, but that only *could* go off. This has *already exploded*."[1]

The ubiquity of American images and references in the Italy of the boom years highlighted the far-reaching nature of change. The rapid process of concentrated industrialization in a country that lacked a genuine secular culture common to all created an enormous cultural gap that only ideas, themes, products, and norms of an American origin seemed able to fill. In this sense the yearning for America so evident in the Italy of the 1950s and early 1960s was an expression of both a real shift in attitudes and expectations and the decline of previously accepted norms and relationships.[2] But Americanization was also an externally directed process; in the eyes of the Americans and the most forward-looking industrial and financial elites, the arrival in Europe of Fordism and mass consumption was part of a long-range design to eliminate social discontent and political instability as well as create new markets for American goods. By diffusing prosperity more widely, Americanization would erode the bases of left-wing support and form the conditions for the construction of a much broader pattern of social consensus than had been possible in the postwar years.

The PCI emerged from a decade of rapid change as a relatively compact and powerful force. Electorally, it even grew over the period from 22.7 percent in 1953 to 25.3 percent in 1963. Yet in virtually every other way the party ceded ground. The end of the "Stalin myth" and the Soviet invasion of Hungary in 1956 profoundly shook the faith of many militants and intellectuals. The cultural vision held out by the party ceased to constitute such a potent rallying point for artists and writers. In addition, demographic changes, the altered nature of the labor force, the new values of the consumer society, and television all undermined political allegiances and established patterns of social solidarity. In consequence, membership fell, the level of activism declined, and left-wing recreational institutions began to decay. Combined with the breakup of the long-standing alliance with the Socialist Party, and the cooptation of the latter into a political design that had as one of its objectives the marginalization and defeat of the PCI, these factors fueled fears that the party's capacity to conserve its influence might be in doubt.

As a whole, it may be said that the PCI moved quite forcefully to change, more so than left-wing and Communist parties in some other European countries. But it was unable to grasp fully the implications of the transformation or go beyond a limited evolution for many years. One chief reason for this lay in the party's rigid vision of Italian capitalism's possibilities for development. This constituted a block to a correct appreciation of the social and cultural changes that were inscribed within the process of expansion. In consequence, reactions to novelty were for a long time unsystematic, provoked by defeat or governed by prejudicial hostility. Where they occurred, innovations in Communist practices were most usually occasioned by the more or less intuitive insights of leading party figures or else they were the fruit of ad hoc responses in particular spheres.

Economic Development and Cultural Change

In the 1940s, both Christian Democrats and Communists envisaged that Italy would long remain a predominantly agricultural country endowed with a few major industrial centers. As Giorgio Galli noted, the world-view of both parties tended to confirm this outlook, with the DC attached to a universalistic vision of the rural world and the PCI to an image of Italy made wretched and colonized by American imperialism.[3] Few indeed were those who could have predicted the transformation that was to take place in the space of just a few years. In 1949–50 salaries were still generally lower than in the rest of Europe and unemployment higher. Agitation on the land and in the factories was widespread. Yet something was beginning to change. In 1949 bread rationing was abolished, and, by the early 1950s, the foundations were being laid for long-term development in both public and private industry. The premises also existed for the spread of private transport with the arrival on the market of the Vespa motor scooter, expanding motorcar production, and, in 1953, the decision to invest in a gigantic production line at Fiat for the new 600cc model, which was to become the first truly popular car in Italian history.[4]

A further innovation was the advent of television broadcasting in 1954. Set up under a twenty-year concession from the state holding company IRI, RAI-TV was subjected in its early years to quite close moral and political control, but this did not impede its success. Thanks to a set of able choices in programming and presentation emphasizing middle-brow culture and family entertainment, Italian television quickly won a reputation for authority and familiarity on a par with the BBC's "Auntie" image ("Mamma RAI"). Perhaps because many of the executives directly concerned with program making had been with RAI since the Fascist period — when they had acquired a feel for popular tastes — sports events, variety, musical entertainment, plays, and quiz shows became broadcasting's staple diet. In its total lack of complexity or criticism, this output conformed perfectly to the dominant ethic of Christian Democratic Italy. No alternative points of view were presented, political discussion was absent, and improvisation was kept at arm's length. In marked contast to some other broadcasting systems, no attempt was made to analyze the problems of society or of its institutions. Difficult subjects were avoided and a generally conformist, conventional image of social relationships presented. In this sense the process of depoliticization, which proved so difficult if not impossible to achieve completely in the cinema, succeeded perfectly in the new medium.

The impact of television was nonetheless far-reaching. It played a dynamic role in completing the linguistic unification of the country, a process already assisted by cinema, radio, and the popular press. Television succeeded in this respect where the school system had failed because it was reasonably immediate in its appeal and because it offered attractive new models of behavior as well as opportunities for shared experience.[5] For this reason, some intellectuals attributed to it a cultural significance equivalent only to that of the *Divine Comedy*. For others, by contrast, including Pier Paolo Pasolini, it signaled the sad eclipse of an autonomous popular world identified with a myriad of local dialects and traditions.

Although the introduction of an ostensibly classless visual culture clearly followed the American pattern, Italian television differed from the American model of broadcasting in many ways. Although Sergio Pugliese, one of the earliest administrators of RAI-TV, undertook a journey to the United States to study its TV broadcasts, and the inspiration behind several early programs was clearly American, the actual output betrayed the influence of different sources. Italian radio, theater, variety, and the popular taste for light music all represented important reference points. Even the quiz shows, which in many respects were completely unrelated to domestic show business traditions, bore some resemblance to the question-and-answer games already popular on the radio.

This point can perhaps best be illustrated with reference to *Lascia o Raddoppia?* (Double or quits?), a program whose enormous popular following contributed decisively to the success of Italian television. The local equivalent of the American *$64,000 Question,* it introduced cash prizes for the first time, awarded to contestants able to respond correctly to questions on a topic of their choosing on a rising scale of difficulty. Presented by an Italian American previously known only to the radio audience of Voice of America, Mike Bongiorno, whose extreme ordinariness and conformism would be subjected to withering analysis by

Umberto Eco in a celebrated essay, the program has been considered a paradigm of development in which everyone could theoretically reach the grand prize.[6] Yet, although it represented something striking and new, any feeling that *Lascia o Raddoppia?* was in some way alien was largely buried by the personalities of the competitors themselves, the characters the program introduced, and the real-life enthusiasms and frustrations that gave it a dimension all its own.

The rapidity with which television was introduced maximized its impact in changing habits and perceptions of the world. The collective element in its first reception reinforced and magnified this aspect rather than undermining it. Despite all the efforts to dovetail television to the dominant value system, its consequences were far greater than even the most perceptive of Catholic observers could ever have imagined. Furthermore, visual broadcasting inescapably reflected and contributed to the emergence of a consumer society whose values and behavioral models were in the long run to prove very difficult to reconcile within the Catholic social model.

Even more than Italian cinema as it became an industry and developed a star system of its own to rival the American one, television communicated urban values and norms to regions of the country and sectors of the population that had previously had little contact with industrial civilization. In villages and towns far removed from the large cities of the North, Italians gathered in bars and recreational centers to catch a glimpse of the new medium. Contemporary observers noted that, because there was no entry ticket to be purchased, television instantly acquired a more inclusive audience that extended even to the old and the very poor.[7]

What fascinated people who had previously only dimly perceived the possibility of a different, more prosperous way of living were the clothes, scooters and cars, modern kitchens, and comfortable homes that appeared on-screen. These could be seen in programs of all types, but advertising played a specific role in sustaining the general transition by persuading, cajoling, and suggesting that people make use of certain products in their lives and in their homes. In particular, it was television advertising more than any other single factor that introduced people who stood outside the mainstream of prosperity into the new way of things. Advertisements were not to be transmitted during regular breaks in programs; rather, they were grouped together into short programs of their own as if to place a sort of cordon sanitaire around them. *Carosello,* the best known of these containers, was broadcast from 3 February 1957 in a slot following the mid-evening news.

To sell these products, advertisers were compelled to invent and entertain the audience with little stories, comic sketches, or cartoons. In this way *Carosello* helped translate the consumer consciousness into a homely, familar setting that could easily be recognized and identified with. In her study of peasants and television, Lidia De Rita found that a great deal of importance was attributed to "knowing" different products, their names, and the slogans and images associated with them.[8] The same phenomenon was also widespread among children, who quickly forced parents to adjust to sending them to bed "after *Carosello*." The success of this container program complete with its own signature tune was such that by 1960 it had become the most popular of all television shows.[9]

Television fueled the aspirations for a better life that led so many Italians from the South and the provinces to move to large cities and especially to the North. As factories expanded and the prospect of a life away from the rigors of working the land became a concrete possibility, a huge internal migration took place. Between 1958 and 1963 around one million southerners changed their places of residence to other regions of Italy.[10]

Between the mid-1950s and the end of the economic boom in 1962, a vast process of cultural change took place. Old values of sacrifice and resignation were displaced by material aspirations and the dream of the good life. Mobility, both physical and social, came to be seen as highly desirable, a fact that was reflected in an enormous increase in private transport. Between 1950 and 1964 the number of motorcycles and scooters rose from 700,000 to 4.3 million.[11] Many of these were Vespas and Lambrettas, cheap but stylish scooters that appealed to the young. For families, the greatest aspiration was to own a motorcar. Films were filled with open-top sports cars and luxury sedans, but, more than anything else, the economical vehicles produced by Fiat marked the arrival of a new way of life to the lower middle classes and to workers. Although the Fiat 600 was comparatively inexpensive at 622,000 lire, this was still a considerable sum for a Fiat worker whose salary stood at 50,000 lire per month or for a white-collar worker earning up to 100,000 lire.[12] Nonetheless, the number of private cars rose from 342,000 to 4.67 million.

Bound up with economic development were changes in social organization. The breakup of established patterns of community life and social solidarity formed a key precondition of the successful socialization of the masses into a new consumer-oriented culture.[13] With the detachment from old habits in work and private life and the uprooting and physical displacement of populations, a new type of social order could take shape in which the family tended to become nuclear, and more emphasis was placed on the home as a distinctly "private" sphere. For those who had lived in close proximity to many others in cramped conditions, the new situations possessed obvious advantages. But, as Alessandro Pizzorno found in the Lombard community he studied in the late 1950s, the escape from suffocation by relatives and neighbors also had a negative side. As the old networks of mutual support and collective living slipped away, families closed in on themselves, and individuals became isolated.[14] This phenomenon was particularly marked among the new middle classes who left city center dwellings for suburban houses and bungalows. But for women a wide range of potential new roles emerged. Even running a home involved new relationships with the mass media and the market. Urban society posed dangers, but it also offered a measure of freedom and, to young women, new opportunities for self-affirmation.

Domestic cultural patterns were so abruptly shaken at this time that the only provider of new models during the period of transformation seemed to be the United States. In the redefinition of habits and lifestyles, American inputs, suggestions, and examples played a decisive shaping role at the same time as the United States represented the ideal society on which a changing Italy aspired to model itself. Although the export of Italian goods to Europe contributed vitally to the economic boom, new products were usually advertised in Italy with reference to specifically American values. Images associated with the United States were the most frequently employed in expanding the market for a given product or, as was more common, in persuading people to buy a product for which no conscious previous need existed.

Intellectuals were not slow to condemn the emergence of what they saw as an American-style mass society. Alberto Moravia attacked the advent of what he saw as a dreadful and vulgar "sotto-Italia" that fed off mass entertainments and collective passions, and Roberto Rossellini likened watching television to chewing gum. The journalist Giorgio Bocca warned that massification would soon lead to "a single Italy of motorcars, advertising, and Coca-Cola."[15] Writers and, above all, film directors consistently and forcefully gave voice to doubts about the transformation the country was undergoing. Although films like *La Dolce Vita*, Fellini's reflection on the moral core of prosperity and the bittersweet myths of a society in transition, and Visconti's powerful melodrama of migration *Rocco e i suoi fratelli* (Rocco and his brothers), both released in 1960, conveyed something of the excitement and freedom the boom brought, they primarily suggested that something more valuable was being lost.

The disorientation of the intelligentsia is understandable. There was much in the boom that was disconcerting and unfamiliar. Moreover, the intellectuals no longer seemed to count for quite as much as they had previously. In the construction of consensus the mass media and the market itself were definitively usurping their role. But this discontentment merely confirmed that an irreversible change had taken place in Italian life and culture.

1956 and Beyond

It would not be an exaggeration to say that all the major political parties were disorientated by the speed and scale of development. Growth was not planned or balanced; rather, it occurred in a spontaneous way that exacerbated existing geographical disparities. Neither at the central nor the local level were the government parties able to meet the extraordinary demands for services, particularly in the areas of housing, health, and other public infrastructures, to which migration gave rise. Although there were many in the Catholic world who regarded change and the process of secularization that appeared to accompany it with alarm, the Christian Democrats were at least able to claim that they were the main promoters and arbiters of prosperity.

The position of the Communists was naturally very different. As would later amply be recognized, the attitude of the PCI toward economic change was marked by an excessively pessimistic view of the possibilities of development. Monopoly capitalism was equated not with dynamism but rather with stagnation and crisis, grinding poverty, and mass repression. Convinced that the bourgeoisie was incapable of setting itself national objectives, the party continued throughout the 1950s to refer to an alternative ideal of development that rested on agrarian reform and

Between Hollywood and Moscow

raised production, unaware that the difficulties experienced by industry at the start of the decade were not a permanent condition but the prelude to a strategy of growth designed to legitimate Italian business directly in society. In the early 1950s, both the PCI and the left-wing trade union confederation, the CGIL, engaged in the sort of large-scale, generic mobilizations designed to unify the working class at the national level that had perhaps been appropriate in the 1940s, but which now bypassed many of the important issues of concern to the most advanced categories of workers. At a time when Italian industry was undergoing the difficult period of restructuring that preceded growth, labor movement activists went to considerable lengths to formulate proposals for increasing production that were put forward at special conferences such as those held by the Metal Workers' Union (FIOM) at Fiat plants in 1951. In this way the PCI believed it was acting hegemonically, involving workers in exploring routes to expansion that it thought Italian industry, concerned principally with the cultivation of foreign markets, was incapable of thinking up. At the union's economic conference in Turin in early 1952, not only was a sectoral plan proposed, but a very precise project was outlined for the development of a popular small car (*vetturetta*) that could be marketed to the middle classes. The idea was based on an analysis of existing products and shaped by the conviction that a lower-priced vehicle could raise domestic demand and stimulate employment. To bring it to wider public attention, a full-size model was assembled by specialized workers and project designers close to the PCI and put on display at the provincial *festa dell'Unità* in Turin in September 1952. Yet bold though the initiative was, it was not a success. So numerous were the similarities between the left's vehicle and the drawing-board Fiat 600 that the company greeted the public unveiling of the model with a denunciation for the theft and circulation of secret documents.[16]

The PCI's difficulties were greatly exacerbated by the crises of the Communist world. Stalin's death in 1953 represented a moment of great importance in the postwar history of Italian Communism. Photographs and documentary film of the ceremonies of mourning conserve something of the great emotion encountered by Paolo Spriano when he took the first copies of *L'Unità* to the Fiat factory gates at dawn on 6 March 1953.[17] As Davide Lajolo confirms, it was not just Stalin the head of the USSR who had died, but the leader of workers and of the oppressed throughout the world, and the mourning touched every house.[18] Given this response, it is quite understandable that the revelation first of the existence and then of the contents of Nikita Khrushchev's "secret speech" to the twentieth congress of the Soviet Communist Party (CPSU) should have provoked shock and bewilderment.[19] These feelings deepened in autumn 1956 as events in Eastern Europe culminated in the Hungarian crisis. Although there were some disagreements in the directorate, the leadership maintained a firm line throughout this period, but as Togliatti and other party leaders rushed to condemn the revolts and justify the Soviet intervention in Hungary, some Communists saw the repression as an intolerable violation of popular will and national sovereignty.

Among the intellectuals, the events of 1956 had a traumatic effect. In Rome, above all, there was a virtually continuous state of friction between university-based intellectuals and the party leadership that began in March in the immediate aftermath of the CPSU's twentieth congress and culminated with the response to the Soviet invasion of Hungary in October. The picture that has sometimes been given of a "liberal" Communist intelligentsia counterposed to a basically Stalinist party hierarchy is not, however, accurate. Just as factory workers were divided in their attitudes toward de-Stalinization and Hungary, so too were the intellectuals. Dissident and revisionist voices have been accorded pride of place in the historiography of 1956, but a significant number of the party's best minds and a good percentage of its educated membership in the country adopted more or less openly Stalinist views.[20]

The first indication that some intellectuals were dissatisfied with the way the question of de-Stalinization was being posed within the Communist movement came in spring 1956, when first the Communist student circle in Rome University and then the academic staff cell criticized *L'Unità*'s coverage of the twentieth congress and called for a wide-ranging debate on the political and ideological implications of the Soviet new course. At the meeting of the cultural commission in July 1956 and in the numerous contributions to the wide-ranging debate on the state of left-wing culture in Italy opened by *Il Contemporaneo,* fundamental objections were raised that were directed not merely against the supporters of Zhdanov but also against the more nationally oriented cultural policy that had been followed from 1952. The PCI was seen as being trapped between Stalinism and a sort of aristocratic provincialism, and its spokesmen were berated for having failed to respond adequately to new needs and to structural changes in society.[21] The writer Italo Calvino articulated this viewpoint most powerfully. In a long speech to the commission he called for much greater attention to be paid to developments in the North of the country where monopoly capitalism was forging new tools to widen the basis of consent in Italian society. It was not enough merely to discuss or to hold occasional conferences such as that for Communist intellectuals within the "industrial triangle" in June 1955, he argued; what was needed was a fundamental reorientation of policy so as to improve the left's knowledge of developments in industry and society and carry its cultural action on to a new, more modern terrain. Only if the party was infused with a "fever of research" designed to put it in touch with a situation in rapid flux could Communists hope to challenge industry and match the intelligence that the latter was accumulating in its own research departments and house magazines.[22] Similar points were made in print by the economist Luciano Barca and the neopositivist philosopher Ludovico Geymonat, both of whom were party members, and by non-Communists such as Norberto Bobbio and Alessandro Pizzorno. As these men saw it, the PCI's emphasis on humanistic culture to the disadvantage of the scientific and the technical, and its reverence for the tradition of Italian Idealism, was impeding an adequate appreciation of the great changes occurring in the factories, in class structure, in ideology, and in the family.[23] Instead of grappling with the new ideas that had been imported and trying to understand how they might be used to analyze the transformation taking place in the structures of the country, left-wing intellectuals, still ensnared within Idealism, had, as Pizzorno bluntly put it, preferred to "study Neapolitan Hegelianism or that of Piedigrotta, Engels' letters to Mr. So-and-So or the minor enlightenment thinkers of Canicattì."[24]

Above all, it was the slavish pro-Sovietism and bureaucratic management of cultural policy that was denounced. Communist and left-wing film critics railed against arid debates and dogmatic positions, the confusion of propaganda with culture, and the transformation of tenets of neorealism into a stale cultural orthodoxy. Led by Paolo Gobetti, critic on the Piedmont edition of *L'Unità*, many deeply regretted the uncritical praise they had showered on Stalinist epics like *The Oath* and *The Fall of Berlin*, which had been passionately recommended to party activists and workers on account of their positive vision of the Soviet Union and stirring themes.[25] Instead of an aesthetic policy being elaborated creatively and collectively, he argued, a cultural line formulated by a small elite had been imposed bureaucratically from above. In consequence, a growing gap had emerged between the sections and the factories on the one hand and critics on the other, and much energy had been used up in campaigns doomed to failure from the start.[26] In defense of the PCI's record, Mario Alicata, who took over as party cultural chief in 1955, conceded that there was a need to recast cultural policy on the basis of a more realistic analysis of state institutions and move toward a less directive approach. In his view, however, it was quite wrong to conflate the errors of the Soviet Union with those of the PCI. Not only had the party never practiced coercion, he said, but there had been a lively debate, and the Zhdanovists were not in the majority. If there had been deficiencies it was not because the party had insisted on identifying and promoting an Italian tradition of democratic and Marxist culture, but rather because it had not done so vigorously enough. [27] This was a fair point. Yet although the PCI could not be blamed for all the defects of Italian intellectual life, it could not be completely absolved, either. The cultural vision of the party had been distinctive and in many respects original, but Zhdanovism manifested itself as much in style as in content. Policies had been handed down from above, and Togliatti, Alicata, and others, with their hectoring and overbearing manner, had fueled the resentments that exploded in 1956.

The political repercussions of the ferment among the intellectuals were considerable. The most dramatic gesture occurred when 101, mainly Roman, Communist intellectuals signed an open letter in which they publicly stated their dissent from official pronouncements on Hungary and demanded a revision of positions inside the PCI.[28] To the consternation of loyalists, the letter appeared in the independent press, and a large-scale row ensued. During the following year virtually all those who signed the "letter of the 101" abandoned the party. In some cases the break occurred over events in the Eastern bloc or the PCI's responses to them. But in others it was a consequence of the clampdown that took place in the party and the individual harassment to which revisionists were subjected.[29]

Against Capitalist Modernity

Although Alicata tried to minimize the departure of many intellectuals, arguing that some of those who left the party had merely been guests, never properly assimilated into the disciplined mentality of the revolutionary militant, it was nonetheless a watershed. It signaled the end of the enchantment between the PCI and more or less the whole of the progressive intelligentsia that had lasted since the immediate postwar period. But it should not be deduced from this that every relationship between the PCI and Italian intellectuals was broken or became strained. Despite the shakeout, neither the basic assumptions of Communist cultural policy nor all loyalties were fundamentally threatened. In the mid- to late 1950s there was no real weakening in the commitment of party spokesmen to a realist aesthetic nor was there a decisive detachment among artists and writers from the positive values that continued to be associated with it. As was shown by the debates on Visconti's historical epic *Senso* and Vasco Pratolini's novel *Metello,* on the one hand, and by the contents of both *Città aperta* and another small literary review, *Officina,* on the other, the neorealist matrix remained in force even if it gave rise to more diverse and heterodox interpretations.[30] Although artists like Pasolini rejected any idea after 1956 that political convictions and creative activity could be mechanically fitted together, they nonetheless continued to strive for some social dimension in their work.[31] Yet the easing of the two camps mentality, scarcely less than development itself, ultimately undercut realism's claim to a dominant position within the aesthetic universe of the left.

Even before the advent of television in 1954, the political partiality of the state radio and the American aspects of its light entertainment programming were an object of Communist protest. Thus the setting up of visual broadcasting under the administration of RAI with the political sponsorship of the DC could not have provoked anything but a wary reaction. In this sense there was a qualitative difference between the Christian Democratic and Communist responses to the new medium. Whereas Catholics engaged in debates on the significance and implications of television, the PCI confined itself to pure condemnation and propaganda designed to highlight the "clerical monopoly" of management and the poor quality of the programs.[32] It also redoubled efforts to persuade its followers to tune in instead to the Italian services of Radio Moscow and Radio Prague. Within the party there was real concern that technology was being bent to very specific political ends. These involved completion of the process whereby critical elements in culture were suppressed and a flat conformist model was being installed in the country.

Writing in *Rinascita* in 1958, in his first serious attempt to come to grips with the new medium, Alicata put it at the center of an article titled "The Degradation of Italian Culture in the Christian Democratic Regime." "In the field of the most modern instruments of mass cultural diffusion (Radio, Television)," he wrote, "the only possible doubt is over whether the discriminatory criteria governing the choice of programs and contributors should be brought to light first or the mediocrity of the results. . . . The reactionary spirit manifests itself in the most vulgar ways and the cultural approximation and superficiality in the most sloppy and grotesque forms."[33] At the ninth congress of the PCI in 1960 broadcasting was considered purely in terms of its propaganda effects. The overriding aim was to expose and combat the falsehoods that were spread by the medium and to break the clerical and state monopoly of RAI-TV in order to secure access for a wider variety of social and political forces.[34]

The purely political way in which television was considered impeded discussion of its long-term implications. There was little or no appreciation of the contribution it was making, for good or ill, to the unification of elite culture and popular culture, or of the way in which it was becoming an important element in everyday life, widening horizons, creating cross-class sources of identity and assisting in the transmission of new tastes and lifestyles. Virtually no help was forthcoming from left-wing intellectuals who, as Francesco Pinto has noted, were unable to grasp the industrial forms of culture that were undergoing rapid development because their own attitudes were preindustrial. Despite the fact that it appeared ten years after the birth of television and was clearly intended to raise the quality of the left's analyses of the medium, even the magazine *Televisione,* briefly published in 1964–65 under the editorship of Arturo Gismondi, was not free of conventional biases. Although the unbending hostility of some circles was absent, the polemic continued relentlessly in its pages against the banal, unproblematic, and excessively cautious nature of RAI-TV programs, "the faithful mirror of a petit bourgeois culture, subaltern and devoid of the ferments of innovation."[35]

The uneven character of Italian development furnished the PCI with new opportunities to criticize the DC and its allies. The decision to invest massively in the construction of motorways was greeted with particular derision. A much more urgent priority, said the party's economic spokesman Giorgio Amendola, was the defense of the land against flooding.[36] At the local level, party organizations joined in particularistic and municipal battles against motorways. The desperate conditions in rapidly expanding peripheral zones of the cities also fueled party propaganda. But these criticisms remained unbalanced by any appreciation of the positive effects of the boom. In 1958, as in 1953, the PCI made the need for a war on poverty a key theme of its election campaign, accusing the DC of being "the party of the privileged rich, of the great capitalists and the landowners."[37] Amendola, moreover, dismissed the very idea of a boom. In June 1960 he wrote that "the truth in Italy is that economic development is not translated into a general improvement of the living and working conditions of the laboring masses."[38] The rich were getting richer, he said, but at the expense of everyone else. Far from resolving old contradictions, the monopolistic direction of development exacerbated them and added new ones.[39]

For all the intellectual support it commanded, the PCI was not good at understanding structural social change. The Gramscians in the PCI were no less dismissive or uncomprehending of the vast transformations associated with the development of a consumption-oriented economy than the Stalinists. Both shared a very pessimistic outlook on Italian and world capitalism's possibilities of development and failed to perceive the scale of the changes that were taking place. Neither the introduction of Fordism in the factories nor the establishment of the premises of a mass consumer economy were even dimly grasped. In the early 1960s, the Communists began to analyze the structural causes of social change. But, up to 1962, the great fear remained that workers, new workers above all, were becoming captivated ideologically by the mythologies of neocapitalism. The "Fiat myth" of high salaries, guaranteed jobs, and paternalist human relations seemed to have had an extraordinary effect. Even where areas of conflict emerged, very often questions of income rather than power seemed to be paramount. Under new conditions not only was the time for political involvement reduced but collective visions of future redemption were eroded by notions of individual well being that were impregnated with material aspirations. Combined with the discrimination to which Communists continued to be subjected, this had a direct impact on party and union organization.

Leading Communists struggled to keep up morale and reaffirm their own vision of modernization. All agreed that the general character of the party's struggles had to be maintained. Despite the fragmentation of social life, the unification of values, obstacles to sustained political involvement, and the diffusion of an "American ideology," Enrico Berlinguer argued, "modernity cannot mean a weakening of the sort of political and moral tension, the sort of human spirit without which there cannot be revolutionary action."[40] Yet if the party was to promote its view with any success, it had to engage in an uphill battle on the terrain of values and ideas, "to set against the pressures that tend to diffuse among the masses certain lines of an American ideology, the new order of values of which Communism in general, and European and Italian Communism in particular, must be the bearers."[41] In spite of the individual status and security that could in some measure be acquired through consumer goods, Communists stuck firmly to the idea that the confidence and self-esteem of workers could only be established collectively through membership of mass organizations. Relentless propaganda was being directed at ordinary people by the press and television, Amendola declared in his speech to the second assembly of Communists active in the factories in May 1961. The aim was to mold the consciousness of workers, suffocate their institutions, and remove their political autonomy. Every aspect of life, from the workplace to the grey and anonymous dormitory zones of the urban peripheries, risked being regulated and controlled under neocapitalism. The threat was grave but it would not succeed, Amendola argued, for workers would not "give up their revolutionary primogeniture as the revolutionary class" for the sake of a "modern-day plate of lentils."[42]

Although Amendola and others made a banner of the revolutionary purity of the working class, factory workers began to see some improvement in their living standards, and poorer, more marginal laborers fell under the spell of mythologies of instant prosperity. The opium of the poor was now more likely to be lotteries such as Sisal or the football pools game Totocalcio than politics, Liliano Faenza noted. "Madonna, with this poverty round here, it would be marvelous to hit the jackpot on Sisal!" a group of bricklayers exclaimed to him.[43] Certainly, consumerism did not lack contradictory and in some respects oppressive dimensions. The goods were highly desirable as practical items and status symbols, but in order to obtain them workers had to take on second jobs or long hours of overtime.[44] Yet evidence shows that even among Communist activists the desire for raised individual living standards was strong. Of the many militants questioned by the researchers of the Cattaneo Institute in the 1960s, only hardened old activists and some young enthusiasts rejected models of consumption. Virtually all others acquired electrical appliances and cars as soon as they could afford them and saved and sacrificed for years in order to be able to buy a flat or small dwelling of their own. Among workers the "passion for the house" also manifested itself in an interest in decorating, do-it-yourself, and gardening.[45]

Consumerism posed a variety of challenges to the PCI. At the most basic level it postulated a vision of life in which the individual and familial accumulation of material goods and not ideology was central. Communist politics rested on diametrically opposed premises. Communist morality also deplored individualism — the pursuit of the selfish and the comfortable — and exalted sacrifice and duty. Close surveillance was maintained over activists and members to ensure their conformity and dedication. "The use of imported alcoholic drinks, an interest in fashion, an unusual touch of elegance and refinement, an outfit in an individual style, any trait that could not be justified by reference to conditions of origin and therefore was to be labeled 'petit bourgeois' could give rise to discredit, irritation, and suspicion," Giuseppe Carlo Marino has written. Even the installation of a private telephone on the part of a modest greengrocer in Messina resulted in a detailed investigation.[46] In time these attitudes evolved, but the tension between party morality and the dominant values of society remained strong.

Nonetheless, the PCI did change significantly after 1956. Togliatti succeeded in ousting the hard-liners — he started to move the party in the direction of "polycentrism" — and he carried forward his plan to develop a strategy based on acceptance of the republican constitution and parliamentary democracy. The cornerstone of the PCI's drive to rebuild and possibly extend its intellectual influence was the Gramscian legacy. After more than ten years in which the only person in the PCI authorized to engage with Gramsci and interpret him had been Togliatti himself, the 1958 Gramsci Institute conference dedicated to Gramsci's thought and action heralded the opening of a long season in which Gramsci occupied a central place in the theoretical and political debates of the Italian left. The variety of views expressed at the conference indicated the development of a genuine interest in his writings that in successive years would spread well beyond the frontiers of Italy. However, although this interest brought new, young intellectuals to the PCI and enhanced its prestige, it must be said that most of the resulting work was of a philological, historical, or theoretical orientation. There was no real applied dimension, and, although ideologically useful, its connection with the actual practice of the party was thus rather remote. Perhaps Ludovico Geymonat was too harsh at the conference when he condemned Gramsci's texts as useless because their author was too close to Croce, and both were cultural expressions of an Italy that had disappeared.[47] But there can be no doubt that new issues and problems had arisen that were far more complex than those Gramsci had considered.

For Communist critics no less than for writers and artists, the traditional intellectual continued to occupy a central position in the Italian cultural system. Yet the status and function of the intellectuals themselves were increasingly subject to redefinition. A great managerial and technological revolution was occurring in centers of cultural production no less than in industry and society at large, and although some sectors survived relatively intact, the scientific and technical aspects of cultural organization became predominant. Industrialization and rationalization significantly increased the numbers of salaried intellectuals, professional technicians, advertising executives, journalists, sociologists, and psychologists. The subordinate role of these indicated a qualitative change in the position of the educated in society. In addition, the extension of public education rendered somewhat anachronistic the pedagogical approach with which the PCI had conceived the political role of the intellectuals in the struggle for hegemony. But most important of all, the expansion of modern means of mass communications, and television in particular, not only coincided with a process of cultural unification on very different bases from those theorized by the PCI but also opened up new channels of information, communication, and discussion that put in crisis the notion of the hegemonic function of the traditional intellectual to which the party had so tenaciously adhered.

Party Culture, Popular Culture, Mass Culture

For rank-and-file Communists, 1954 was not only the year that saw the advent of television. It was also the year in which the Scelba government, having succeeded in eliminating the remaining elements of neorealism from the cinema, stepped up the campaign it had begun in 1952 to oust workers' organizations from properties that they had taken over from the Fascists at the end of the war. In some cases the buildings had belonged to Socialist circles or associations before 1922, but such claims proved almost impossible to establish legally. Despite a tide of protest, numerous Case del popolo were closed down or turned into schools or barracks for the Carabinieri.[48] This grave attempt to undermine working-class organization and strike a blow against the influence of the left in leisure was broadly a failure. Barely a few months after the evictions, work began to construct new Case, carried out by volunteer labor and paid for by local subscriptions. These buildings stood as symbols of the combativeness of activists, of their determination to resist any offensive designed to weaken working-class solidarity.

Precisely this defiant attitude conditioned the first grassroots responses to television. Whereas the DC installed television sets in party sections in towns and villages, local PCI federations sometimes forbade their sections and Case del popolo to do likewise.[49] The more Stalinist militants denounced the output as "priest's garbage" and tried to dissuade others from having anything to do with it.[50] As an alternative, much stress was put on the use of propaganda slide shows, with party organizations being encouraged whenever possible to purchase a projector. However, despite the interest they aroused in rural areas, such initiatives were inevitably unsatisfactory and short-lived, like "pursuing an aeroplane on horseback," according to Galluzzi.[51]

Judgments in the party press on the contents of some of the most popular television programs emphasized their supposed "cruelty" and "dehumanizing" influence. In particular, it was the quiz show *Lascia o Raddoppia?* that gave rise to objections. "In a country such as ours, with a very low standard of living, waving a 'plate' of these proportions under the nose of some poor devil is an offence to all," wrote a *Vie Nuove* correspondent. "Accustomed to importing its programs from America, the television does not realize this. Nor could it do so, far removed as it is from the life of normal people, from taste, and from the intelligence of the Italians."[52] By employing foreign models that some felt were ill-suited to Italy because of their high emotive content, RAI laid itself open to the charge of failing to play a positive cultural role. If American ideas were to go on being adopted, "then television would become an instrument for dehumanizing human events. . . . the sense of its proportion in relation to society would be lost," it was said.[53]

Yet among workers and their families, including many party members, television quickly acquired great popularity. Despite strong party reservations, most Case del popolo, sports clubs, bars, and even some party sections rushed to acquire sets in order to head off competition from Catholic and state-owned circles, DC sections, and commercial establishments. This had positive and negative effects. It meant that left-wing and labor movement organizations participated fully in the new collective ritual and bustled with renewed life most evenings. But such was the appeal of the sports events, variety shows, and quizzes that made up mainstream output that it became very difficult on some occasions to hold party or union meetings before 10 P.M. The level of attendance in consequence began to drop alarmingly.[54]

Despite the watershed year of 1956 there were few signs in the late 1950s that Communist and left-wing critics were succeeding in eliminating the obstacles that had prevented them from shaping or even understanding popular taste. Although public figures regretted the demise of neorealism and deplored the output of television, the popular cinema of the 1950s and the new quiz shows attracted widespread interest. The female stars of the period appealed to working-class Communists not just on account of their beauty but because of their strength of character and humble origins. Several of them, notably Silvana Mangano, Gina Lollobrigida, and Lucia Bosé, had made their first screen appearances in popular neorealist films, but all were considered broadly to belong to a left-wing, popular cultural universe that was flexible enough to include glamour as well as grit.

While the Catholic press ignored or attacked these stars and the values they embodied, *Vie Nuove* was one of the first magazines to grant them ample publicity. In return, Gina Lollobrigida or Silvana Mangano would pose for photographs reading the weekly, and in 1954 Sophia Loren acted as "godmother" of the annual Miss *Vie Nuove* contest.[55] The popular Communist press was also able to insert itself in the interstices of the new passion for television by springing to the defense of personalities who fell victim to the ire of the moralists, such as the sexy singer Abbe Lane, well known for her small-screen appearances alongside her bandleader husband Xavier Cugat, or Maria Luisa Garoppo, a famously busty tobacconist from Pordeonone whose embarrassingly long string of successes on *Lascia o Raddoppia?* drew barbed comments from Catholic commentators and various self-appointed defenders of decency. Given the general party attitude toward the quiz, there were strict limits to this sort of appropriation. But whereas critics, intellectuals, and militants appeared to loathe it, many ordinary party members and sympathizers could take a little pride in the fact that Edy Campagnoli, the glamorous assistant of the show's Italian American presenter Mike Bongiorno, was a former Miss *Vie Nuove* finalist.[56]

Although the PCI seemed unable to grasp the general significance of mass culture, or understand the reasons for its great success, it would be wrong to suggest that the party failed to appreciate its impact on the actual practice of politics.[57] In terms of its own system of communications, it showed an acute sense of the need to adapt, breaking with a marked tendency in previous years to underestimate the potential value of mass communications.

Adaptation to the cultural model that was gradually becoming a regular part of popular consciousness was a feature of all those sectors of the PCI that directly encountered mass taste. The popular Communist and left-wing press had of course begun to adapt several years before, but only from the mid-1950s were the highly successful and progressively expanding *feste dell'Unità* affected. RAI might have been unreservedly condemned, but if it helped attract large numbers of people the party was only too happy to include television personalities and middle of the road performers straight from the San Remo festival in the program of its own festivals. Instead of the Resistance songs and choruses of rice weeders that had once held exclusive sway, popular singers like Nilla Pizzi, Claudio Villa, and Luciano Tajoli (only a few of whom identified politically with the PCI) became star attractions, exhibited with scarcely less pride than the painters and intellectuals who patronized the *feste* for little or no financial reward.[58] In this process the gatherings lost a little of their political identity and something of their spontaneous character, but the party was pleased to accept such compromises to ensure that its festivals were never isolated in a ghetto. In this it was undoubtedly successful. Over time the *feste dell'Unità* would become a vital entertainment network, indispensable to a music industry keen to promote its stars before large live audiences.

For *Vie Nuove* the reduction in the level of political tension and the reorientation of social goals posed a particular set of problems. To render the magazine more popular and enhance its appeal to women, Maria Antonietta Macciocchi, who had edited *Noi Donne* for six years, was appointed as editor in 1956. Over the next three years she introduced various changes, simplifying the language, making wider use of photographs, and in general abandoning the high cultural pretensions that had to some extent marked the magazine under Fidia Gambetti, its previous editor.[59] The degree of success, however, was limited. Although Macciocchi insisted in an internal report that real sales (rather than the print run) increased by ten thousand per issue between 1956 and 1959, the overall trend from 1953 was a downward one.[60] In contrast to *Famiglia Cristiana, Vie Nuove* did not prosper during this period. From 1954 it began a slow but inexorable decline that ended with the magazine's being ceded first to the publisher Teti in 1969 and then to a cooperative before it finally closed in 1978. The reasons for this were various. Despite Macciocchi's efforts, *Vie Nuove* failed to attract a real following beyond the ranks of the party faithful. Attempts to raise sales by seeking distribution through news kiosks flopped because the magazine retained a strong party profile that, although it was not generally borne out by the magazine's contents, was underlined by "the sudden narrowing of certain numbers, under the sign of a strong party imprint."[61] Moreover, the organizational dependency on the party meant that *Vie Nuove* never shook off its predominantly male image, nor did it attract more than a very modest amount of advertising.[62] At a time when interest in new durable goods was expanding rapidly among workers and their families, this weakness diminished its appeal with respect to independent publications. The articles that appeared on television programs and popular cars and other products also tended not to share the enthusiasm of ordinary people or to illustrate their uses but rather to be highly critical in tone.[63] In this sense *Vie Nuove* failed to reflect adequately the evolving desires and curiosities of its readers.

Those in charge of the Communist press did make some effort to latch on to the fascination with new household appliances and means of transport and combine it with a collective vision of social improvement. Radio sets, sewing machines, typewriters, scooters, and even Fiat 600 cars were offered as prizes to those who excelled in the constant drive to maintain and increase sales and subscriptions to party papers and magazines. But insofar as such prizes could only be acquired thanks to the efforts of entire PCI federations, or at the very least a whole section, they contradicted the individual and familial emphasis of the conversion to consumerist aspirations. The incentives dangled before single activists tended, especially in the early 1950s, to be mainly ideological in nature.

Marino reports that in Alessandria a sales competition was held in which the first prize was a signed photograph of Togliatti, the second a signed photograph of Longo, and the third a signed photograph of Secchia. The consolation prize was a second-class return rail ticket to Rome.[64] At the national level the pattern differed little. The activist within each federation who sold the most copies of *L'Unità* in 1950 received a two-day break in Bologna as the guest of the PCI federation (traveling on a third-class rail ticket), and five hundred runners-up were tempted with ownership of a small library of Marxist-Leninist texts.[65]

It was no less difficult for the PCI to make the language of mass culture its own in the propaganda campaigns it was constantly engaged in. From the mid-1940s it had been recognized that the party often failed to convey its message to poorer workers and peasant women, especially in areas where its oral propaganda did not penetrate. Yet despite the great numbers of comics and photoromances consumed by these groups, there were strong ideological resistances to the adoption of such tools of communication because they were perceived to be corrupt and of American derivation.[66] In the late 1950s this attitude began to crumble. After a successful experiment with a "progressive" photoromance in Sicily, Giuliana Saladino of the PCI federal committee in Palermo argued that form and content were not inseparable. If there was to be any chance of reaching sectors of the population lacking basic education, for whom even a magazine like *Noi Donne* was remote and difficult, then a more flexible attitude was needed. The idea was subsequently taken up in some localities in the form of election materials. For example, in Bologna in 1956, some use was made of attractively presented party photoromances (two of them were titled "Stronger than Destiny" and "The Great Hope") that featured a love story just like *Sogno* or *Bolero Film* but also a strike or some illustration of the benefits of left-wing local government. In the final frame the hero and heroine found themselves not before an altar but a polling station.[67] In case anyone had missed the point, it was suggested explicitly that the achievement of happiness would be greatly assisted by voting PCI.

On other occasions the party timidly latched on to entertainment formulas. In the 1958 election campaign, the DC used songs and sketches from television in its propaganda. The PCI, for its part, coined a slogan to suggest that, instead of extolling a nonexistent prosperity, the prime minister Fanfani should be invited to come down from cloud-cuckoo-land (*scendere "dal blu dipinto di blu"*) in the manner of Domenico Modugno's hit song *Volare*.

The above examples were but small aspects of a broader change. It was acknowledged that because people were better informed it was no longer enough to stage generic public meetings. The focus of rallies had to be topical and specific if audiences were to be attracted and their interest maintained. Moreover, the erosion of the stark language and inflamed imagery of the late 1940s necessitated a different style of communication more directed to immediate needs and seductive rather than alarmist in tone.[68]

Naturally, the party flagship was also affected by the developments. Throughout the 1950s the party daily *L'Unità* struggled against the odds to maintain its high daily print run of around four hundred thousand copies.[69] The reports and memos on the paper conserved in the party archives refer constantly to the situation of financial crisis in which it and other Communist papers found themselves. Indeed, many flanking newspapers, including the prestigious (and, in the eyes of some, excessively independent) *Nuovo Corriere* in Florence, edited by Romano Bilenchi, were forced to close in the mid-1950s. A variety of local supplements to *L'Unità* was also suppressed. The paper sought to combat adverse political conditions and a decline in its volunteer sales force with a more lively and diversified presentation. Red ink was introduced, along with local news features and a women's page (although the latter was described in an internal note in 1960 as "still being of poor quality").[70] Toward the end of the decade it was recognized that changed conditions of life and the success of television and the popular press necessitated some adjustment and adaptation. Given the important political role of the paper in maintaining inward and outward cohesion in the party, its essential character could not be subject to change. The Turin and Genoa editions of the paper were closed in 1956, the Milan and Rome editions of the paper were unified under a single direction, and in 1962 a new national edition was launched under Alicata's editorship. The paper ceased to be directed so much at the political collaborator and instead sought to address the varied needs, including cultural interests and desires for distraction, of a potentially wider audience of client-readers.[71]

If the PCI continued to view television mainly as a tool of enemy propaganda, it was because there was no democratic control of the me-

Between Hollywood and Moscow

dium through parliament or even through a committee of guarantors such as the BBC's board of governors. News broadcasts were unctuously pro-government in orientation and, on occasion, scandalously biased. Not until 1960, moreover, when election tribunes were introduced, did any Communist appear on the screen. Togliatti himself was seen by viewers for the first time in April 1963, a full nine years after broadcasting began. Yet, limited though the opening was, the creation of election tribunes was a godsend to the PCI, for, as Giorgio Galli observed, it enabled the party to use television to reinforce partisan attachments.[72] Using its own well-developed system of communications, the PCI could focus attention on the rare appearances of its own leaders and then influence perceptions of those appearances by commenting on them and diffusing watchwords launched during broadcasts. Particularly skilled in this respect was Giancarlo Pajetta, the first Communist to appear on *Tribuna politica,* whose capacity to invent slogans and distribute humiliating putdowns to adversaries and journalists became legendary.

Leisure and Social Integration

From one point of view the PCI's own system of communications was rendered more modern and efficacious through the adoption of new techniques. But there were also other possible viewpoints. For some, this adaptation was a further sign of the decline in left-wing popular culture that was a marked feature of the late 1950s. With mass emigration and the onset of development, the whole "southernist" perspective on progressive folklore that had been championed by De Martino lost force. Just as the peasant question slid down the party's agenda, so the South lost much of its cultural fascination. In the North and Center the drive to promote a network of organized cultural activities associated with the labor movement was undercut by social and political trends. Emigration left rural Case del popolo with fewer people to cater for in the depopulated countryside; in the cities, migrants often settled in sprawling peripheral areas distant from the traditional centers of working-class leisure. However, even flourishing Case del popolo found that there was diminishing interest in the vast range of collective activities that they organized. With the spread of Vespas, motorcars, and the consequent development of "mobile privatization," the great moments of diversion, feast days, and holidays were spent less and less in organized trips to the country or seaside. Young men who had joined the PCI after the war settled down with their families, and a younger generation preferred to invent its own leisure through informal activities and spontaneous forms of group association.[73] To be sure, the addition of television sets, juke-boxes, pinball machines, and, later, bingo all helped stave off the decline of circles and clubs, but only temporarily, and in any case the adoption of such entertainments was often flavored with the bitter taste of defeat.[74] In the North, local administrations extended their range of activities by instituting public libraries and sports and recreational centers, thereby taking over, particularly in left-wing areas, some of the specific functions of the Case del popolo and even of the PCI itself.

The deep anxiety of left intellectuals about the vulnerability of the working class to the perils of neocapitalist society was evident even in reactions to Visconti's powerful film *Rocco e i suoi fratelli,* which of-fered a view of the economic boom seen from below, through the eyes of an immigrant family from the South adapting to life in the dangerously corrupting metropolis. As the Communist director par excellence, each of Visconti's works had provoked extended discussion and had been interpreted in some way as a comment on the prospects for revolution in Italy. Yet, far from being a forward-looking work, *Rocco* was infused with nostalgia for the South of the recent past, which the director had brought to the screen twelve years previously in *La terra trema.*

To clarify his position and set aside misunderstandings, Visconti was persuaded to write an article for *Vie Nuove.*[75] The positive personality of the film, he stressed, was Ciro, "the brother turned worker who has not only shown a nonromantic and unsuperficial capacity to seek a position in life but also acquired consciousness of the various duties that follow from various rights." To those who felt that the nostalgic Rocco (played by a splendidly charismatic Alain Delon) was the director's real hero, Visconti firmly restated his political beliefs: "Overall, and, I must say, without my realizing it, the finale of *Rocco* has turned out as a symbolic finale, emblematic I should say of my southernist conviction: the worker brother speaks to the youngest member of the family of a vision of the future of the country that represents the ideally unitary one of the thought of Antonio Gramsci."[76]

The hostility to passive entertainment and in particular to anemic light music was so strong that some intellectuals decided to take it upon them-

Between Hollywood and Moscow

selves to provide an alternative. Comprising Franco Fortini, Italo Calvino, and others, the *Cantacronache* group furnished music and words to songs that it hoped would counteract the bland output of the song festivals. Although the operation, unsurprisingly, was not a resounding success, in part because it was too overtly political, a large number of songs were eventually recorded, some by well-known artists including Milly and Ornella Vanoni.

For all its occasional eccentricity and not infrequent elitism, the reaction of the intellectual left to mass culture was not only motivated by the concern to preserve the privileges of a category of declining influence. Problems in the left's ability to occupy a stable place in the organization of working-class leisure were compounded by the failure to make any progress in the campaign to democratize ENAL, the state recreational organism that supplanted the Fascist OND at the end of the war. Following the decision of the Catholics and the Republicans to found their own associations, the left found itself increasingly isolated in its battle against government control of an organism that was highly bureaucratic and committed to an "apolitical" use of leisure (no political activity or political newspapers of any sort were allowed in ENAL circles). The situation was made worse by the attempt on the part of leading enterprises in the North to set up recreational circles of their own that were run along paternalistic lines for employees, and the gradual detachment from ENAL of circles that tired of its chronic immobilism. Concern about these trends among left-wing parliamentarians, intellectuals, and trade unionists led to the foundation in 1957 of ARCI, the Italian Recreational and Cultural Association.[77] The first objectives of the association were to secure the dissolution of ENAL and to win recognition of the "welfare character" of ARCI itself so that it could enjoy the same rights and legal benefits that were once the sole prerogative of ENAL, but which subsequently had been granted to the Catholic and Republican associations. In fact, ARCI would at first be denied legal recognition on the grounds of its allegedly political nature. Only in 1967 would it overcome this obstacle. But despite this handicap it succeeded in uniting the circles that had left ENAL and in winning support from a variety of Case del popolo, recreational circles, cooperatives, film and cultural clubs, sports organizations, musical bands, amateur theatrical groups, and choirs.

In the first years of its existence ARCI campaigned vigorously against ENAL and sternly defended the autonomy of circles, to which it offered a number of publications, much practical guidance on administration and bookkeeping, and encouragement in the organization of cultural and sporting activities. It was hoped that in this way the labor movement could enhance and enrich its recreational dimension and thereby combat organizational decay.

The problem of leisure (*tempo libero*) in industrial society was addressed first by industrialists, sociologists, and psychologists. In the late 1950s the term was rejected out of hand by many labor movement spokesmen as a neocapitalist mystification. However, by the early 1960s it was widely recognized that, as a result of economic and social change, there had been a massive increase in expenditure on culture and recreation.[78] Cinema, television, theater, and sports events, as well as the jukebox and other entertainments, had greatly altered how vast numbers of people, not only urban dwellers, organized their social life. At the national cultural convention organized by ARCI in 1961 the implications of this development were discussed by representatives of all branches of the labor movement (trade union, political, recreational, cooperative). It was acknowledged that the old dichotomy between elite and popular culture had been obfuscated by the spread of mass culture.[79] But at the same time it was argued that the process of cultural unification that was taking place was merely artificial. For it to be dynamic and genuine, ordinary people had to be protagonists, not subaltern components. Although "apocalyptical" views of the massification of culture were on the whole avoided, many contributors to debates within ARCI and the PCI regarded television, the mass circulation press, and cultural industries in general as a distorting element that distracted people from reality. The task was to try to bring about some form of cultural unification from below in which the grassroots activities of an autonomous, federally organized ARCI would play a leading role.

At the third ARCI congress in 1962 a concerted attempt was made to broaden the association's role in the light of this more critical perspective. Whereas previously in the tradition of the workers' movement Case del popolo and recreational circles had not contributed directly to the political work of left-wing parties and still less had they been connected to cultural policy, new conditions, it was felt, called for a change. A revamped network of varied grassroots centers and activities could help counterbalance the erosion of the collective dimension and inducements to live in accordance with the values of consumerism. To achieve this "the autonomous and specific action of all the democratic organizations of the popular workers' movement" was held to be "indispensable."[80] The role of ARCI was to lead the way in elaborating a critical outlook: "It must give the bulk of its attention to the demand for leisure, promote the creation of particular services, and overcome the primitive phase of its existence in which it was mostly limited to the circles and their problems."[81]

At a local level, ARCI circles often helped the left's recreational network supersede the fortress mentality that took shape in response to the repressive atmosphere of the early 1950s. By taking over the organization of cultural activities from such groups as the Italy-USSR association they overcame a narrowly political approach that in the post-1956 era made little sense. By promoting, like the Leopardi circle founded in the Casa del popolo Corazza in Bologna in 1959, recitals of popular music, film shows, theatrical events, and debates, they also combated the tendency of some Case del popolo to merely latch on to the dominant currents within the new media-transmitted culture and of others to lapse into a monotonous routine of wine drinking, card games, and bowls.

Yet ARCI was perhaps too ambitious. What was held out in its lively and certainly fruitful debates of the early 1960s was nothing less than the possibility of a fundamental reversal in the emphases of the PCI's cultural policy such as to put questions arising in everyday work and leisure on the political agenda for the first time. Great difficulties were encountered in lending this grand design a practical dimension. The surge in recruitment of the early years dropped slightly when, after 1962, attention shifted away from the campaign against ENAL and defense of circles. Moreover, the membership was extremely unevenly distributed and, owing to lack of resources, rather thin on the ground even in left-wing strongholds. In 1964 the association claimed to have 432,000 members belonging to 2,910 circles, but if it could boast 36,000 members in Bologna and 55,000 in Florence, then these constituted relative exceptions even in Emilia-Romagna and Tuscany.[82] An indication of the picture elsewhere may be gleaned from the fact that only 457 people belonged in Genoa and that no circles at all existed in such important cities as Rome, Naples, and Palermo or in much of the South as a whole.

Further obstacles came from within the PCI itself. Although there was great interest in ARCI and, indeed, a desire to use it to help break the sectarian stance of many Case del popolo, the association's policy proposals found a lukewarm response among the PCI leadership.[83] For most leading Communists it was not the place of recreational associations to theorize a political role for themselves or interfere in cultural policy. Nevertheless, through ARCI the labor movement began in some small way to occupy a critical place in the changing texture of social and cultural life. Through its debates the essential elements of a response were mapped out, a response that, although never more than marginal in global terms, would become gradually more important and condition approaches to cultural problems in successive years.

Overall, it would appear that those sectors of the PCI and the Communist sphere most directly affected by changes in the pattern of social life developed their own responses, making provision for new conditions. The style of political communication became more pragmatic and sophisticated, the press endeavored to adjust to new demands in the market, and the network of circles found a possible outlet to its crisis in ARCI. In this sense one might say that the organization reacted well and confirmed its capacity to respond, within certain limits, to movements in the society of which it was a part. This was no mean achievement. The problem, however, was that the isolated aspects of social change that the PCI's antennae picked up did not fully correspond to all the changes that were occurring, which themselves added up to more than the sum of their parts. The one-way channel of information and decisionmaking in the PCI prevented completely open discussion of novelty. In addition, the party leadership only partially grasped the overall sense of the phase of transition through which the country was passing, with the result that incremental adjustments were often late and neither coordinated nor translated into political innovations.

Working from a set of assumptions about economics, politics, and society that were not constantly measured against reality, the PCI either misunderstood or failed to recognize many of the most significant changes of the 1950s. Confusion over tendencies toward technological rationalization in industry, perplexity over an economic growth thought to be impossible, and, later, uncertainty about how to interpret the possible inclusion of the Socialists in the government area were only the most visible signs of this. Yet how far were the difficulties of the boom years specific to the PCI and not simply a generic problem of adaptation? As one Communist official, Emanuele Macaluso, was to point out at an organizational conference in 1964, "It is a fact that for every large organization, and for our party also, adapting to a new situation requires time."[84] It was above all the rapidity of change, he argued, that had thrown the PCI into a phase of turmoil and uncertainty. Up to a point this observation was valid. But the economic boom and the process of political realignment, in addition to the great cultural changes, posed enormous problems for the PCI and undermined several of the fundamental premises on which the party's strategy was based. No longer could it argue that the potential for expansion in the economy was held back by the residues of feudalism or that Italians were destined to remain forever poor without the enactment of structural reforms. No longer could Catholicism be considered the only impediment to Communist hegemony over the lower classes. The vision of life in terms of the multiplication of consumer goods also became a factor. No longer could the PCI propose a cultural policy hinging on the recruitment of writers, artists, and academics when the spreading mass communications were taking over many of the functions in organizing hegemony once ascribed to intellectuals. No longer could official social norms be considered valid for the whole of society at a time when questions about the role of women and secular values were beginning to emerge. Each of these factors called into question the political line and the relationship with society that Togliatti had elaborated for the PCI after the war. The effort of renewal and revision embarked on by the PCI leader from 1956, significant though it indisputably was, failed even to begin to address many of these problems. As a result, the PCI lost credibility on the left. In the 1960s, when the party embarked on far-reaching debates about economic development and its strategic implications, important innovations occurred, but at the cost of lacerating and unprecedented internal divisions. It was perhaps fortuitous that these were not solely directed inward but were also the consequence of a social context that was markedly more disposed to protest and conflict than the 1950s.

4

From Elvis Presley to Ho Chi Minh

Youth Culture and Cultural Conflict between

the Center Left and the Hot Autumn

The first Center Left government, formed with the abstention of the Socialists in March 1962, heralded a new phase in Italian political life. After a formal gestation period lasting six years and discussions lasting even longer, the PSI was brought into the orbit of the DC, and the basis of consensus on which government rested finally extended. On the surface the objectives of the Center Left could not have been clearer. The aim at one level or another of all the forces involved was to modify the political equilibria of the early cold war years and find more modern ways of managing public affairs suited to the imperatives of industrial society. In this sense the Center Left held out a promise of change. It also signaled a reduction in the level of tension that had marked society since the late 1940s. This development was greatly facilitated by Pope John XXIII's rejection of the stridently political style of his predecessor and the emphasis on reform and social justice of the new American president, John F. Kennedy. Beneath the surface, however, a variety of other objectives were being pursued. Although hopes for reform were encouraged by the process of political change and the measures adopted by the government to nationalize the electricity industry and raise the school leaving age to fourteen, the overriding aim of a majority of the DC was to minimize change and concentrate on the political goal of isolating the PCI and reducing its influence in society.

In contrast to the increasing immobilism of the Center Left, Italian society was dynamic and turbulent in the 1960s. Early in the decade the labor movement resurfaced and, in 1962, gave rise to the largest strikes the country had seen for over a decade. Young people, who were judged by nearly all to be conformist and passive, increasingly found themselves embroiled in civil and public strife. As urban Italy asserted its dominance, foreign influences became more systematic and widespread, in popular music and fashion for example, complementing critical impulses in cinema, literature, and theater. In this process of deprovincialization, expanding cultural industries came to play a prominent role, albeit reorganized in accordance with the requirements of an integrated, increasingly bureaucratically run society. In consequence, artistic and intellectual roles were redefined through the mediations of the market. At the same time, older forms of cultural mediation, strategies of separation between elite and popular culture, and conceptions of the intellectual function gradually disappeared. These transformations interacted with other changes but also generated tensions and responses of their own that reached a point of explosion toward the end of the decade.

For the PCI the period was one of great risks in which changes in politics and society presented some opportunities but also exposed the party to challenges it had not previously had to face. The end of the monolithic unity of the international Communist movement provoked by the Sino-Soviet split and the death of Togliatti in 1964 both signaled in different ways the passage to a new era. Even before the death of the man who had effectively led the party since 1926, a process of policy renewal began in which discourses were reworked, old approaches reelaborated in light of new conditions and new problems considered. In particular, the catastrophic perspective on capitalist development was dropped during 1962, although deep disputes both inside and outside the party took place over the nature of the line to be adopted in its place. In cultural policy new departures were occasioned by the final demise of the neo-realist aesthetic and the emergence of new modernist currents, and by the increasing role of mass communications in popular leisure. These innovations were significant, but the party's grasp was seldom sure, and its stances seemed increasingly inadequate to groups on the far left and student activists who bombarded the PCI with ever sharper critiques during the mid-1960s. Although the Communists were able to confront the issues raised by political protest at the end of the decade, they were less able to appreciate underlying cultural themes. These would give rise to serious difficulties in the 1970s as the party sought to put itself at the head of a new social bloc.

Youth Culture and Political Socialization

The changes that took place in the conditions of young people in Italy in the 1950s and early 1960s were by no means identical to those registered in Britain and America. Certain comparable shifts, bound up with economic growth and the spread of the values of a consumer society, did occur, but within a cultural context that exhibited marked differences. For the 1950s and much of the 1960s Italian youth remained substantially more integrated into the family unit, both financially and culturally, than their Anglo-Saxon counterparts. They were consequently more subject to social controls and enjoyed fewer opportunities for freedom of expression. Yet some things were changing. Thanks principally to wider education (even before the school leaving age was raised in 1962, more young people were staying on at school than ever before and the level of absenteeism, once endemic in the South, was in steep decline), television, and the consolidation of a national and increasingly industrialized popular publishing industry, the adolescents of the boom years were the first generation in Italian history to be broadly homogeneous in terms of language, tastes, and cultural reference points.

Together, television and other mass media contributed to the long-term process that was to wed the young to a vision of modernity in which the city and urban styles of life were seen to be more attractive than rural or provincial alternatives. One 1964 study of the effects of television on peasants found that the medium furnished young people with aspirations far removed from both their origins and daily life in the countryside.[1] An inquiry published in *Vie Nuove* in the same year left no doubt that both the premises and the promise of change were widely accepted. "I hope to have a fiancé more educated than myself, and who is not a peasant," declared one female interviewee. "My parents are peasants and I know just how unpleasant it is to live in the country."[2] The new generation was in any case more likely to be growing up in the large cities of the North than in the backwaters of the southern countryside, but with the spread of Vespas, Lambrettas, and the poor man's version of the previous two, the *ciclomotore* (a bicycle with a small motor added), even rural youth could more easily reach the towns to visit the cinema, go dancing, or buy comics and illustrated magazines. Of all the themes that captured the imagination of young people at this time, mobility was perhaps the most important.

Less attached to preceding cultural models and more exposed to the messages of the mass media, youth most readily responded to new trends and ideas.[3] The domestic entertainment industry was not slow to respond to new demands. From the late 1950s a series of radio shows, including *Il Discobolo* and *Bandiera Gialla,* and television programs such as *Alta pressione* provided a regular, if by no means continuous, diet of pop music. In the same period, the replacement of the old 78-rpm record with the more manageable 45-rpm single, which was first used in marketing rock-and-roll and pop genres, coincided with the boom in record buying. From five million in 1953 sales rose to eighteen million records in 1958, twenty-two million in 1963, and over thirty million in 1964.[4] Musical entrepreneurs proved to be ingenious inventors of new ways to promote pop and carry it to audiences even in the most backward of provinces. One of the most remarkable was the *Cantagiro* competition, which involved contests between singers in every town along the route of the immensely popular *Giro d'Italia* cycle race. Other competitions were strictly associated with the summer and took place mainly in seaside resorts. A great number of musical films (often flimsy, low-budget efforts thrown together around one hit song) also carried the music far and wide and helped make its performers into stars.

The enthusiasm with which young people adopted the products of mass culture directed at them tended to confirm the impression that the youth of the early 1960s accepted the world of consumerism as it found it.[5] Many Communists shared the view that the apparent disinterest of adolescents in social issues and collective struggles was due to their cultural integration into the pastimes and behavior models of industrial society. This conviction, however, was widespread. One foreign observer writing in 1964 of a new set of Italian pop stars expressed the view that "for Italian adolescents the great dream of the future must surely settle in being another Bobby Solo, Little Tony, Peppino Di Capri, Adriano Celentano, or Rita Pavone."[6] Two sociologists even coined the phrase "the youth of the three Ms" to put a label on the apparent conformism. By this it was intended to suggest that young males rejected politics and were concerned only to secure a car, a trade, and a wife (*macchina, mestiere, moglie*) for themselves.[7] Guido Baglioni, another sociologist, also came to the conclusion that "young people of today give the distinct impression of accepting the society in which they live just as it is. . . . These young people do not want to change radically the present institutional and social arrangements; they are not competitive, ambitious, daring, or at all rebellious."[8]

With the benefit of hindsight, it may be said that it was mistaken to view the popularity of American-inspired music and fashions as a sign of passive integration. Rather, such things provided youth with a clear-cut means to identify with the new and the modern, as well as a channel for the formation of cultural preferences different from those of older people. Even though pop was imported into Italy in a preconfectioned form and bore no relation whatsoever to established musical traditions, it still provided sound, mood, and feeling that gave a recognizable shape to a variety of interpersonal and group experiences that distinguished the young from their elders. More generally, however, pop in Italy was an important element in the transition from a traditional society that was rural and largely reliant on the Church for its values to a type of society in which behavior models were derived from the mass media. Through pop music and from their participation in it, young people formed a worldview that was unlinked to tradition, was more oriented toward the peer group than class or family ties, and favored spontaneity over planned activity, immediate over delayed experience, and pleasure over sacrifice.

As early as 1961 Togliatti voiced concern about the PCI's ability to relate to the needs and aspirations of the young. The occasion for this warning was furnished by a letter sent to *Rinascita* by a youth expressing dissatisfaction with a view of life limited to "the rush for money, the steady wage, television culture, etc."[9] The letter's author deplored the "emptiness of ideals" in contemporary society and stressed his need for "something to believe in; something that is worth living for." In his published reply, Togliatti seemed struck by a rare moment of public doubt. He asked himself if the party was sufficiently able to harness the enthusiasm of youth before it became dissipated in uncertainty and discouragement.

To make the PCI a force better able to act as a guide for youth, Togliatti called for inquiries to be set up and debates to take place at all levels of the party. The traditional channels of party communication had to be renewed and reinforced. The first priority was to encourage "prestigious men" to visit youth centers and clubs, not just on special occasions but as a "continuous process of mutual comprehension, clarification, and guidance." Well intentioned though this approach was, its very paternalism vitiated any prospect of success. Moreover, neither the basic assumptions of the party's cultural policy nor the heritage of orthodox Marxist criticism of mass culture made for a good grounding in approaching youth culture. Precisely the qualities of entertainment and distraction that critics of an earlier generation had found to condemn in cinema and mass circulation magazines were now the most visible hallmark of youth culture. Hence it tended to be seen inside the party as a grave sign of "integration," "depoliticization," and "Americanization" to be counterbalanced in some way at all costs.

Similar views also found their way into the PCI's publications. *Vie Nuove* spoke of the popularity of jukeboxes and tenpin bowling as sources of the Americanization of youth that could only be worrying for the "old continent."[10] A few years earlier the FGCI's organ *Nuova Generazione* published photographs of Elvis Presley accompanied by captions that denounced the "hysteria and paroxysm" he appeared to cause.[11] James Dean, popular in Italy as elsewhere thanks to the films *Giant* and *Rebel without a Cause,* was also subjected to attack for his portrayals of a youth "who puts off his transformation into a man by every means," avoiding reality by "indulging in a protracted escapism and using all his energies to resist inclusion in the great crowd of adults who inspire fear in him and whom he detests."[12] Much the same resistance to any flight from rationality marked reactions to other currents as well. The beat movement was accused of being "a mind-boggling mixture of mysticism, escapism, jazz, and marijuana, the latest and most exasperated example of that banality and fear of facing up to reality, that 'infantile' complex that is sapping the great objective possibilities of the new generation in the United States."[13]

The strongest condemnations of youth culture in the Communist press appeared in *Noi Donne*. An article on the Piper Club discotheque in Rome published in March 1965 contained the following summary judgment on pop music:

> The world of pop and the shake is filled with false models taken from the world of show business. . . . Is this where the independence of youth is to be found? Not a chance: adults have already laid their deceitful hands on

it. The "grown-ups" have built up a gigantic commercial gearwheel that makes millions from the tastes and fashions of adolescents. . . . So the revolt associated with pop is prefabricated by the adult world. It is a prefabricated revolt that, as far as we are concerned, carries the stamp of official approval. So much for rebellion.[14]

These criticisms reflected real concerns. Although party commentators were skeptical of the hastily put together sociological inquiries into youth that were broadcast on television or published in magazines, the PCI felt the impact of change directly at its base.[15] From the late 1950s, youth seemed to be attracted only by the dances at the *feste dell'Unità*; they shied away from political involvement and the sacrifices it entailed. In contrast to the youth of the 1940s, their outlook, shaped by music and entertainments, was oriented toward the present, not the future. For this and other related reasons, Pietro Ingrao noted in 1964, some youngsters saw the party in terms of restrictions (discipline, routine activities, officialdom) rather than as a creative, democratic force.[16] Another problem, it was felt, lay "in the indifference of some of our rank-and-file members toward the problems young people raise, and even toward their attitudes and behavior."[17] If a young person was likely to be made fun of or criticized for wearing a particular hairstyle or unconventional dress, he or she was not going to be easily attracted to the party section.

It should not be deduced from this, however, that the PCI was completely divorced from youth culture. In areas where party structures were profoundly intermeshed with community life, the PCI or the broader institutions of the labor movement offered young people opportunities and spaces that were to facilitate the formation and diffusion of new interests. While the Church continued to stigmatize dancing, the *Casa dei giovani* (youth club) opened next to the PCI federation in Modena in the mid-1950s organized the first discotheques in the town. Moreover, the Bolognese Gianni Morandi, a fresh-faced teenage idol of the mid-1960s whose popularity, amid ups and downs, would be undiminished over three decades later, was a PCI member who began his career singing in the Case del popolo under the watchful gaze of portraits of Marx, Lenin, and Gramsci.[18]

For some, the solution to the party's problems lay precisely in building up the Case del popolo and recreational circles. If the young could be involved first in these structures, they would be less prone to fall victim

Between Hollywood and Moscow

to the temptations of the wider world.[19] However, here a further difficulty arose. If a generational break was opening up in the left, then one reason lay in the decision to close off an important channel of socialization into voluntary activity in 1960 when API, the Association of Italian Pioneers, was wound up on the orders of the PCI leadership. This organization, a sort of Communist scout group based on the Soviet pioneers, was enormously popular in Emilia-Romagna and Tuscany. But from the earliest days, its very existence was a source of friction with the Church, which adopted an extremely antagonistic attitude toward any organization that challenged its near monopoly of children's recreation. In 1949 the association's leaders were excommunicated, and Bologna's Cardinal Lercaro founded "The Friends of Jesus," an organization formed "to expiate the sins of the Pioneers," whose members aged between six and thirteen slept with stones in their beds or walked with them in their shoes and subjected themselves to other mortifications.[20] The propaganda campaign continued throughout the 1950s until Togliatti decided that the damage done by the polemics outweighed any advantages to be gained from maintaining the existence of the association.[21] The children's paper *Il Pioniere* continued for a number of years as a supplement first to *L'Unità* and then *Noi Donne,* but gradually the remaining local Pioneer organizations petered out. When it was eventually disbanded in the Santa Viola quarter of Bologna in 1964, the local branch of the Pioneers had seven hundred members.[22] It would be an error to make too much of this, but there can be little doubt that it was a factor in the breakdown in communications between the labor movement and youth.[23]

What role was played by the FGCI during this difficult phase? The Communist youth organization's ability to grasp changes in the condition and aspirations of young people was handicapped by an apparently irreversible decline in membership that was far more serious than that of the PCI itself. By 1962 the organization counted just 183,600 members, whereas its membership had stood at 358,000 in 1956 and 230,000 in 1960.[24] In part this decline was due to changes in the pattern of social life, new leisure attractions, and the sapping appeal of traditional political militancy.[25] Yet at its thirteenth congress in 1953, the FGCI had made important innovations in its structure designed to bring it nearer the specific interests and activities of youth. Circles replaced sections as the key organizational unit, and youth evenings took the place of assemblies. If an internal problem may be singled out, then, it must be said that this lay in the unspecified mediatory role that the Communist youth organization was supposed to exercise between the party and young people. This question, which was a thorn in the side of the FGCI throughout its existence, first emerged sharply at this time. Youth leaders, who in any case were often men in their late twenties or early thirties, found it difficult to latch on to new trends in society because they felt obliged to play to the gallery, to take the adult party and its leadership, in other words, as their point of reference.

At the first sign of a political awakening of youth, perceived in the mass involvement in protest against the Tambroni government's opening to the neofascist right in 1960, the FGCI reverted to a more highly ideological type of existence. As Achille Occhetto, secretary of the organization in the early 1960s, subsequently admitted, debates from this point on became more strictly oriented to a party audience. They were, he said, "designed to be put at the service of the party as a whole."[26] Virtually no mention can be found in the magazines *Nuova Generazione* or *La città futura* of the everyday experiences of teenagers or family problems, and the few tentative attempts to raise questions relating to love and sexual relationships in official circles were rebuffed on the grounds that they were not political.[27] In private, of course, young Communists often shared the habits and tastes of their peers, but the public posture of revolutionary purity prevented this from being fruitfully put to use. Although some would later speak of the fascination they felt for John Kennedy, there was little evidence at the time that they shared the collective emotions of a generation enchanted by the myth of the New Frontier. The publications of the FGCI contained only revulsion for the United States, and articles invariably highlighted the negative aspects of its role in the world.[28] The Soviet Union, by contrast, was held up as an example of social progress and technical achievement, much play being made of the leadership it established in the field of space exploration following the launch of the first sputniks in the late 1950s and the first manned space flight by Yuri Gagarin in April 1961.

Diversification on the Left

During this period the sort of relationships that had prevailed between party and intellectuals since the war finally dissolved, and the aesthetic of realism lost its place at the center of left-wing debates about art and society. Although efforts were made to revise the PCI's cultural policies in light of social and political changes, they came too late to prevent a general fragmentation of interests and loyalties on the left that was perhaps in any case inevitable. Both the party and intellectuals oscillated at different levels between strategies internal to the cultural apparatuses of neocapitalism and ferocious rejection of them. The result was a dissolution of old alignments and the emergence of new cleavages that divided the left culturally in a variety of ways.

Undoubtedly, one of the most significant developments of the early 1960s was the emergence of a broad, heterogeneous area of left-wing cultural and intellectual activity outside and beyond the reach of the PCI. In part this arose because shifting alliances in the political system loosened old affiliations and stimulated a demand for new analyses. But there were at least two other motivations. First, after approximately twenty years, the perspectives and watchwords of the postwar years had lost much of their appeal. The ethic of commitment accompanied by recognition of the primacy of the party on the cultural plane commanded few supporters among those for whom 1956 was a more vivid landmark than 1945. Second, the waning appeal of Marxist-Leninism and the declining relevance of the received variety of Gramscian Marxism meant that, for the first time in its history, the PCI found itself gripped by a crisis of ideas. At a time when social and political developments raised many new problems and the opportunities for direct intellectual intervention were multiplying, this was a major handicap. It meant that the process of rejuvenation and reorientation in the culture of the left inevitably accentuated strategic diversification.[29]

Within the party, a major debate occurred in 1962 when the Gramsci Institute held a conference titled "Tendencies in Italian Capitalism." It was recognized that monopoly expansion, although it had exacerbated old contradictions and added new ones, had also signaled a form of development of capitalism. But there was little agreement over how far the party should embrace new schemes of interpretation. Whereas Bruno Trentin of the CGIL union, Lucio Magri, and Vittorio Foa readily employed concepts such as "consumerism," "alienation," "mental conditioning," "mass society," and "affluent society" drawn from modern Catholic sociology and radical American social theory, Amendola, the party's chief economic spokesman, dismissed them as futuristic. In his view the backward elements in the Italian system were still strong, and neocapitalism was a long way from having resolved them. Albeit with some modification, the national task of the working class in seeking to propose solutions to long-standing problems and forge alliances with other strata to force their realization was as valid as ever.[30]

These differences could be contained as long as Togliatti led the PCI. After his death in 1964 the first public fracture in the Communist leadership of the postwar period occurred when a left-wing headed by Ingrao explicitly challenged the theses of Amendola and the center right of the party at the eleventh congress in 1966. At issue was the exhaustion of the reformist impulse of the Center Left government. For the bulk of the leadership this signaled that the Center Left had failed and that the PCI could present itself as the sole champion of change. The left, by contrast, argued that the design had succeeded because a part of the labor movement had been sucked into the government area. Ingrao warned that the ability of neocapitalism to accommodate progressive demands might even lead to the integration of the PCI into the system unless it adopted a radical alternative strategy founded on an alliance of anticapitalist forces forged through mass struggles in the factories and civil society. The left was heavily defeated at the congress, but the issues it had raised did not go away. On the contrary, they found a loud echo in a far left area, which took shape inspired by the resurgence of conflict in the factories, Chinese criticisms of the PCI, and the Vietnam war.

Journals such as *Quaderni Rossi, Classe Operaia,* and *Sinistra* regarded the explicit conversion to constitutionalism operated by Togliatti after 1956 and the PCI's desire to use its political and organizational weight to influence the direction of the Center Left as a capitulation to social democracy. Instead, they sought to forge the necessary elements of an antagonistic strategy designed to explode the capacities for integration of neocapitalism. No less than the sociopolitical strategies of the PCI, the critique invested its cultural policies. Writing in *Quaderni rossi* in 1962, Alberto Asor Rosa first formulated the condemnation of the postwar culture of the left that he would subsequently develop in *Scrittori e Popolo,* the book that, together with Mario Tronti's *Operai e Capitale,* would constitute one of the key texts of the new workerism of the 1960s.[31] In essence, Asor Rosa attacked the PCI for having assumed an uncritical position in relation to bourgeois culture and for stressing those elements of its own culture that most conformed to an existing national tradition. Instead of seeking to build a new culture of the working class, it had emptied Marxist theory of its most radical contents and embraced, in the Gramscian concept of the "national popular," a backward populism that might have had some relevance in the second half of the nineteenth century but was entirely redundant in a context characterized by capitalist development and large-scale industrialization.

Like others who sought the wholesale renewal of left-wing culture, Asor Rosa objected not to the politicization of culture as such but rather to a certain brand of party dogmatism that, he argued, had diverted creative activity from real problems and trapped it in sterile, generically progressive forms. The task was to break definitively with old methods and find new, more specifically Marxist, methods of work that might be promoted through the independent self-organization of intellectuals.

The intellectual ferment on the left was considerable in the 1960s, as different groups and journals, often with very small circulations, struggled to find new sources for a cultural and political revival. Only from 1967 would *Quaderni Piacentini* (founded in 1962) and other publications including *Giovane Critica, Ombre Rosse,* and *Nuovo Impegno* begin to find a wider readership. But their early history is significant because it signaled the emergence of new energies in provincial localities (like Piacenza) once regarded as sleepy backwaters and also because they often published the first Italian translations of authors such as Herbert Marcuse, Max Horkheimer, and Jürgen Habermas. The young editors of these reviews dismissed entirely the perpetual search for alliances that had characterized PCI cultural policies in the 1950s, substituting a more rigorous theoretical approach that relied on historical and international alternatives to the dominant Italian and orthodox Marxist sources. Their endeavors were not universally appreciated. In finding them guilty of "beatnik Stalinism," Pasolini coined a memorable, if inaccurate, epithet that conveyed a deep distaste for both their high moral tones and uncompromising political extremism.[32]

Certainly, for a good many of the writers and intellectuals who had reached maturity in the 1950s, the voices calling for a new poetic of commitment were highly irritating. Rather, their concern was to break free of all the restrictions and limitations deriving from any close relationship between politics and culture. Alberto Arbasino, Umberto Eco, Eduardo Sanguineti, Nanni Balestrini, and others belonging to the mainly northern "Group of 63" brought a new vein of modernism and experimentalism to Italian letters that affected all forms of language and communication. By refusing to conceive of literature in terms of ideology and writing in terms of politics, the "new vanguard" did not reject politics as such, but merely insisted on the autonomy of cultural discourses.[33] In contrast to many artists and intellectuals of an earlier generation, moreover, they did not conceive their role in isolation from cultural apparatuses, the market, modern techniques of expression, and mass communication. Instead, they functioned as a new literary establishment that, while striking an aggressive, nonconformist posture on many questions, aimed to achieve cultural power through group solidarity, media intervention, and coordinated editorial policies. Some of the individual members of the group were very radical but, as Gian Carlo Ferretti has argued, they were objectively internal to the new structures of Italian neocapitalism, not just because they took a positive view of the economic boom and prosperity as the basis for a new literature but because they themselves were often integrated members of the apparatuses they sought to control.[34]

Crisis and Transition in Cultural Policy

To assess the reactions of the PCI it is necessary to bear in mind three points. First, the party was divided on problems of culture as well as politics, and there was disagreement over the degree of renewal felt to be necessary. Whereas the center right tended to defend the status quo, the left demanded revision and greater pluralism. Second, the alliance mentality was still strong; consequently, the primary task was often perceived to be that of "recapturing" intellectual loyalties on whatever basis possible. Third, the development of mass culture demanded responses at broader levels than had conventionally been the practice in cultural policy.

Togliatti was aware that the cultural axis on which he had founded the "new party" in 1944 was no longer fully adequate, nor were old methods of intervention. In the final years of his life he promoted changes that dovetailed with the determination to render more distinctive and autonomous every aspect of his party's profile.[35] To cater for the widening basis of intellectual activity and the debates occasioned by changes in both party ideology and society following the rapid process of development, *Rinascita* became weekly instead of monthly, and a more heavyweight journal *Critica marxista* was also started.[36] As a sign that the party no longer intended to dictate its views, the cultural commission in its old form was done away with at the tenth congress in 1962 and intellectuals were urged to converge on the Gramsci Institute as a focus of research and discussion. Finally, in the Yalta memorandum the commitment to liberalization was confirmed. "We must become the champions of freedom in intellectual life, of free artistic expression, and of scientific progress," Togliatti wrote.[37]

To underline the significance of this departure, the PCI leader chose Rossana Rossanda, a dynamic and relatively young woman cadre from Milan who had headed the city's House of Culture and was at home with new intellectual concerns and debates, to replace Alicata as the party's cultural chief in 1963. Given the controversy surrounding her relatively brief tenure in the post, it is worth examining her policies and reactions to these in a little detail.[38]

Like Lucio Magri and others, Rossanda favored a radical opening-up process.[39] They took the view that, in order to overcome the crisis of orthodox revolutionary theory and effectively analyze transformations in technology, the organization of production, and industry and society generally, it was necessary to reach outside the Communist tradition and make use of the work of John Kenneth Galbraith, Paul Baran, and Paul Sweezy, Joseph Schumpeter and Theodor Adorno. The demise of *Il Contemporaneo* as an independent publication at the end of 1964 may be read as a step in this direction. On one level it concorded with the decision taken at the tenth congress to abandon old methods of direction and surveillance. But on another it indicated the impossibility of preserving a common theoretical denominator among Communist intellectuals. Recent debates had produced "fragmentations of positions (often of an antithetical or mutually polemical nature)."[40] Clearly, if the PCI was to benefit from the revival of interest in Marxism and to avoid simply being eclipsed by the detachment from established currents of Communist theory, a radical response was required.

Writing in *Rinascita* in August 1965, on the first anniversary of Togliatti's death, Rossanda reviewed the manner in which the PCI leader had opted for a national-progressive perspective on the problem of cultural renewal in 1944 that bypassed many of the more recent developments in "international democratic culture."[41] The result was an impoverishment of the culture of the left, she suggested, that would not have occurred if more weight had been given to the positions of *Il Politecnico* and *Studi filosofici*. In keeping with what she took broadly to be Togliatti's final wishes, Rossanda aimed to renew completely the discourses and reference points of PCI cultural policy and establish new bases on which the party might forge a relationship with intellectuals without in any way seeking to intervene in technical controversies over the value of this or that painting, film, or scientific theory.[42]

The reactions to this attempt to open a new phase in cultural policy and liberate the party of the oppressive weight of a tradition that had outlived its usefulness were numerous. For Alicata, a man profoundly attached to the Gramscian-Togliattian tradition, the desire to reread recent history in this critical way was tantamount to heresy. In the debates preceding the eleventh PCI congress in 1966 he mounted a determined campaign to preserve continuity in which he was joined by other members of the "Togliatti generation," including Ranuccio Bianchi Bandinelli and Renato Guttuso, who attacked Rossanda for wanting to effect a "liquidation of the past."[43] Various accusations were leveled against her. In discussing past errors, she was accused of simply embracing the views of one-time adversaries. Instead of practicing the "critical" openness encouraged by Togliatti, it was suggested she merely surrendered to the theses of the "new experimentalism." But it was a sign of the confusion of the times that Rossanda was criticized not only for capitulating to the modernists and the experimentalists but also for adopting perspectives hitherto associated with a left that was external to the party proper.

The variegated nature of the criticism to which Rossanda was subjected suggests that she became a scapegoat for the collapse of the conventional cultural power of the PCI. Rather than acknowledge the sickness some found it more convenient to damn the doctor. Apart from her relative inexperience at the national level and her close identification with Milan, Rossanda suffered from two further handicaps. First, she failed to win the trust of the very people her critique was most designed to appeal to: the intellectuals who had drifted away from the party since 1947 and especially after 1956 on the grounds of its dogmatism and provincial outlook. For reasons of their own, a number of former Communist writers chose to suggest that the PCI was guilty of opportunism in passing from what Remo Cantoni called "an indiscriminate closure to an indiscriminate opening up."[44] Following the desertion of the artists, Oreste Del Buono asserted, the PCI merely aimed to reach them wherever they were.[45] Second, by identifying herself with the left and lining up with Ingrao at the eleventh congress, she left herself politically exposed. It was no surprise that she was one of the first victims of the limited purge that followed the outcome of the congress.

The attack on Rossanda within the party was symptomatic of a general resistance to change in the PCI.[46] Instead of recognizing that profound social changes produced a need for cultural reorientation and revision, middle-aged cadres on the center right of the party preferred to vent their fury by denouncing Communist spokesmen who failed to uphold the universal validity of party tradition. Yet, with or without her, it proved impossible to uphold a "party point of view" on the arts and philosophy, and the party press could do no more than register the real fragmentation that had occurred in the positions and viewpoints of the Communist intelligentsia. Alongside antihistoricism, antirealist and experimental aesthetic positions long resisted by Togliatti and others soon penetrated the party and acquired citizenship there.[47]

In many ways the reevaluation of the postwar cultural options of Togliatti was but a necessary premise to a broader innovation in cultural policy by means of which Rossanda hoped to "dedogmatize" PCI positions; forge links with men such as Elio Vittorini, Franco Fortini, Italo Calvino, and others who had left the party in earlier years; and create the conditions for a new organic influence of the party in the cultural sphere. Unfortunately, the storm of protest raised by Alicata and others served to conceal what was the real core of Rossanda's proposal: a "political program" for culture in which the vision of a reorganization of the national culture would take the form of a set of policies oriented toward reform of the educational system, public broadcasting, and other cultural agencies.[48] In addition, the party would seek to defend and promote the interests of left-wing intellectuals employed in these agencies and connect their demands with a more general alternative outlook on national development.

In the PCI of the 1960s, schizophrenic attitudes prevailed toward mass culture. On the one hand, it was recognized that the decline of the network of recreational and mutual support structures developed in the Center and North, consequent upon demographic changes, greater prosperity, the expansion of municipal services, the diversification of leisure and other factors, while widely regretted, matched a similar process in Catholic-controlled leisure activities. In this sense the supplanting of old forms by new channels of mass cultural diffusion contributed to a general reduction in the frontal conflict between Catholics and Communists that had been widespread in the 1950s. Under the Center Left, moreover, this relaxation produced an easing of cold war tensions at other levels. With the entry of Socialists into RAI, news programs ceased to be so stridently partisan, several programs were broadcast on the Resistance, and some of the neorealist films of the 1940s were brought to the attention of mass audiences for the first time. In 1965, screenings of *Ladri di biciclette* and *Miracolo a Milano* (Miracle in Milan) were viewed by 10 million and 8.5 million people, respectively. Furthermore, the extension of books, magazines, encyclopedias, and television brought new ideas to popular attention and helped stimulate cultural interests. For these reasons Rossanda and Luciano Gruppi, a close collaborator of her successor (Paolo Bufalini), moved beyond the tendency to demonize cultural industries.[49] The fact that Italy was a highly politicized society in which the labor movement and its parties were significant forces meant that there was no danger of a shift to an "American style" model of mass culture in which the lower classes formed a passive, captive audience, Gruppi affirmed.[50] The left, by means of cultural and political action, could impede any flattening process. To be effective it should not seek to promote alternatives to existing industries but rather to bring pressure to bear to promote new, alternative contents.

This shift of policy heralded a new approach to cinema. Ever since the late 1940s the party had preferred to deal with film directors as single creative intellectuals rather than engage with the commercial and industrial apparatuses in which they worked. It had defended creative freedom and the national industry, promoting the cause of realism without excessive dogmatism. It also criticized Hollywood's tendency to invade Italian screens wherever and whenever possible. In consequence, it succeeded in winning the sympathies of many directors and screenwriters of only the most generically left-wing convictions. In the mid-1960s this stance was set aside. Instead, it was argued that one of the most vital conflicts was internal to Italian cinema itself. On the one hand, there was a profit logic that involved indiscriminately making films designed to please the widest audiences and maximize box office earnings regardless of content; on the other, there were filmmakers whose authentically creative and critical capacities needed to be encouraged and stimulated.[51] One result of this policy shift was a campaign led by Mino Argentieri against the increasing dominance of a profit mentality in cinema. With support from a younger generation of filmmakers, most of whom made their debuts in the early 1960s, PCI spokesmen demanded a much greater measure of consistency from directors than had been the case in the past, insisting, for example, that it was not right that someone should make public declarations of opposition to the war in Vietnam and at the same time accept the involvement of American finance in Italian cinema. Directors such as Michelangelo Antonioni, whose film *Blowup* was shot on location in London with an English-speaking cast, were singled out for particular castigation; they were, Argentieri wrote, "Hollywood collaborationists who do not even dare to denounce their own servitude."[52]

The stance was the outcome of an increasing conviction that neorealism had failed because the PCI had not been sufficiently vigilant in pulling up directors such as Giuseppe De Santis and Pietro Germi who had corrupted and diluted the original poetic by making recourse to the tools and conventions of American cinema.[53] In this way entertainment criteria had substituted the sociopolitical impulse at the core of the first wave of the movement, and a passage had occurred to a more conventional type of cinema almost without anyone being aware of it.[54] This view was reinforced by the new focus on industrial mechanisms that followed the attempts of Alicata and Rossanda to redirect cultural policy. For the first time detailed inquiries into the state of the film industry were published in the party press and the degree of penetration achieved by the U.S. majors analyzed.[55] Unless there was a revitalization and expansion of the state's role, it was argued, there was a risk of nonconformist filmmaking being squeezed out altogether and of cinema ceasing to reflect the specific impulses of Italian society.

This perspective was informed by a mixture of real concerns, old prejudices, and new sectarianism. Insufficient account was taken of objective processes of industrialization and internationalization in culture or of the strength of Italian cinema in the 1960s with respect to Hollywood, which, while still powerful, was in steep decline. Moreover, it was simply not true to imply that the presence of American capital lowered the quality of production. Films such as Federico Fellini's *Otto e mezzo* (8½), Marco Bellocchio's *La Cina è vicina* (China is near), and Elio Petri's *I giorni contati* (Numbered days) were all coproductions; the low-grade films featuring Italian pop stars, the films of the Sicilian comedians Franchi and Ingrassia, and many spaghetti westerns were financed by

Italian capital.[56] Although Italian producers found it useful to draw on American support for large-scale spectaculars like *Sodom and Gomorra,* directors were often glad to be able to turn to foreign production companies in order to escape the tyranny of the petty-minded bureaucrats and industrialists who had made life so difficult for them over the previous twenty years.

The contradictions faced by filmmakers who from one point of view wished to maintain a high public profile as creative artists and socially concerned intellectuals, while from another faced industrial pressures and tempting offers to make lucrative commercials for television, were just one feature of the tensions accumulating in Italian society that would explode in 1968.[57]

1967–69: Social Movements and Culture

Throughout the advanced industrial world protests took place in 1968 involving mostly young people and students. The conflicts of that year, despite their brevity and intensity, signaled the end of a certain paternal culture and its system of values and the explosion of new demands for participation and self-determination. In Italy, the movement was part of the international cycle of protest and also the outgrowth of domestic pressures that had been building up since the middle of the decade. The outbreak of unrest in the universities in 1967–68 and the workers' agitation of 1969 marked the end of the attempt to modernize the country without permitting any major changes in social and economic equilibria. Because these conflicts have been analyzed in detail in several studies in English, the treatment here will be brief and specific.[58]

Young middle-class people who had been inspired by Pope John XXIII and President Kennedy in the early 1960s became disaffected as the decade wore on. More open attitudes toward love and sexuality, expressed in part in pop music, repeatedly came into conflict with the bigoted attitudes of the establishment. The influence of far-left intellectual debates was small but not insignificant; the issues of the Vietnam war and the colonels' coup in Greece gave radicals a chance to reach a wider audience. However, protest was initially triggered by an attempt to reform higher education. First presented in 1965, but only discussed in parliament in 1967, the plan formulated by the Christian Democratic

Education minister Luigi Gui for reform of the university aimed in some way to reconcile growing demands for wider access to higher education with industry's need for a more versatile, better trained labor force. Innovations were planned in the internal organization of faculties, teaching arrangements, and course development as well as, most significantly, the imposition of a ceiling on student numbers.[59] Far from satisfying, the proposed reforms did not seem to please anybody. Economic development and raised expectations had placed the educational system at a crossroads between what were incompatible interests, such that any proposal for change, solicited in one form or another in all quarters, would risk firing latent hostilities. The students found their aspirations reflected least of all in the reform and quickly denounced the attempt to tighten selection procedures as contrary to the ideals that supposedly animated the Center Left. Protest began in the major northern cities, as well as Pisa and Trento, in 1967. By early 1968 strictly educational issues had been displaced by increasingly general questions.

The actions of far-left groups, the role of neofascists within the student body, and the repressive response of the authorities all contributed to the broadening of conflict. "Global contestation" became the watchword of spring and summer 1968, as agitation spread throughout civil and political society. All established institutions, traditions, and privileges were subjected to uncompromising criticism, and contradictions and hypocrisies ruthlessly exposed. After the universities, protest spread to festivals, exhibitions, conferences, and museums as the critique of hierarchy, and separation was carried to the cultural system as a whole.

The apparatuses and exponents of high culture were not the sole subjects of attack. Light music festivals and other examples of the lowbrow entertainment furnished by RAI, publishers, and the film industry were also sharply criticized. The example of Luigi Tenco, a singing star who polemically committed suicide in early 1967 after the jury of the San Remo festival preferred an insipid love song to his own entry, was important here. But so too were more ideological considerations. Goffredo Fofi argued that, by means of what he called a "televisual mishmash" (*pappetta televisiva*), the bourgeoisie imposed on the proletariat a culture that was functional to the maintenance of its power insofar as it contained models of behavior and proposed values that conflicted with the true interests of workers.[60] Yet although a stern opposition to what was seen as a conformist low culture was maintained for a number of years, the alternatives were few. Compared to students in the United States, where an alternative culture developed before the university conflicts, Italian students did not look like lifestyle revolutionaries. Mostly they were quite conventionally dressed, and they were austere in their attitudes. That many lived at home did not help experimentation, but the influence of "old left" politics and theory probably counted more. Only later, as the movement became a moment of bonding and consciousness-raising for the participants, did a rejection of bourgeois norms occur. Freer dress styles, communal living, and sexual experimentation become part of the way the movement expressed itself. Women, who by 1968 accounted for one-third of the university population, participated in great numbers in the protests but often in subordinate roles.

Despite these limitations, the student movement represented the eruption of cultural change under the nose of the PCI. The novelty and intensity of the eruption forced the party to act, respond, interpret, discuss, and engage in dialogue, as well as change certain perceptions, in a way that it had not previously had to do. In terms of the actual relations between the PCI and the movement, two spheres need to be distinguished. The first concerns the responses of the party as a complex political entity marked internally by generational and policy divisions as well as a plurality of organizational articulations. Second, beneath the often difficult political relations there is a need to examine the impact of the student unrest on the cultural networks of the PCI and assess how far it contributed to their renewal and rejuvenation. It is the second area that is of primary concern here.

By the late 1960s, the cultural area of the left was much more heterogeneous than it had once been. Moreover, at the grass roots the old networks of popular recreation no longer occupied the central place in popular leisure that they once had. But if in some respects these processes implied a decline in Communist cultural hegemony, there were also countervailing elements. The left did not merely undergo the effects of cultural change passively but developed responses that allowed it to assert its influence in new ways.

It is significant that at this time ARCI began to adopt a bolder line, more autonomous and less defensive, that led to it successfully drawing in more young people and providing a cultural infrastructure for important sections of the student movement. Although in the long term this would enable it to act as a useful bridge between the various components of the extraparliamentary left and the PCI and assist the party in regaining the allegiance of many of the cadres of 1968, in the short term it tended to produce a gap between ARCI, which generally favored an "alternative" cultural approach, and the PCI, which did not.

By 1968 ARCI could count on 3,145 affiliated circles, 62 provincial committees, and 451,000 members.[61] Some of the circles were little more than recreational outlets, but a substantial number functioned inside the Case del popolo, where they shared facilities with trade unions, sports clubs, and (to a diminishing extent) political parties. As television ceased to be a collective phenomenon and entered private homes, with the result that traditional working-class leisure activities went into decline, ARCI circles contributed to the revitalization of grassroots culture by offering a rich program of films, musical events, debates, and lectures. The Leopardi circle, for example, formed in the Bolognese Casa del popolo "Corazza" in 1959, organized evenings of jazz and popular music, and weekly film shows at theatrical events.[62] In the mid-1960s it also held special meetings and shows dedicated to the third-world liberation struggles of Vietnam and Latin America. Circles such as this were not widespread (in Bologna there were three), but, unlike the Case del popolo, they tended to draw an audience from a whole city rather than a well-defined quarter. Thus, when the student movement began to take shape, they were not caught unprepared. Through their activities the Case del popolo as a whole opened up and came to accept the diversity of positions on the left, abandoning their collateral relationship to the PCI. They became centers of activity once more, places where students could relax or participate in evenings of protest songs, watch a performance of avant-garde theater, or listen to a debate involving speakers from a variety of factions and groupings.

At a national level ARCI had begun, from its fourth congress in September 1966, to formulate a cultural policy of its own. Having finally won a promise of ministerial recognition some months previously, the association aimed to make the most of newly favorable conditions characterized by a revival of interest in politics, a demand for culture among youth that was not catered for by the market, and union requests for a reduction in the length of the working week to develop a new texture of cultural associations that might subtract free time from control and exploitation by the culture industry and the employers. In ARCI's view, it was essential that if the continuing battle to prevent the establishment of a capitalist monopoly of leisure was to succeed, then it was not sufficient merely to bring pressure to bear in favor of a general transformation of cultural institutions as part of a revitalization of the structures of civil life. It was also necessary to form an authentically antagonistic culture of the left that drew on the tradition of working-class organization represented by the Case del popolo and circles.[63] The entertainments typical of the recreational movement were thus inserted in a context that saw a variety of courses, seminars, and lectures flourish in which all the major problems of society were studied and discussed. These endeavors assisted students and workers engaged in protests or struggles in understanding their situation and connecting it to a wider context. Courses such as those organized by the Leopardi circle on Marxist theory, workers' councils, the Paris commune, psychiatry, and Chinese medicine contributed significantly to the development of a left-wing consciousness among the mass of students who took part in the occupation movement.[64]

In contrast to the first fifteen years after 1945, when the recreational dimension of the left had been oriented principally toward structuring working-class leisure, often without regard to the content of the initiatives undertaken, the 1960s saw a general process of revision in which the cultural level was raised and a distinctive antagonistic edge added. It would be unwise to exaggerate the extent of this process. Not only did many Case del popolo not have an ARCI circle, but even in those that did a clear separation often obtained between a new range of activities, in which students and some acculturated workers took part, and traditional games of cards and Saturday evening dances that catered to the needs of the conventional clientele. Moreover, it was during the 1960s that television conquered a permanent place in the leisure of the working-class family. But, following the raising of the school leaving age, the average educational level was rising, and it was no longer unheard-of for the sons and daughters of workers to continue their studies. The attempt at redefinition was therefore to some extent favored by events and was essential if leisure was not to be given up altogether as a terrain of competition and conflict.

Television was one of the first areas in which the new line of ARCI made its effects felt. Within ARCI circles "television control groups" were born that monitored RAI-TV's output, and demonstrations were organized from time to time against what was seen as an authoritarian usage of the means that combined lowbrow entertainment with a partial and biased political coverage.[65] This complemented the more general campaign of the PCI for the democratization of television that culminated briefly in a bill for the reform of RAI presented jointly by the Communist and Socialist Parties in April 1970. Founded on the principle of nationalization of RAI, this bill envisaged wider access to public broadcasting and an end to government control as well as the abolition of all advertising and wider use of independently produced material.

Closer to ARCI's own strategic conception of its function was the construction of alternative circuits in cinema and theater. In a major departure from what had been the dominant approach to the cinema in the PCI in the 1950s, ARCI set up its own distribution network for which it produced special 16-mm versions of Italian and foreign classics (the first, in 1960, was Visconti's *La terra trema*). The aim was not to close off left-wing culture in a ghetto but rather to engage in activities capable of stimulating involvement and participation against the dominant atomizing logic of the culture industry.[66] In this commitment to action from below concerned with ownership and control of the means of cultural production, ARCI developed an approach that student activists found extremely congenial. It was natural therefore that, following 1968, the movement of film clubs should expand greatly and undergo a process of revitalization led by young cadres drawn from the protest movements.

The theater was in many ways the scene of the most problematic initiatives in 1968. From the middle of the decade ARCI had considered ways to create a circuit of its own that would break the monopoly of mainstream theater and permit actors to perform before audiences with little or no previous experience of theatrical activity. Around the same time Dario Fo and Franca Rame broke with the bourgeois theater and proposed a stable collaboration with ARCI. The result was a company, Nuova Scena, that in 1968 began touring in the North and Center of Italy, performing in Case del popolo, factories, open squares, and recreational circles. By any standard the enterprise was a success. Using texts written by the company and adapted to local requirements, Nuova Scena undertook 250 performances in its first six months of activity, reaching 105 centers, of which 93 were small villages.[67] An estimated 140,000 people saw its shows. Not only did ARCI's membership rise in consequence, but new circles were even formed to organize further activities.

Despite these fortuitous circumstances, political frictions emerged rapidly. Nuova Scena's statute proclaimed that it was a revolutionary collective that rejected any attempt to reform the bourgeois state and sought to promote the direct assumption of power by the working class.[68] As a result, very explicit political polemics were regularly included in its shows in which the organized parties of the left including the PCI were mercilessly lampooned. Following sustained criticism in the Communist press, many Case del popolo in Emilia and Tuscany closely allied to the PCI refused to accept further bookings for the company.[69] The matter was resolved only toward the end of 1970, when Fo and the members of Nuova Scena most associated with him abandoned both the company and ARCI, leaving others to continue with productions of a more sober type for three more years.

There can be little doubt that ARCI was influenced by the Chinese cultural revolution and far-left thinking, as some Communists suspected. It sought to create a culture based on direct and unmediated contact with the people, and to this end it employed tools of communication such as the wall newspaper that belonged to a bygone era. These were defended on the grounds that they were more likely to be read by ordinary people than books and magazines. But to Adriano Seroni and others they smacked of an inappropriate third worldism.[70] This impression was confirmed by the Maoist flavor of some of the slogans propagated in the wall newspapers, notably "free time as a time for revolution." On one occasion a worker was depicted dragging an intellectual down from his platform (*cattedra*); a slogan printed under the illustration invited readers to "shoot down intellectuals who behave like the priests of cultural rituals."

Despite the oversimplifications of some of ARCI's analyses, it was inaccurate to describe the association's activities as either irrelevant or defensive. Alternative circuits were conceived not as a means of withdrawal but rather as the best means of bringing pressure to bear on existing institutions. Moreover, in latching on to leisure as a key terrain of conflict, the association encountered the approval of the trade unions and of the Catholic and Republican recreational organisms. The dispute with the PCI continued into the early 1970s, with ARCI insisting repeatedly that it was the party that had failed to grasp the novelty of the situation.[71] By 1970 it was claiming the right to occupy not merely a cultural space but a political space too.[72] Between the destructive fervor of the revolutionary vanguards and the continuing concern of the PCI to use culture as a terrain on which class alliances might be forged, ARCI drew on new and old instruments to elaborate what it saw as the socialist culture of the near future.

To a large extent the hopes of ARCI were linked to the specific impulses of the late 1960s. In the long term it would prove impossible to break the hegemony of television and cultural industries.[73] But more than any other sector of the labor movement it was well placed to benefit from the across-the-board revitalization of grassroots organizations that occurred at that time. In consequence, it mediated between the established left and protest movements, assisting in the construction of a broader and more heterogeneous area of the left in society capable of outlasting the gradual downturn in the cycle of protest. At the same time it effectively did away with a variety of old myths and lent cultural policy a mass antagonistic dimension for the first time.

The Political Response of the PCI

At a more general level the Communists initially found the unrest a pleasant surprise, proof that the consolidation of industrial capitalism did not necessarily imply the passivity and conformism that had been so widely feared. As Giuseppe Chiarante, one of the Communist leaders most directly concerned with educational questions, wrote in a topical book on 1968, previously this new sensitivity was "expressed only in anarchic revolt, individual rejection of integration, destructive attitudes, and passive negation of current values."[74] However, by no means the whole of the PCI or the workers' movement viewed the burgeoning protest in such a positive way. Not only did student activists display an easy extremism and cosmopolitanism that irritated party members; they were also arrogant and intolerant of the established left, despite the fact that they were often of bourgeois families and had no experience of grassroots political or industrial struggle. Thus any indulgence was a mistake for some senior figures on the right of the party.

It is probable that the imminence of the June 1968 elections prevented the right from winning out. The PCI was fearful that student leaders might call for abstention, as had occurred in West Germany; in addition, the desire to end the isolation of the party was strong. Against this background, Togliatti's successor Luigi Longo undertook a personal initiative and met with student leaders in Rome. Although the latter, like many other student activists, regarded the PCI as something of a political dinosaur, they were pleased to win an acknowledgment that the student movement was "an aspect and a moment of the Italian revolutionary movement."[75]

The student movement was in many ways a brief phenomenon. But during 1968 two sectors of society other than university students began to show signs of unrest; high school students and workers. The former were obviously particularly receptive to the impulses of protest in higher education, to which older brothers and sisters often contributed. School students rebelled against selection, demanded grants, and called for open discussions, the right to hold assemblies, and the right to make an input into the curriculum. They rejected the policy of cutting schools off from societal influences and politics. However, as Lumley observes, the schools' movement was also characterized by a more explicit rejection of respectable bourgeois society than its senior counterpart. An instant repertoire of insubordination derived from British and American youth cultures was much more readily drawn on; long hair, garish clothes, pop music, disrespectful behavior. It was at this level, much more than in the 1968 of the universities, that the potentially subversive implications of the spread of a foreign-inspired mass youth culture were worked out.

Contacts between workers and students in 1968 were limited but not insignificant. Workerism was one interpretative paradigm adopted by the student movement in Pisa and Trento, and the idea of the university as a factory was widespread. As systematic police raids in spring 1968 rendered continuation of the university occupation movement problematic, many demonstrators moved in the direction of the industrial sphere. For the most part students joined pickets outside factories or public marches, where the enthusiasm and additional numbers they brought were mostly welcomed by weak unions denied access to workplaces and eager to create an impression of general social support for their cause.[76] Some of those with applied professional skills (students of medicine and law) aimed to render themselves useful to the working class in a more practical way; a minority sought to shake off embarrassing social origins by seeking factory employment.[77]

Between autumn 1968 and the closing months of 1969 a new cycle of industrial conflicts unfolded in Italy that reached its zenith in the "Hot Autumn," a brief but explosive season that witnessed one of the largest strike movements in twentieth-century Europe. Whereas earlier agitation was initiated by experienced workers with long experience of union activity, semi-skilled and unskilled workers contributed decisively to the radicalization of protest. In factories such as those of Fiat in Turin, of Montedison in Porto Marghera, and Pirelli in Milan, where unions were weak and elements of paternalism strong, years of pent-up hostility burst into the open. The subaltern position assigned to the working class in Italy's postwar development was radically overcome, as control over the factories slipped from the hands of management. The authority of foremen and squad leaders was completely undermined by a new spirit of shop-floor solidarity and the widespread use of brief but highly disruptive "hiccup" strikes.

The concentration of the strikes in the North and the drawn-out nature of the protest cycle meant that no revolutionary crisis occurred, even though this was fervently hoped for and promoted by the far-left militants who were so important in extending conflict. However, activists nevertheless remained firm in their convictions. Because the entry on the scene of the workers' movement prolonged the wave of social conflict begun in 1967 and absorbed some of the themes that had been put in circulation by the student movement, there seemed to be little need to interrogate the appropriateness of the analyses of society that had gained credence at the height of the student agitation. Yet although the revisionist Marxist writings of the early 1960s, on which the activists of 1968 drew, were closely concerned with the factory and the changing composition of the working class, these were not the only source of the ideology of the students. From Marcuse, the French movement, and the liberation movements of the third world, they derived a global critique of the Western model of economic development and of established patterns of left-wing opposition. In reality, however, the critique developed in the student movement not just of the oppressive nature of old institutions and values but of the moral corruption perceived in the newer consumerist ideologies of the family car and the refrigerator did not at any point find a sympathetic audience among ordinary people. This was not due to an innate insensitivity to any discourse of a qualitative nature (the struggles over the organization of work and production in the factory were proof of that). Rather, it may be attributed to the fact that the critique itself was based on inaccurate assumptions about Italian society.

In his book on the Italian working class published in 1968, Amendola argued that the whole thematic of the "affluent society" as "mass consumer society" was a false one in Italy.[78] This was not entirely true, because the fascination of consumer durables was sufficiently strong to have provoked significant changes in the practice of the PCI itself by the end of the 1950s and to have acted as an impulse to the migratory wave from the South. But he was undoubtedly right to point out the low levels of average consumption that still prevailed in Italy, where growth had been led more by exports than an expanding internal market. Moreover, the Italian road to development, far from leading to the integration of the major organizations of the working-class movement, had been predicated on their exclusion. Thus the PCI and the unions, for all the criticism to which they were subjected, possessed reserves of credibility far greater than many on the far left wished or imagined.

Although the PCI was ultimately the main political beneficiary of the whole protest cycle and in consequence saw its national political standing much strengthened in the mid-1970s, it would be an exaggeration to claim, as did one of the leading figures on the center right of the PCI, Gerardo Chiaromonte, that the movements merely accelerated processes of economic, social, and cultural transformation already in progress and to which the party had made a great contribution.[79] In reality, the movements were much more than an expression of continuity — indeed, in a very real sense, they abruptly ended the model of modernization followed up to that point in Italy — and the role of the PCI was frankly less. Not by chance for Chiaromonte the greatest crime in 1968 was committed by those intellectuals and Communists who flirted with extremist currents instead of vigorously disputing their theories and wrongheaded assumptions.[80] Yet neither the workerist Marxism of the early 1960s nor the groups that propagated it were external to the real trajectory of Italian development. Had the PCI as a whole opted for confrontation, the risk of finishing up like the PCF, which neither understood nor was renewed by the events of 1968, would have been considerable. In 1969 the PCI expelled Magri, Rossanda, and other leftists who had founded the factional journal *Il Manifesto* in the belief that revolution was once more on the agenda in the West, but in other ways, and particularly in the area of grassroots cultural activities, it maintained some sort of dialogue.

A multipurpose float calling on people to vote Communist, support the peace campaign and beware of television. (From the archives of the Istituto milanese per la storia della Resistenza e del movimento operaio.)

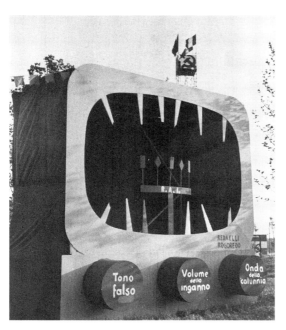

Antitelevision propaganda at a Communist festival. (From the archives of the Istituto milanese per la storia della Resistenza e del movimento operaio.)

Under the gaze of Engels, Gramsci, Stalin, and Lenin: a Saturday evening dance in a Casa del popolo. (From the archives of the Istituto milanese per la storia della Resistenza e del movimento operaio.)

Scouting Communist-style: a group of young Pioneers. (From the archives of the Istituto milanese per la storia della Resistenza e del movimento operaio.)

Prosperity reaches the workers: a Milanese family aboard a Lambretta scooter. (From the archives of the Istituto milanese per la storia della Resistenza e del movimento operaio.)

An American-style skiffle band performs at a *festa dell'Unità*. (From the archives of the Istituto milanese per la storia della Resistenza e del movimento operaio.)

"Bobo" and "Molotov" mourn the passing of the PCI. (From *L'Unità*, 18 February 1991, 10; reproduced by kind permission of *L'Unità* and the author, Sergio Staino.)

5

Crisis, Austerity, Solidarity

The Question of Hegemony in the 1970s

For Italian public opinion the 1970s became a decade to forget, almost as soon as it was over. The dominant images of the period conveyed by press and television were ones of terrorism, economic crisis, political immobilism, ideological saturation, social disintegration, and cultural disorientation. Such a picture was not, and is not, entirely false. During this period Italian democracy faced several serious challenges that it did not always appear able or willing to respond to. Yet the specificity of these should not be exaggerated, for the country's basic problems were similar to those of most industrial societies. They were, however, exacerbated by the effects of rapid and uneven growth, rising expectations on the part of a complex variety of social strata, cultural lacerations arising from the erosion of a traditional authority structure, and the sudden spread of a modern industrial culture to the population as a whole. The country was, in short, caught in a situation in which tradition and modernity combined and conflicted in unprecedented ways at different levels of society. Yet to picture the period only in negative terms would be inaccurate. For many people the 1970s were unquestionably a positive decade. A variety of new groups gained recognition as active participants in the political process. Important reforms were passed affecting civil rights and social services (which reached a level of provision quantitatively equal to that of other advanced societies). Society as a whole became less intolerant, and the material fruits of the economic boom were extended more widely than ever before.

The period between the divorce referendum of 1974 and the election of June 1976 was in many ways the most fruitful and fortuitous phase in the whole history of the PCI. Its membership and its electorate both grew; it attracted support in new quarters, acquired recognition and respect as a potential force of government, and occupied a central place in political debate. One key to its success was its multifaceted appeal. Somewhat paradoxically, the PCI in the 1970s was perceived as a force both for the preservation of order and for change, for moderation and at the same time for revolution. This image evidently did not displease the party leadership, which cultivated it by its proposal for a Historic Compromise between Communists, Catholics, and Socialists: the three great currents of opinion and political forces whose ideas and organizational expressions were seen to encapsulate civil society.

The PCI's disappointing experience on the fringes of government between 1976 and 1979 was extensively analyzed and debated during the 1980s.[1] Yet, if the causes of the party's failure are to be grasped, it is not sufficient to examine lacunae and distortions in its action at the governmental level or to scrutinize the reasons why it proved so difficult to hold together the coalition that supported it in 1976. Close attention must also be paid to the PCI's cultural activities and to the means whereby it sought to establish a new pattern of hegemony in the country. The party's attempts to harness the energies of the intellectuals who flocked to its side and to reorient popular culture by extending the institutions of working-class leisure were in many ways impressive. However, they rested on certain assumptions that were either faulty or incomplete. Thus not only were the PCI's adversaries able to outmaneuver the party on the terrain of government where they were historically strongest, but they were able to forestall its design for cultural hegemony and manipulate modernization in such a way as to undermine the credibility and appeal of the left's project. Unable to grasp this, or to free itself of procedures and commitments that had once seemed appropriate but that became less so in the late 1970s, the PCI saw a decline in its cultural influence that by the end of the decade was actually greater than its loss of political support in the 1979 election.

Modernization, Marxism, and the Intellectuals

By the end of 1969 the protest cycle that began early in 1967 had reached its conclusion. With some gains achieved, especially by the industrial working class, and the energies of many exhausted, protest waned and the traditional organizations of the workers' movement began to rebuild their authority and prestige. But 1968 had been no temporary or superficial phenomenon in Italy. It had fundamentally shaken social and cultural relationships, created a culture of protest, turned thousands of students and workers in activists, diffused expectations of political change, undercut old values and norms, and diffused new ideas about the factory, the school, and the family. It broke a given model of modernization, or so it seemed; one based on low salaries, steady erosion of the collective influence of the working class, and the reconciliation of consumerism with conventional values and patterns of social control.

Italy was still in many ways an intolerant society in the early 1970s, but pressure for change was stimulated considerably following 1968 by the circulation of themes and suggestions born of the youth and student movement and the continuous attacks on convention maintained by the film industry and popular publishers. The fragmentation of old models and values in the wake of the protests, and the simultaneous erosion of the ability of public institutions to act as the transmitters of norms, contributed to the emergence of what might be called an antiauthoritarian common sense. This diffuse insubordination was most noticeable in the public domain. Urban protests over housing, public transport, health facilities, and other services, for example, disrupted everyday life for much of the 1970s. But traditional authority relations were also disturbed by changing attitudes and behavior even in the home.

The declared goal of the PCI in the 1970s was to seek to organize a new pattern of hegemony in Italian society around the working class. After being expelled from spheres of influence in the late 1940s, the labor movement asserted itself powerfully at every level from 1969. After declining steadily during the economic boom, the number of blue-collar Communists in Italy's factory town par excellence, Turin, rose from 13,700 in 1967 to 27,600 ten years later; the white-collar membership increased from 60 to 5,200.[2] Around one-third of the party membership in Turin was signed up in the workplace in the early 1970s, a figure that reveals the remarkable extent of the PCI's resurgence as a factory organization. In 1969, Hellman notes, there was just one section in each of the city's six largest industrial plants, with a total membership of 1,000. In 1973 there were thirteen sections in these plants with 3,900 members. By 1978 the figures had risen to twenty-four and 6,300.[3]

These developments were matched by an expansion of the culture of the labor movement, which became a pole of attraction for quite diverse social strata. Students and young intellectuals threw themselves into organizing courses of history and theory for workers who, under the provisions of the Workers' Statute, were entitled to 150 hours study leave per year. Buoyed by the great season of collective action, many of the institutions and rituals of the left-wing subculture also underwent a significant revival. Not only the unions and ARCI, but the cooperative movement, Communist press, publishing activities, and the *L'Unità* festivals all expanded and grew in appeal. Somewhat to the consternation of the PCI, a great variety of left-wing initiatives also flourished outside the official labor movement.

Because they enjoyed substantial resources and were an integrated part of a stable subculture, the institutions and cultural activities of the PCI did not share the weaknesses that Lumley has identified in the counterculture of the far left.[4] As the great season of collective action unfolded, these structures drew in new blood, and, when the far left began to falter around 1973, they expanded further. There was still a very marked regional imbalance, with many areas of the South remaining completely outside the left's networks, but the level of development was nonetheless impressive. The expansion of ARCI was quite rapid after it gained the same legal privileges that had been granted earlier to the Catholic and Republican associations and as factory recreational circles left the declining ENAL to affiliate with it.[5] For its part, the League of Cooperatives owned no fewer than fifty-eight theaters, one-quarter of the total in the country; the *L'Unità* festivals, which increased in number from 4,700 in 1972 to 7,000 in 1975, constituted a larger circuit than any organized by the domestic entertainment industry.[6] By any standard, these were enviable resources. The integrated nature of the mainstream left's circuits, moreover, meant that in some spheres, such as live popular music, it could compete effectively with, and sometimes even displace, the private sector.

It was not only at the level of popular culture that the left experienced a widening of its influence. Cultural legitimation increased at every level as the tradition of antifascism flourished in the face of the deadly threats of the extreme right. In the early 1970s left-wing novelists enjoyed a new heyday, and the prince of Communist film directors, Luchino Visconti, was accepted without reserve as an exponent of national culture (his funeral in March 1975 was accorded full state honors). The Resistance

Crisis, Austerity, Solidarity   **141**

won a central place in all mainstream accounts of recent Italian history, and the publication by Einaudi of a critical edition of Gramsci's prison writings in 1975 was a major event.

Yet, at the same time as Marxism triumphed, it also diversified further. Although Gramsci and Lenin were widely referred to, it was not always the official versions of their thought that prevailed. In the 1960s, Mao, Leon Trotsky, Rosa Luxemburg, and the council communists all acquired an audience, as did the Frankfurt School and the structuralist Marxists Louis Althusser and Nicos Poulantzas. In the 1970s, currents that had always been minoritarian within the PCI, like those associated with Galvano Della Volpe, or that had flourished outside it, like those of the (ex) *ouvrieristes* Mario Tronti, Alberto Asor Rosa, and Massimo Cacciari, gained a wide following inside and outside the party. Even within the PCI, mainstream intellectuals such as Giuseppe Vacca and Biagio De Giovanni in Bari constituted a "school" of their own, publishing their work not through Einaudi or Editori Riuniti but through a local left-wing publisher, De Donato.

Although the Communists were the eventual political beneficiaries of this blossoming interest, it is probably true to say that the majority of senior figures in the party and long-standing activists never really accepted, and probably never properly understood, the diversification of Marxist culture. For Luciano Gruppi, as for other cadres, the alternative currents to emerge in the 1960s were scarcely more than petit bourgeois deviations to be combated simply by citing a few corrective passages from the classics.[7] But the men who were mainly responsible for Communist cultural policy in the 1970s, Giorgio Napolitano and, from 1975, Aldo Tortorella, recognized that, in part at least, the party had to learn lessons rather than impart them. If it had lost control of Marxist culture in the 1960s, it was because its own brand of Marxism had proved inadequate as a tool for analyzing the structural changes taking place in Italian society. It was clear, for example, that at the end of the 1960s protest had exploded in ways and in quarters of society that were quite unexpected.

At a pathbreaking Gramsci Institute conference held in 1971 on the theme "Italian Marxism in the 1960s and the theoretical-political training of the new generations," Communist intellectuals and politicians for the first time examined the background to the student movement and the emergence of a far-left critique of the labor movement and the established parties of the left.[8] The debate touched on every aspect of the PCI's theoretical and cultural profile from 1956. The question of reform, social and cultural change, and the role of world events in contradicting some of the assumptions embedded in the party's intellectual and political tradition were reviewed. The whole affair, it might be said, was an admission, remarkable for a party that was still in many ways convinced of its own supremacy, that Communists had fallen out of touch with society and that, to recover a fruitful relationship, lessons needed to be learned from the "heresies of the 1960s."[9]

Two strategies were pursued to facilitate renewal. First, the party opened up to the representatives of the Marxist dissent, not merely tolerating them but welcoming them into its ranks. In addition, Della Volpe's insistence on the need to strengthen the materialistic foundations of Communist ideology and come to terms with the natural sciences was largely accepted. A crucial role here was played by Enrico Berlinguer's brother, Giovanni. A professor of physiology at Rome University as well as a party official with responsibilities for culture, he was a rare example of a Communist intellectual with strong links to the world of science. As such, he was well placed to heighten awareness of scientific research in the party and to extend its influence into a new area. He opened up the Gramsci Institute to scientific issues and helped promote conventions such as that held on the theme "Science and the organization of work" in Turin in 1973, which brought some scientists into contact with the labor movement for the first time. Second, any attempt to dictate to intellectuals was abandoned. The commitment to pluralism and freedom of research first set out at the tenth congress in 1962 was strongly reasserted, and *Rinascita* was encouraged to host a wider range of viewpoints.

These positions were sternly criticized by traditionalists. Carlo Salinari, Renato Guttuso, Ranuccio Bianchi Bandinelli, and, later, Giorgio Amendola all attacked the lack of direction that resulted and the concessions that these positions seemed to be making.[10] But Napolitano denied that the party's own specific Italian-Marxist tradition was being liquidated. "It was, in substance," he stated in 1973, "a matter of making an effort to safeguard the vital nucleus of our 'historicist' conception — defending it from certain hasty detractors — while at the same time overcoming the intrinsic limits that it has revealed." Moreover, tolerance was not an option, to be debated or revoked at will, he asserted, but a principle to which the PCI had to show it adhered.[11]

In terms of quantitative recruitment, the 1970s saw an expansion of membership that was comparable only with the 1943–45 period. It was as though the "wounds" of 1956 and 1968 were overcome in one bound.[12] Naturally, this extraordinary conversion provoked anger in some quarters. Although the leading independent newspapers noted that two out of every three intellectuals seemed to have become a Communist, *Il Giornale* and the DC's daily *Il Popolo* denounced those who aligned themselves with the PCI as opportunists. No doubt this was an appropriate judgment in some instances, but there were many factors that contributed to a process of realignment that involved intellectuals of a Catholic and lay background as well as a Marxist one. The crisis of the New Left and disgust at the corruption of the DC both counted. So too did the campaign on divorce, which brought the PCI into contact with groups such as the *cattolici del No* (Catholic dissenters), some of whom, including Raniero La Valle and Mario Gozzini, stood as independents in the Communist lists in 1976. Other factors included the erosion of the neocapitalist ideology of permanent growth and the reemergence of long-standing problems not tackled by the stop-start reforms of the Center Left, the degradation of institutions, and the PCI's adoption of a more liberal stand on questions of culture and politics. In addition, anticommunism was rapidly losing force. In many quarters, people could for the first time express support for the PCI without bearing any career or social penalty. Finally, many intellectuals were attracted by talk of the need for a new organization of culture and the promise of a preeminent role in reshaping society along more collective lines. Subject to a long-term decline in their real influence and deprived of any autonomous or creative role by institutions and apparatuses that had long since taken over the main functions of social and cultural integration, they saw in the PCI a vehicle of their release from an intolerable but unavoidable subalternity.[13]

As Communist influence grew, the party's cultural chiefs were presented with an opportunity to shake off the subcultural aspects of their practices and to seek to condition the culture of society as a whole. The latter had always been the preferred policy of the party hierarchy, and this was reflected in the changes that took place in the *L'Unità* festivals. From 1972 the larger provincial festivals and, above all, the annual national festival changed in character.[14] They ceased to be events directed exclusively at PCI members and loyal supporters and became a key aspect of a wider cultural strategy. They became gigantic in size and more professional in their construction. The festivals showed what could be achieved by volunteer labor motivated by political passion and a collective spirit; they showed the PCI as a model of efficiency and a proponent of "a new way of governing"; they also showed that the Communists could take, and indeed to a large extent had taken, over the best in bourgeois culture and made it available to all. The holding of the annual national festival outside areas of extensive and solid Communist support in the 1970s (Rome 1972, Venice 1973, Naples 1976, and so on) underlined the growth of the PCI's force in the whole nation.

Among purists and politicized artists there was much criticism of a policy shift that seemed to deprive the festivals of their specificity. In particular, the appearance of commercial stands, it was argued, had turned the most important cultural event in the left's calendar into a version of the Milan fair, a sort of giant supermarket in which every visitor could admire the goods on display, make his or her selection, and leave without experiencing any particular elevation of class or political consciousness.[15] However, the potential for hegemony in the middle of the decade was strong enough to persuade even ARCI to abandon "alternative" policies and make a bid for general influence. The expansion of ARCI, the creation of the regions, strong pressure for the reform of culture, the erosion of the DC's dominant position, the disintegration of the challenge of the far left, and finally the conquest of power by the major parties of the left at the local level all created the conditions for a qualitative leap. The leaders of ARCI first promoted the unification of their association with the sports association UISP (already in force on a de facto basis at local level) in 1975; a year later they unveiled a new line that proposed to exploit the political and institutional opportunities of the moment to institute a new phase of planning of culture and recreation at the local and national level. This involved the conceptualization of a new role for the state in tourism, leisure, and sport as well as more established cultural activities. However, ARCI spokesmen were careful to stress that planning should be carried out jointly by the institutions and social forces, among which they counted principally ARCI itself and the other components of the left's cultural network. The aim was neither a paternalistic provision of services nor a restriction of choice but a new framework in which citizens participated actively and determined collectively the needs of their city or quarter.[16] This emphasis on decentralization, participation from below, and the role of social actors was important, for it distinguished ARCI's approach from social democratic ones followed

Crisis, Austerity, Solidarity

earlier in northern Europe by aiming to keep the initiative within civil society.[17] As part of this process it was intended to extend the texture of grassroots organization by making the cultural and recreational circuit of the labor movement into a resource for the whole community.[18]

Reaching for Hegemony

With its emphasis on work and responsibility and its evident disapproval of the liberalization and commercialization of sex that occurred in the mid-1970s, the PCI appeared to some to be old-fashioned and puritanical. The repeated references to private consumerism as a "distortion" and to the need to substitute it with a more positive, social variety also struck a negative chord. But, in the context of the oil crises of 1973 and 1975 and the more general difficulties of Western capitalism, the Communist interpretation of social and economic development won ground. With the embroilment and defeat of the United States in Southeast Asia, it seemed that the whole "American way of life" as it had been adopted in postwar Italy was destined to disappear. It was up to the working-class movement to step in and offer to lead the country in a different, more collective direction.

At a central committee meeting dedicated to culture held in January 1975, Napolitano sought to register formally the advances that had been made and address specifically how the PCI might begin to construct a new framework of hegemony. Underlying Napolitano's address were two assumptions. First, there was a conviction that bourgeois hegemony had substantially dissolved. By its neglect of education, scientific research, and Italy's historical and cultural heritage, he asserted, the country's elite had revealed its incompetence ("We have had a ruling class not only incapable but unworthy of running the country").[19] Taken in the broader context of the objective crisis of neocapitalist ideology and the Center Left, this neglect was tantamount to a confession of bankruptcy. Second, there was a conviction that, although the crisis created the conditions for a struggle to assert the hegemony of the working class, there were also dangers of an involution within the situation. In other words, there was a risk that the collapse of the American-derived idea of development and progress as a process of monopoly-led economic and technological growth would lead to mistrust in the possibility of any idea of progress. In this case, regression, disorder, and the disappearance of any sense of the public good were the likely outcome. Thus it was not just subjectively desirable for the PCI to engage in a broad-ranging cultural struggle, it was essential if the party was to promote a new pattern of class hegemony. Only in this way would it be possible to affirm an alternative view of progress.

How exactly was this new framework to be constructed? It is significant that emphasis was not placed purely on the party or on the intellectuals as individuals, as had been the case in the 1940s. Drawing on Gramsci's previously neglected writings on the organization of culture and Althusser's extensions of these, cultural spokesmen highlighted the importance of ideological apparatuses, which were seen as crucial to the transformation of society. As Giovanni Berlinguer put it in October 1975, "they contain a greater flexibility, permeability, and possibility of self-determination of ends and methods with respect to other institutions."[20] In other words, educational institutions, broadcasting, cultural and scientific institutes could be modified much more easily than the police, the bureaucracy, or economic structures; to this extent, their position in capitalist society was potentially contradictory.

The education system was of particular interest. After 1968 this came to be viewed within the PCI as a sphere of general political relevance, not just a central concern of cultural policy, the position to which Mario Alicata had promoted it in the 1950s. This was because an old system of university education geared to the reproduction of a narrow elite had been dramatically undermined by the educational expansion of the 1950s and 1960s, and, by their inaction, the ruling forces showed that they could neither control this process politically nor supply a new vision of the purposes of education and the role of knowledge in an advanced industrial society. As a result, an institution that, in Giovanni Berlinguer's words, had been "one of the bourgeois bunkers up to now impregnable by the workers' movement," vacillated and ceased to function as a simple transmitter of bourgeois ideology.[21] This provided the PCI with an unprecedented chance to intervene and mobilize on this terrain and to offer an alternative vision of the role of education in society. The party began purposefully. In contrast to the far left, which rarely went beyond a repeated call to "destroy the school" and eliminate cultural and intellectual hierarchies, and whose exponents in any case largely abandoned educational institutions as specific fields of struggle after the demise of the student movement, the PCI invested much energy in reinforcing its presence in precisely this area. Napolitano explained in 1971 that the PCI wanted "a school system open to the need for transformation in Italian society, to the interests of the working class and the popular masses, to the conception of the world and the cultural positions of which the working class is the bearer."[22] In other words, the party wished to promote Marxism as a source of inspiration and creativity in a variety of disciplines and advance it as the ideal modern historical, scientific, and technical axis of a reformed school system. It also wished to open up educational institutions to the idea that only the working class in its given organized form could lead the process of social change. By 1975 these ideas were being articulated differently. In keeping with its strategy, the party advocated a new normative framework that ostensibly was not Marxist but pluralistic, including all democratic, lay, and Catholic currents. The stress fell on antifascism, on the promotion of rational attitudes and a modern scientific consciousness, and on the democratization of institutions. However, reference continued to be made to the ideas of equality and international solidarity as well as to the recognition of the role of labor in society and to the rejection of war and racism.[23]

The crisis of schools and cultural institutions was seen as an important aspect of the more general crisis of social organization and the political direction of the state. The role of Communist intellectuals in helping develop a solution was twofold. First, they were encouraged to contribute to a new vision of progress by elaborating the practical and technical aspects of it. They were to explore the role of science and technology in a new type of development, debate the appropriate form of educational reform, and conceptualize a new organization of work and of cultural activities; in short, to shape a new culture. In doing this they were encouraged to break out of their insular practices and debate with the representatives of other currents, especially Catholics. They were also urged to overcome once and for all the limitations of a tradition in which both the social and natural sciences had occupied a negligible place and to examine and engage with the advances of non-Marxist strands of thought. For Asor Rosa this change involved intellectuals aligned with the labor movement "making the leap" from a minoritarian intellectual attitude to the hegemonic attitude of intellectuals who participate in a "project of government."[24]

Second, intellectuals were encouraged to contribute to the education and cultural advancement of the common people. To overcome "pro-found distortions in the habits, patterns of consumption, and use of lei-sure of the popular masses" they were urged to act, not just individually but collectively, to mold public opinion and win support for new styles of living. They were expected to do this through the schools, universities, and other public institutions and through collaboration with the party and popular organizations. From 1975 great stress was placed on the mass dimension of cultural policy. It was seen to be crucial to the success or otherwise of the PCI's struggle to effect a shift in the culture and values of the population at large. Napolitano referred to the role of the cooperative movement, of local government, and also of ARCI (now that it had over-come its previous attachment to class-based alternatives), in making culture an "aspect of a different and higher way of life."[25] But he recog-nized that intellectuals, if they broke with "residual aristocratic atti-tudes," had a crucial part to play — for example, in filling large gaps in the left's knowledge of the real nature of mass cultural life by studying popular literature and television programs.

In general, the PCI may be said to have successfully effected a measure of theoretical renewal and recuperated a relationship with broad groups of intellectuals on the basis of a perspective of institutional and cultural change. Under Napolitano and Tortorella, most of the remaining traces of dogmatism were eradicated from the party's policies along with the sectarianism of more recent stamp, which had crept into some areas such as cinema in the late 1960s. Great attention continued to be paid to to the men of letters who to a large degree still acted as the prima donnas of Italian culture, but more interest than before was shown in the wider intelligentsia. It was recognized that this was a vast and heterogeneous stratum whose members were central to the functioning and to the cohe-sion of advanced industrial society.

Ultimately, though, the PCI failed to realize its goals. Some of the rea-sons for the Communists' failure to give rise to the new model of hege-mony that its spokesmen theorized and sought to articulate were bound up with the political events of the 1976–79 period. But significant mis-conceptions and errors of judgment undermined their aspirations even before they were presented with an opportunity to realize them.

One problem was that the workplace was seen as the only fulcrum of identity and variations in values as explainable solely in class terms. Communists were not sensitive to "private" questions, and they reacted awkwardly to such issues as divorce and abortion. Feminism was at first dismissed, in the words of a leading woman Communist, as an "heir to the youth movement and its errors."[26] It was seen as an imported phenomenon of American origin that was of concern to middle-class women with no experience of the world of work, more an expression of social unease than a social movement.

By 1976 such attitudes had softened markedly, but the party's whole encounter with the women's movement and the feminist problematic was governed by a total faith that it, like other "new subjects," would "flow into the river of the workers' movement," adding new dimensions to its battle for emancipation without in any way undermining this project.[27] It was not understood that feminism was the bearer of a universal point of view that tendentially broke the system of solidarity on which the left's political strategy was founded by prioritizing the contradictions between the two sexes at the expense of the labor movement's concern with the conflict between capital and labor. Nor was there any sense that society's developments and the complexity of its contradictions might in some way render the social leadership of the party vulnerable or fragile. There was perhaps no reason why there should have been in the short term, because no group detached itself from the PCI in the triumphant run up to the elections of 1976, and women did not do so afterward either.[28] "The crisis of double militancy for Communist women never led to a break with the party, as happened with the activists of the New Left," Gloria Zuffa has written, "because they still derived from the life of the party a rich experience of interaction with reality, education, and personal realization." Unlike the women of the extraparliamentary left, they did not equate the "personal" with the merely private, nor did their criticism of the tradition of emancipation pass over the fact that they had themselves benefited from its achievements.[29]

More fundamentally, most Communists tended to interpret Italy's economic crisis unilaterally. Unlike the country's economic elite, which regarded the situation as one of grave but fundamentally conjunctural difficulties, they saw it as one of irreversible decline unless "elements of socialism" in the form of planning, public investment, and democratization were introduced. They failed to understand how crisis acted as a stimulus to industry, which responded by decentralizing production to the small factories of the "third Italy" and by making recourse to the twilight "black economy" that escaped official regulation and that drew

Between Hollywood and Moscow

on women, youth, and immigrants for its piece-rate labor. Here costs were low while profits and productivity were high.

Inevitably, these developments undermined the power and leverage of the organized working class. In 1974 Paolo Sylos Labini revealed that Italian society was characterized by an ever greater presence of the commercial and white-collar middle classes, which constituted half the active population.[30] The manual working class, by contrast, was declining. At a cultural level, too, the picture was less encouraging than it first appeared. Although party rituals drew in vast numbers of people once they were directed to the population at large and ARCI benefited from an influx of students and from the affiliation of circles that had previously been associated with other labor movement associations, the core cultural institutions of the labor movement declined. The Case del popolo lost their characteristics as alternative and autonomous centers of collective mobilization and recreation, as the PCI scaled down its involvement in them and as left-wing administrators at the local level sponsored public structures and events geared more toward "the people" in general than to a class.[31] They were services open for use by undifferentiated citizens rather than aspects of the collective solidarity of a class. As Giorgio Triani has noted, "the recognition of the state of crisis of the functions traditionally performed by the Case del popolo was inserted in a design that, although it claimed a leading role for the working class, assigned to the Case del popolo a role of linkage and thus of mediation between citizens and institutions."[32] In other words, the bid for hegemony by ARCI accorded a subordinate function to the institutions that had been the primary centers of self-organization of the class.

Communists, although they spoke of the working class in revered terms, tended to conceive of it somewhat statically, thinking primarily of the skilled male workers of the large engineering works of the North. They were slow to see that it was becoming more diversified and that the crisis was creating new divisions. Nor did they appreciate that its cultural "otherness" with respect to the structures and institutions of capitalism had been undercut by social and cultural change. Although there was talk of uprooting consumerism and defeating the ideologies associated with it, the reality was that these had already permeated the mental horizons of workers and their families.[33] The processes of reprivatization of workers' leisure that had begun in the 1950s continued apace in the 1970s and was only temporarily interrupted by the collective action of 1968–73.

The lack of social and economic analysis conducted by the party, and of which some of its representatives complained, harmed it because it produced a comfortable attachment to familiar dogmas and beliefs. It also meant that new themes were rarely anticipated or given proper consideration. The mass media offer a useful example here. From 1970 a mainly left-wing movement promoted the reform of RAI in view of the forthcoming exhaustion of its twenty-year contract with IRI. Angry over biased news, the exclusion of the extraparliamentary left from the election tribunes in 1972, and the domination of broadcasting by government, the left led action from below, in which ARCI played a notable part. The aims of the movement were to develop RAI's public-service dimension, removing it from the control of the DC, decentralizing it, and promoting the involvement of social forces in its management while preserving its monopoly position. In keeping with traditional labor movement concerns, there was a desire to eliminate advertising and enhance the educational aspects of broadcasts.[34]

Despite this activism there was little sign that PCI leaders really understood the importance of television. Although there was hostility to the vision of life conveyed by the medium,[35] far more attention was paid to the formative qualities of the party and the education system. Thus the PCI leadership did not perceive that its project for hegemony was damaged when a law reforming RAI was adopted in 1975 that took little account of the reform movement's proposals. Control was subtracted from the executive and passed to a parliamentary commission (which in turn nominated ten of the sixteen members of RAI's council of administration), as the reformers had urged. Under the new system, broadcasting was also reaffirmed as a public service and a state monopoly, with the exception of local radio and cable television. But no real democratization of management or access occurred.[36] Instead, a system of party partition that had first emerged under the Center Left in the 1960s was entrenched as the parties shared control, with the DC and the PSI retaining the lion's share. In the share-out even the PCI received posts, and after 1978 it was accorded a position of command within the new shoestring regional channel RAI-3. For their part, the main parties of government began to move away from pure attachment to the doctrine of state monopoly broadcasting. Thus party political interests won out as positions were shared more widely in compensation for the failure of more far-reaching drives for reform. The result was a consociational diversion that would set the tone for the reforms in other areas of the subsequent period.

Why did this occur? It was not merely because the reformist forces were weak. It was also because the PCI accepted a political compromise and failed to push for measures it itself had not articulated. Instead of real reform it was happy to accept a measure of political influence. This in turn occurred in part because mass communications were not understood. Many of the prejudices of the past were overcome in the first half of the 1970s, as intellectuals began to look at the media sociologically and as RAI and the press were opened up to contestation from within by journalists and to the intervention of the left and the labor movement.[37] But, as Enzo Forcella pointed out in 1976, no Marxist theory of mass communications had ever been formulated. As a consequence, there was little intellectual coherence to the PCI's positions.[38]

All this suggests that several of the key assumptions of Marxists — the fragility of capitalism, the inevitability of socialism, the leading vocation of the working class, the perception of hegemony, the progressive simplification of industrial society — were rapidly losing or had already lost validity. This was understood by sophisticated Marxists like Leonardo Paggi and Valentino Gerratana, who called for a more open and fruitful interaction with other currents of contemporary thought.[39] The situation was exacerbated by the growing popularity of libertarian ideas and the decline of the appeal both of Eastern Europe and of the Chinese example that earlier has fascinated the far left. As a result, the intellectual hegemony of Marxism, which had seemed so decisive in the first half of the 1970s, proved ephemeral. The cracks in the edifice were exemplified by some notable defections. Lucio Colletti was a striking example of a front-rank exponent of Marxism who put himself outside the Marxist tradition and became a sharp critic of it.[40]

The attacks on Marxism and the debates on the democratic credibility of the PCI that multiplied in 1976–78 were regarded by most Communists as instrumental polemics, spurious diversions designed to prevent the PCI from acceding to power. Yet in fact the PCI leadership itself occasioned debate by rejecting the Soviet example and embracing Eurocommunism. To strengthen their position, Communists referred explicitly to Gramsci, who was considered to have corrected the defects of Marxist-Leninism and offered a democratic strategy for socialism. However, such stances occasioned further heated debate over the nature of Gramsci's strategy for hegemony. For the PCI, this was a democratic path, a means to extend support for socialism within a pluralist context; for its adversaries, it was no more than a means to party domination.[41] For all these reasons, it may be said that, in the mid-1970s, conditions at once favored the PCI and made it exceptionally difficult for the party to consolidate the support it won. The moment of its greatest electoral triumphs in this sense coincided with the beginning of its definitive decline as a cultural force.

California Dreaming: Youth Culture in the 1970s

Following the demise of the student movements of the late 1960s, all the frictions and demands that had initially been denied an outlet by the movements' highly politicized character came to the fore in their own right. Since the only view of society and culture to be generated by the extraparliamentary left was one marked by a narrow workerism, it was not well placed to respond to the resulting pressures. Yet, more immediately and directly than the PCI, it was forced to react not only to the civil rights lobby and to feminists and homosexuals but also to the hippie counterculture that came to exercise a notable influence on youth. The problems this raised were greatly complicated by the much broader base the youth movement acquired in the mid-1970s.

Given that the student protest that fueled the New Left was the off-spring of a society in which the mass media and consumerism had already begun to exercise influence, it is probably true to say that the militant culture to which the vanguards subscribed never catered to all the needs even of the first wave of activists. What is certain is that even in the very early 1970s many school and university students no longer actively identified with the far-left parties, although these still constituted a reference point of sorts. The main reason for this lay in the apparent inability of the political forces born of the student movement to offer any outlet to burgeoning cultural needs. For the first time, youth in the early 1970s seemed to represent a genuinely distinct category in Italy. The preceding years had seen a progressive detachment from the framework of ideas and behavior of older generations, and it now seemed possible to talk of a recognizable pattern of youth culture. This could be identified in a series of tastes regarding music and clothes, certain left-inclined political attitudes (although the extent of these should not be exaggerated), an open approach toward sex, and hostility toward careers and the idea of integration into society. It may be said, in short, that in the early 1970s Italian youth found itself in much the same situation to that of American or British youth in the mid- to late 1960s. As a result, rock music, drugs, and alternative lifestyles found a ready audience.

The cautious adaptation of the far left to these themes did not herald its resurgence but rather coincided with its decline. Although the more authoritarian Leninist organizations born in the late 1960s began to dissolve in 1971–73 when the cycle of protest turned downward, and were subsequently dealt a death blow by the women's movement, the role of the Italian equivalent of a politicized hippie movement should not be underestimated. *Re Nudo* — a magazine heavily influenced by American hippie culture and its ideas of communal living, sexual liberation, drugs, and mysticism — prospered as its claimed readership doubled from fifty thousand to one hundred thousand between 1975 and 1978, and tens of thousands of young people converged on Milan for its annual festivals of the "youth proletariat."[42] For a generation of young people who could lay claim to very few centers of social aggregation outside a by now largely mythical "movement" while being deeply committed to a collective sense of "being together" (*stare insieme*), these festivals, like pop concerts, took on great importance. This was partly because the music provided an outlet to a cultural need, but also because the concert and the festival offered a way to escape the sense of isolation experienced at school, in the family, and even, according to some accounts, in the political group.

In the 1970s individual or group frustrations intermingled with feelings of cultural displacement to explode in an unmediated form as civil disturbance and violent protest. Nowhere was this more apparent than at *Re Nudo*'s annual *feste,* which began as small-scale events before mushrooming in the middle of the decade. Mixing an idea of Woodstock with some features of the *L'Unità* festivals, the *feste* simply could not deliver what they promised. Trouble broke out at several popular summer festivals and cultural events in the mid-1970s, but it was at the 1976 gathering in Milan's Parco Lambro that things finally got out of hand. The few hundred people deeply committed to finding the bases of an alternative lifestyle were heavily outnumbered by the thousands of mostly male youngsters who had come along seeking simply a good time. It mattered little to them that food and drink stalls were cooperatively run; theft and raids were commonplace. Following one mass assault on a refrigerated van hired by the organizers, youths were even seen playing football with frozen chickens — an image that was long to remain fixed in the minds of those who attended the festival.[43]

The sudden mushrooming of interest in music and countercultural festivals caused concern within the PCI, for it showed that the advances of the PCI on the electoral plane were not matched by similar trends in culture. The PCI had absorbed relatively easily the light music of the 1950s and the Italian pop of the 1960s. Popular singers regularly appeared at local and national *L'Unità* festivals. But foreign rock groups and their Italian equivalents were regarded with disapproval because rock was seen as being lifestyle oriented, and its exponents were associated with deviant social behavior (drugs, long hair, etc.). In the minds of older Communists it was a phenomenon to be lumped together with the deviations of 1968.[44] Only after ARCI organized a successful tour by the exiled Chilean group Inti Illimani did some begin to appreciate the political potential of large-scale concerts. Nevertheless, the sudden surge in the popularity of rock and of jazz festivals in the mid-1970s caught both the PCI and the FGCI by surprise. Compelled to catch up in a hurry, the young Communists staged their own festivals, first at Pincio in 1975 and then, more memorably, at Ravenna in September 1976.

Proclaimed as open to all, the Ravenna Festival, Gianni Borgna has written, "was the first and perhaps the only attempt by the Communists to make contact with the 'freakish' and 'wild' world of the concerts and of the 'youth counterculture.' "[45] The theme of the event, "Liberty is not a festival," indicated the desire of the PCI to connect the "personal" themes of rock with politics and impede any ebbing of the alignment with the left expressed at the polls. The balanced program reflected this. Alongside the Italian rock groups PFM and Area and mainstream singer-songwriters including Lucio Dalla, Angelo Branduardi, and Eugenio Finardi were Inti Illimani, dialect singers, exponents of Neapolitan popular music, and the "politicals" Giovanna Marini, Ivano Della Mea, and Paolo Pietrangeli. However, although massive crowds converged on the festival site, the event was not a success. Far from opening a new dialogue, the FGCI festival signaled the end of their season. The bizarrely named Wastock, organized in 1978 by the remnants of the extraparliamentary left, was merely a farcical epilogue.

To understand the difficulties of the PCI fully, broader aspects of the question need to be considered. During the 1970s youth movements became progressively detached from the workerism that had marked the student movement of the late 1960s, although they retained an attachment to autonomy, the other key concept born of the contestation. The far left had always preferred the unskilled, mass worker as a reference point to the skilled worker of the Socialist and Communist tradition. As the economic crisis made its effects felt and the black economy grew, the mass worker tended to be replaced by yet another subject in the writings of the ultra-left theorists like Toni Negri. Now it was the socialized worker (*operaio sociale*) that was singled out as a possible bearer of the revolutionary project.[46] This category included students, student-workers on the fringes of the labor market and the unemployed as well as irreducible marginals like vagabonds and thieves. These groups, together with the fallout from the extraparliamentary left (Potere Operaio dissolved in 1973, Lotta Continua in 1976), mixed in the late 1970s in the "area of autonomy." In a city like Milan this included the squats and self-organized circles of proletarian youth that blossomed from the mid-1970s as well as other elements of the counterculture, such as naturists, the centers of yoga and alternative medicine, feminist circles, and so on. These did not share the cult of violence that distinguished the hardline Autonomia Operaia but rather an ideology that combined postcollective individualism with a rejection of preexisting political mediations.

Communists were perplexed and disorientated by the waning of interest in politics and the emergence of personal questions. Although there was an attempt through music to reconstruct a relationship with the mass of youth, the emergence of the individual and the displacement of a theory of revolution (identified by Communists with the Italian Road to Socialism) with a theory of subjective needs was held to signal a disturbing process of Americanization that was confirmed by the spread of drugs, mysticism, and communitarianism.[47] The emphasis on the public-private debate, which extended out of the women's movement and the hippie left to the New Left as a whole, contrasted with the puritanism and rigor that still constituted a key element of Communist morality.[48] To some degree this was a generational matter. But events would prove that the Communists were right to perceive serious dangers in the situation and among the attitudes of youth toward the end of 1976. Unfortunately, the actions of the PCI leadership at this crucial juncture did nothing to defuse these.

National Solidarity, 1976–79

The period between the election of June 1976 and the first half of 1979 was one of the most complex and challenging in the whole history of the PCI. It was also a critical one for the country and its institutions. Against a backdrop of severe economic crisis and a mounting terrorist threat, the Communists played a key role in the formation of "national solidarity" governments, first by abstaining and then from March 1978 to January 1979 by actually forming part of the parliamentary majority that sustained the government in office. Much has been written about this experience and the often disturbing events of the period; on the whole, judgments have been negative. Seeking to furnish a balanced view, Michele Salvati and Paul Ginsborg have given the Communist leadership credit for helping the country find a way out of the economic crisis and for assisting the passage of several significant reforms.[49] More widely, the PCI's role in defending democratic institutions against the challenge of terrorism has been praised. Yet overall the period has come to be seen as one of failure and utter disappointment. The PCI succeeded neither in enacting an intellectual and moral reform nor in reforming the state in the way it had argued was necessary. The party lost support among groups that had rallied to it in 1975–76, took the blame for unpopular measures, and suffered highly damaging blows to its credibility.

Sensing that the PCI was in danger of losing the initiative, Enrico Berlinguer intervened with a series of speeches between October 1976 and January 1977 to restate the fundamental themes with which he had identified himself since 1974.[50] He stated that the working class was now in a position to condition government action at all levels. If it was prepared to accept sacrifices provided these were spread fairly and shared by all, it was not because it was weak or because it accepted the priorities of conservative forces. It was willing to do so because the old neocapitalist model of development was in crisis, and thus through sacrifices it was possible to wage a war against waste and for equity, efficiency, and a

Between Hollywood and Moscow

rational use of resources. Austerity was synonymous with a new quality of development, Berlinguer argued, in which the emphasis was to be shifted from individual consumption, seen as artificially induced, wasteful, and alienating, to collective needs expressed in terms of health, education, and effective democratic administration. It was envisaged that its adoption would coincide with a profound modification of economic and social structures, a shift in the way the state functioned and a transformation of values and lifestyles.

Napoleone Colajanni has suggested that Berlinguer's scheme was generic and impractical, laced more with moralism and socialist messianism than good economic sense.[51] Yet the PCI leader did call specifically for public spending to be cut and for its perverse clientelistic dynamic to be halted. Moreover, to facilitate the consolidation of the hegemony of the working class, he aimed to mobilize the intellectual talents available to the left. At a remarkable gathering of the cream of the intelligentsia at Rome's Eliseo Theater in January 1977, he urged intellectuals to collaborate in the project of renewing Italy in two ways: first, by organizing and promoting the shift in a collective direction of public and private values; and second, by contributing to the practical articulation of socialist proposals and policies.

Potentially, this was one of the most fruitful moments in the long history of relations between intellectuals and Communism. Such was the presence of writers, philosophers, university teachers, scientists, and professionals at the meeting that right-wing commentators openly bemoaned the conformism of the intelligentsia in throwing its lot in with the new force of authority in the country. Yet in fact the actual extent of this realignment was superficial, and neither of Berlinguer's appeals produced a satisfactory response. His insistence on justice and parsimony in opposition to the hedonism of the consumer society was ridiculed in the press. More importantly, it encountered sustained criticisms from Colletti, Norberto Bobbio, and others.[52] Bobbio in particular contrasted Berlinguer's views with Marx's emphasis on the satisfaction of needs.[53] The party's attempts to rally the talents on a programmatic basis ran into a number of difficulties. The intellectuals most closely identified with the party were generally of a humanistic background and poorly equipped to provide practical solutions. Much better placed were the technical experts and scientists who threw their support behind the party in the 1970s. Yet here other problems arose. Politicians with a general culture and a global outlook found it difficult to work with intellectuals whose expertise was specific and who tended to produce complicated briefing papers not readily accessible to the layperson. The absence of formally constituted research staffs, or any other institutionalized means whereby the contribution of these experts could be channeled systematically, rendered the problem more complex.[54] Although various sectoral conferences were held (some of which, such as that on the state held in May 1977, provoked wide debate), and there were many public and private meetings, the results were on the whole unsatisfactory. The much maligned *Proposta di progetto a medio termine* (Proposal for a medium-term project) published in July 1977, which was supposed to represent a serious attempt by the PCI to seize the initiative and offer a vision of the purposes and aims of National Solidarity in terms of values and reforms, did not in reality move much beyond the general vision Berlinguer himself had set out.[55] Thus the intellectuals who had been so enthusiastic about the PCI finally achieving great influence if not actual power quickly became disillusioned. However, disaffection with the party was still more marked among youth.

Protest first took the form of a university occupation movement that arose in response to the publication by the education minister Malfatti in December 1976 of proposals to restrict university entry. However, the protest quickly spilled over into general opposition to the Historic Compromise and in particular to the conduct of the PCI since the election. Berlinguer's emphasis on austerity provided a particular focus of attack. Most young people never shared, and in many cases never even understood, Berlinguer's idea. Having grown up in, or at least having been continuously exposed to, the cultures of consumerism, they were not persuaded of the transformative potential of the concept. It smacked not of something new but rather of something that belonged to the past. The detachment from austerity was exacerbated by the economic crisis, which had among its principal effects the exclusion of young people from the labor market. The result was a certain downward leveling of youth of different strata who increasingly took on the characteristics and consciousness of a disadvantaged subgroup that lacked the institutional guarantees and the secure status that the working class had enjoyed since 1973. Young people converged on the universities or were confined to casual work within the black economy, or both. In the 1960s student workers had been relatively few and far between; by the mid-1970s they accounted for 49 percent of students.[56]

The PCI was slow to appreciate these changes. It also failed to foresee the devastating impact that Malfatti's proposals would have on the young, for whom university entry had ceased to be largely an elite option and had taken on the status of a right. By any standard this sloth was shocking; after all, the Communists had spent much of the period after 1968 debating university and school reform and insisting on the central importance of this theme to the struggle for working-class hegemony.[57] There are basically two explanations for the PCI's immobilism. In the first place, it must be recognized that, on this terrain as on others, the PCI leadership was outmaneuvered. It proved impossible to advance reform to either the university sector or the school system, as powerful interests linked to the DC obstructed change both in institutions and to the cultural axis on which education in Italy was founded. The second explanation concerns the PCI's own attitude toward higher education. As Communists saw it, the Italian education system was organized on the basis of negative and outdated hierarchical divisions between the arts and the sciences and between intellectual and manual skills. If the working class was to assert its hegemony and productive labor be established as the primary value of society old hierarchies and privileges needed to be overcome. Thus Communists did not view the intellectual unemployed with much sympathy. The hostile attitude of the PCI was reinforced when the registers opened by the largely ineffectual law of 1977 on youth employment revealed a broad rejection of manual and agricultural jobs on the part of those who enrolled.[58] Communists deplored this refusal of manual labor as a sign of the continuing dominance of the values of the urban middle class in wide sectors of society. What they did not, and perhaps could not, appreciate was that it was also evidence of the declining appeal of the working-class movement as an alternative pole of cultural attraction in an increasingly postindustrial order.

It is against this background that the extraordinary clashes of February–March 1977 should be seen. For the first time a social movement developed that regarded the PCI not as an ally but as an enemy. In marked contrast to the evenhanded attitude shown in 1968, the party sharply criticized the student movement as a source of disruption and destabilization. No effort was made to distinguish between the violent fringe and the bulk of the movement; nor were the real dissatisfactions of students appreciated. Instead, full support was given to the raids on bookshops and forced closure of radio stations, including Bologna's Radio Alice, which had allegedly helped coordinate street violence with its broadcasts, and to the wave of arrests that followed the events of mid-March. Although the DC and the PSI distanced themselves from the campaign, the former because it feared the long-term consequences and the latter for more opportunistic reasons, the PCI whipped up a "moral panic" designed to remove legitimacy from the movement.[59]

The "movement of 1977" was short-lived, a brief resurgence of protest after the end of the most vibrant and long-lasting protest cycle in the whole of postwar Europe. The absence of any clear goals, the increasing circulation of hard drugs, and the presence of many bitter and disillusioned people lent the whole movement a desperate air. Yet in spite of the economic crisis and in very deliberate contrast to the ideology of crisis, the movement was also permeated by a curious joie de vivre. At one level, this involved the theft of costly foodstuffs from delicatessens and supermarkets and a refusal to pay full price in first-run cinemas and restaurants. At another, it involved enthusiasm and creativity in a strangely modern cultural mix that, unlike the previous left-wing alternative cultures, did not hark back to a simple rural past but rather celebrated the metropolis, modern technology and mass communication, consumption, and so on.[60] By its disrespect, the movement of 1977 revealed just how far the ideals and values of the left had worn thin. It also contributed decisively to the deconsacration of the labor movement and the PCI. Yet it could achieve little in its own right. As the year wore on and the question of repression overtook all others, the violent neo-Leninist components increasingly set the agenda for the movement as a whole, eventually leading to its demobilization. Four years later scarcely any trace at all remained of the youth centers, assemblies, collectives, radios, and bookshops that had constituted the archipelago of autonomy.

From the point of view of the students, the PCI's attitude and the "repression" it sponsored signaled a number of things. First, it demonstrated that the Communists were now a full part of the power elite and that they had joined not only with the other parties but also with the coercive apparatus of the state to oppose dissent. Second, it showed that this meeting of forces covered all possible political mediations and that no other forms of expression were allowed. Third, it indicated that the accentuation of the authoritarian character of the state reduced the possible space for nonauthorized ideas and forms of collective or individual action. Fourth, it signaled that, as the labor movement became a part of the state, working-class culture lost its alternative, antagonistic character and became a force for moderation and conservatism.

The PCI's harsh response to the movement was motivated by genuine concerns about violence but also by anger at what appeared to be deliberate maneuvers to discredit the party and undermine the assertion of a new pattern of hegemony. For Gerardo Chiaromonte, the explosion of protest was evidence that "in this period, as often in periods of crisis, the sense of the real historical process becomes attenuated."[61] The PCI revealed a strain of humorlessness in 1977 that reflected the dogmatic, preconceived way in which it read social and political developments. Despite this, in 1977–78 Communists did engage in efforts to understand a phenomenon that was not easy to decipher, and some individuals often showed an acute awareness of how the cultural influence of the labor movement, far from being consolidated, was actually undergoing a reversal.[62] Unfortunately, these insights did not find expression in any flexibility or change of direction at the top of the party.

After the end of the phase of National Solidarity in 1979 various leading Communists recognized that the party's perspectives and behavior had been defective.[63] However, no full examination of National Solidarity or of the Historic Compromise occurred, nor would it occur as long as Enrico Berlinguer lived. This was unfortunate, for the behavior of the Communist leadership revealed an understanding of the evolution of Italian society that was at best partial. Relying excessively on conventional Marxist-Leninist assumptions about capitalist development, Communists failed to perceive the vitality and flexibility of Italian capitalism. In addition, they underestimated the impact of structural change on class relations and the rise of a consumerist and media-related culture. Even if the economy had proved as fragile as leading Communists assumed, there could have been no simple return to the cultural and political order of the 1940s. In a context in which the aspirations shared without exception by all strata were those of individual well being and familial prosperity, the prospects for a new pattern of hegemony founded on frugality and collective solidarity were dismal. Noble though Berlinguer's project unquestionably was, it ultimately lacked the structural and superstructural conditions necessary for its deployment. Perhaps the most serious flaw of the Historic Compromise was the excessive faith in politics that underpinned it. Conceiving society primarily in terms of the political parties and traditions that it expressed, the PCI failed to sustain the impulse for participation and decentralization at the expense of a mere consolidation of the dominant position of the political forces. Yet, despite the result of the 1976 election, events of the 1970s showed that in many ways society had outgrown the traditionally dominant political forces. Events also indicated that the heyday of the mass party as such was over. This was not immediately apparent to many even in 1979, but during the 1980s it would be amply demonstrated as both major parties lost support and the PCI struggled to remain a central force on the political scene.

6

Welcome to Prosperity

Economic Growth and the Erosion of Left-Wing Culture

Throughout the Western world the 1980s saw the return of questions first raised in the 1950s. The rise of neoliberalism and the declining intellectual appeal of Marxism, the difficulties of left-wing parties and the appeal of individualism and consumerism all led latter-day partisans of the "end of ideology" thesis to suggest that between them liberal democracy and consumer capitalism had succeeded in creating a value system and style of living capable of integrating the vast majority of Western populations. All historical alternatives, whether state socialist or even social democratic, were therefore either invalid or unnecessary. In Italy the first debate produced only a limited echo, for, despite the crisis of 1956, economic growth, the decline of political activism, and the formation of the Center Left, modernization did not result in any erosion in the electoral support of the PCI. On the contrary, as the profile of the country changed so the electoral standing of the party improved. But in the 1980s, a new phase of growth, the extension of prosperity, the restoration of stable government in the form of a five-party coalition centered on the PSI and the DC, the decline of the collective movements of the 1970s, the intellectual eclipse of Marxism, and the massive extension of a culture based on television and mass commercial entertainment all led to the reproposition of the argument. Although the PCI remained a powerful force, controlling between a quarter and one-third of the vote, counting a membership of 1.6 million, and retaining influence among important sectors of society and of public opinion, it lost both votes and members, found itself politically isolated, and could no longer command the central position and widespread attention of the 1970s.

Having been saved from collapse in part by emergency measures that the PCI supported, Italian capitalism expanded significantly in the 1980s and was well placed to exploit the upward swing in the international trade cycle in the middle of the decade. The new capitalism was like the old in some ways, but its base was broader and it was accompanied by the technological and industrial revolution that deeply affected the tertiary sector and marked Italy's emergence as postindustrial society. With ideological concerns displaced and politics a discredited activity, Italian business was able to legitimate itself directly in society for the first time. Untroubled by the presence of vibrant countercultures and assisted by compliant politicians, entrepreneurs established a concentration of ownership in publishing, newspapers, and the unregulated private television sector, and peddled images and ideas that were at once conformist and brashly commercial. More subject to the influence of the mass media than at any time in their history and possibly more exposed to foreign (especially American) archetypes, many Italians lived in a vicarious imaginary world that offered some pleasure but no autonomy and only one type of stimulus — the stimulus to buy. For better or worse, the cultural specificity of the country was sharply undermined by its absorption into global networks of communication almost exclusively as a consumer of material produced elsewhere.

All this struck at the heart of Communist culture. The PCI found not only that it was unable to organize a broad-ranging cultural battle around a working class that was pushed onto the defensive, internally divided, and numerically in decline, but that it was unable to identify itself with progress and modernity. As a consequence, it was not well placed to resist the attacks that were launched, not only by the center right but also by Bettino Craxi's Socialists, on its ideology and national function as well as the broader values of antifascism and the Resistance. Moreover, the leadership was compelled to come to terms with its inability to control either values or the flow of communications within the party itself. These difficulties were compounded by a situation of political impasse. In the 1960s the PCI had responded to the Center Left by demanding that it fulfill its promise of reforms; it had done this in the awareness that the working class was recovering from defeat, that the PCI shared a common culture with the Socialists, that Communism was advancing on a global scale, and that anti-Americanism commanded growing support among youth. In the 1980s there was no reform program, relations with the PSI reached a nadir, Communism was discred-

Between Hollywood and Moscow

ited internationally, America emerged powerfully under Reagan from the economic and political crisis of the 1970s, and the working class encountered new defeats. To cap off matters, the PCI was unable either to recover a convincing oppositional profile after its experience of close identification with government or to articulate convincingly the new themes of environmentalism and pacifism that had gained ground among young people.

Overall, it is impossible to avoid the conclusion that, although it preserved most of its electoral strength, the PCI experienced a historic defeat in the 1980s. Yet it should be borne in mind that, despite adverse circumstances and, at times, poor leadership, the party remained a vital force. On a cultural level, the PCI became much more pluralistic as well as open to a variety of previously rejected mass cultural forms. For some, the latter reeked of opportunism or surrender, but as a result popular culture was often reelaborated in interesting and original ways.

The Second Economic Miracle

Like other Western societies, Italy prospered in the 1980s. The defeat inflicted on the trade unions in the dispute with Fiat's management in November 1980 was undoubtedly a contributor to recovery and growth as well as a vitally important signal that the balance of forces of the post-1969 period had been decisively altered.[1] Although many on the left, including the PCI's national leadership, refused for a number of years to acknowledge the historic defeat of the labor movement, the consequences soon became apparent on the cultural plane as well as the industrial one. Divided by conflict, fragmented by automation, and diffused in an archipelago of small firms, the working class lost not only its numerical primacy but its ability to act as force of attraction. As Gad Lerner notes, even left-wing intellectuals reconciled themselves to the idea that it was a race nearing extinction.[2] For its part, the trade-union movement was compelled to accept that it had alienated some categories, especially of white-collar workers, and that it had failed to pay sufficient attention to the problems of efficiency and productivity.

Overall, this period has been described as one in which a new social paradigm was exchanged for an old one, in which an era marked by public involvements and collective concerns came to an end and was replaced by a new, less ideological phase in which there was a privatistic, consumerist focus.[3] In Italy, the late 1970s did not merely witness the natural ebbing of the new social movements, something that occurred elsewhere in Europe and preceded the emergence of parties espousing a "new politics"; rather, they saw a dramatic shift of paradigm that to some extent canceled the explicit heritage of the movements.

The resulting change of cultural climate destroyed the interpretative scheme privileging collective action that had held the stage for a decade and canceled much of its legacy. Even the women's movement, the last truly mass movement of the 1970s, was forced off the streets, excepting a brief reappearance at the time of the 1981 referendums on abortion. Instead, its adherents went into the institutions and the parties or underground into insular cultural and theoretical work. The various structures of the extraparliamentary countercultures collapsed. *Lotta continua* ceased publishing in 1980, the vast majority of the political radio stations closed, left-wing bookshops and cafés shut or changed stock and clientele, small publishers such as Savelli, Bertani, Mazzotta, and De Donato that had published many of the sacred texts of the youth movements and the left wound down and went out of business; even large publishing houses identified with the left, principally Einaudi and Feltrinelli, encountered difficulties and were forced to restructure.

It was not just the heritage of the New Left that was undercut but the cultural legitimacy of the whole of the left. Marxism, which had constituted a vital reference point and source of stimulation for intellectuals even outside the left since the 1940s, fell out of vogue. The oft-cited names of the 1970s — Louis Althusser, Galvano Della Volpe, Walter Benjamin, and Paul Baran and Paul Sweezy — disappeared; in their place, once despised liberals were lauded. The publisher Adelphi captured some of the intellectual high ground with its republications of Heidegger, Nietzsche, and even Croce. There was no real hegemony of the right, but the "crisis of ideologies" seemed only to affect the left. Its language, concepts, terms, and shared assumptions all entered a far-reaching crisis.[4]

It is striking that several of the more successful cultural events of the period seemed to want to turn the clock back, as if to erase the whole phase of contestation and crisis and begin again from the boom years of the early 1960s. The grand relaunch of the Festival of San Remo song contest in 1982 after years of decline, and the astonishing resumption of rituals thought to have been abolished forever, such as the debutantes' ball in Monza, added to the sensation that the 1970s had never existed. Yet although customs and conventions unfashionable in the recent past could easily reemerge in the climate of conformism and amnesia, the clock obviously could not really be turned back. The monopoly of broadcasting by RAI had ended, the sexual revolution had occurred, the women's movement had altered consciousness, and individuals had asserted their autonomy from institutions. Levels of education, moreover, as well as standards of living, had been raised. Thus any reknitting of the hegemony of dominant groups would have to be on a new basis or at least would have to take account of these things. In fact, the obstacle represented by themes and ideas that had their first airing within the extraparliamentary left was not so great. Indeed, in many ways the erosion of old institutions and values and the growth of new privately oriented individualism created an ideal terrain for the advance of commodification and consequently for the affirmation of postindustrial capitalism.

The passing away of the political initiative from the left, the mood of deradicalization and its practical consequences, and the firmness with which employers attacked and defeated a weakened and divided union movement brought about a set of circumstances that, Forgacs writes, "favored oligopolistic power in the cultural industries: press and publishing concentrations, broadcasting deregulation and the rise of the private networks."[5] Global changes in communications, new strength and integration based on economic recovery, and tremendous resources deriving from the massive increase in the capitalization of the Milan stock market from 1982 further facilitated the passage of cultural power directly into the hands of the economic elite. There was no greater proof that the culture of enterprise had become hegemonic than the way Fiat, Montedison, and Olivetti seized control of the leading newspapers and magazines while Silvio Berlusconi moved from construction to advertising to the independent television sector, before ousting his publisher-competitors there to establish a monopoly and branch out into the retail industry (by taking control of the Standa department store and supermarket chain) and finally publishing (winning most of the Mondadori empire after a prolonged battle).

It has been argued by Alberto Asor Rosa, Paul Ginsborg, and others that the victory of capital was accompanied by an extensive "cultural revolution" at mass level.[6] The attractions of consumerism and individual mobility that won the middle class to solid support for a moderate, democratic order in the 1950s and 1960s was extended in the 1980s to encompass the entire society. In consequence, support for liberal democracy and neocapitalism was wider and firmer than at any previous time. If this is true, then the most important element in the cultural revolution of the period was the development of private television networks, since it was these that, despite their precarious legal position, won a dominant place in the cultural system and that, through their advertising and programming, transmitted a new way of looking at the world to a vast public. Berlusconi's idea of television was quintessentially American. He saw viewers not as citizens but as consumers to be delivered to advertisers. The purpose of programs was to hold the attention of viewers over as much of the day as possible with images that were as alluring and as immediately accessible as possible. It was entirely natural, therefore, that he should have constructed an American image for his flagship, Canale 5, using old American films and popular television series, most notably *Dallas,* which he took up in 1981 (when it was dropped by RAI) and used as the cornerstone of his assault on the ratings of rivals.

Catholics and Communists looked with horror on what they saw as the devastating cultural effects of the "anthropological revolution" effected by Berlusconi. Youth especially, they thought, was being lobotimized and Americanized by the relentless spread of consumerism and lowbrow mass culture. This argument was not a new one, of course. It had been voiced in the early 1960s as well. But the apparent conformity and willing integration of young people after a long season of collective action lent new relevance to an old theme. Were young people really as uncritical of the surrounding society and its values as media images suggested? Or was there a process of industry "filtering" as in the 1950s and 1960s that concealed and softened a more complex reality? Certainly, constructing an overall picture of a differentiated and shifting youth world is a difficult task and perhaps an impossible one. But there are indicators and surveys to which reference may be made. Alessandro Cavalli and Antonio De Lillo, the authors of two full-length studies of youth published in 1984 and 1988, noted that the young became progressively more accepting of the social and moral order even if they tended to be more tolerant than their elders. Their interest in formal politics also declined between the two surveys, although this was not linked to the spread of consumerism, since those who consumed less tended to take a less active part in a broad range of leisure and voluntary activities. Insofar as young people took part in society actively they did so in informal, spontaneous ways on specific themes such as the environment, disarmament, and conditions in the schools.[7]

The PCI after the Historic Compromise

For the PCI the early 1980s were a discouraging time. Goals that the party had put forward confidently in the 1960s and 1970s and that had won wide support appeared problematic and of questionable relevance. Intellectuals, in particular, adopted this view as the previous climate of sympathy and participation gave way to a more distant and critical relationship. The renewed appeals to intellectuals that emanated from the party following a 1981 session of the central committee dedicated to culture (the first since 1975), at which they were identified as a "new subject" to be involved in the project of the left, fell on deaf ears.[8] The early 1980s witnessed not a new wave of mobilization but rather a quiet demobilization, as a substantial number of the intellectuals who had joined the party or collaborated with it, in some instances to the point of working for it full time or assuming elective office at national or local level, withdrew.[9] In some cases the withdrawal was accompanied by bitterness and frustration about the general course of events, in others about the party's failure to make full use of their talents. Some of those in the latter category returned to private life while others were seduced by promises of jobs and influence advanced by the Socialists.

This was a significant phenomenon, but its scale should not be exaggerated. Certainly nothing took place like the sea change in the political alignments of intellectuals that occurred in France.[10] Overall, the PCI retained the support, albeit without enthusiasm, of a remarkably large number of university professors, technicians, specialists, artists, and writers. It was still quite easy to find intellectuals willing to stand as independent Communist candidates in elections or contribute to its journals and conferences. In part this pragmatic, political alignment occurred because there was no other progressive force capable of attracting them; but the skill of leading Communists should not be underestimated. The problem was that the nature of the alignment was sometimes so loose as to be of questionable value. For the first time there was talk of a "Communist area" of intellectuals, outside and substantially free of the party yet referring to it. This consisted of those grouped around institutions such as the Gramsci Institute, the Communist Economic Research Center, and the Center for Reform of the State, and critical independent publications like *Laboratorio politico, Il centauro,* and *Pace e Guerra,* which were tolerated in a way that would have been inconceivable as recently as the 1960s. In addition, there was the Independent Left group in parliament.[11] In this area various political sensibilities and intellectual currents coexisted. Although Marxism and Leninism (but not the Stalinist synthesis Marxist-Leninism after 1979) continued to be proclaimed as the sources of the PCI's principles, intellectual interest in them declined sharply. The same fate befell Gramsci, who had risen to intellectual favor in conjunction with the PCI's ascendancy and had been seen, largely as a result of the efforts of a handful of organic intellectuals, as the intellectual architect of Eurocommunism.[12] Instead, many intellectuals in and around the party began to pay systematic attention to the mainstream social sciences, in their Anglo-American progressive version, or to some variant of German-historicist "weak thought."[13] Developed in substance by Massimo Cacciari in 1976 (the year he was elected to parliament as a Communist independent), the concept of weak thought was extended and popularized by Gianni Vattimo and Pier Aldo Rovatti.[14] Seen as the most typical intellectual development of the 1980s, it questioned the idea that history was a unitary process and that truth was born of a single rationality such as class or science. In contrast to "strong" ideological or religious truths, it suggested that existing realities should not be opposed but that possibilities and solutions should be sought within their complex and pluralistic interstices.

For the PCI it was disturbing indeed that Marx and Gramsci ceased to be sources of interest not merely to intellectuals in general but to left-wingers and Communists. In the past there had always been a solid nucleus of organic intellectuals willing to defend the PCI's theoretical patrimony and sometimes elaborate it at the highest intellectual level, but now the contradictions and theoretical traditionalism of the leadership group were singled out and attacked precisely by some of those who might have been expected to be loyal. Inspired largely by Asor Rosa, *Laboratorio politico* conducted a penetrating analysis of the servitudes of the Historic Compromise in the absence of any formal party reflection. Another journal in the Communist area, *Democrazia e diritto,* also exposed the inconsistencies and weaknesses in Eurocommunism.[15] The exhaustion and crisis of many core Marxist forecasts were highlighted by such luminaries as Eric Hobsbawm, Althusser, and, in a speech to the sixteenth PCI congress marking the centenary of Marx's death, by Cesare Luporini. "It must be recognized that many things he said are no longer valid," Luporini judged, after having assessed Marx's role and indicated his contribution to the intellectual patrimony of all Communists.[16] In such circumstances it became difficult for the party to defend itself convincingly against its ever more numerous adversaries among liberals and conservatives. To reconcile traditional Marxist commitments to the overcoming of capitalism, the exercise of unchecked power on the part of the working class, and the state as a tool of social transformation with a negative judgment on East European socialism and approval of Western bourgeois values and procedures became an increasingly difficult and, ultimately, perhaps impossible exercise. The party's very strategy in these conditions, and the specific formulations of it that were advanced from time to time, lost the grandeur that had enveloped them in the past and exposed them to assessment according to more pragmatic criteria.

Many of these problems were confined in the early 1980s to the higher planes of the PCI's political culture. But some were not. All large left-wing parties in Western Europe with roots in the working-class movement faced a historic challenge at this time, and the PCI was no exception. At issue was the ability of a left born in the convulsive processes of the first wave of industrialization at the end of the nineteenth century to evolve so as to represent the interests of the broad mass of people in a society that was rapidly assuming postindustrial coordinates. This did not necessarily involve a traumatic break with tradition, but it did require a genuine review of the goals and methods of the left in light of altered circumstances. Although he was widely perceived to be a defender of the PCI's domestic tradition, Enrico Berlinguer recognized that the party needed to reexamine its attitude toward social movements and draw from the legacy of autonomy of those of the 1970s. Verbally at least, he was highly receptive to the questions that women above all raised, and he frequently made reference to the revolutionary significance of the women's movement. Somewhat belatedly, he argued in 1981 that the PCI should not seek to impose its schemes and conceptions on the movement but rather learn from them.[17]

Ordinary Communist members and activists were not on the whole sensitive to intellectual anxieties or to new issues and demands (although it should be remembered that the recruits of the 1970s were more educated than older activists and that *L'Unità* covered cultural and political debates regularly). Although contradictions and elements of uncertainty inevitably crept into even routine elaborations of official ideology,[18] most militants and cadres believed what they were told; namely, that Marxism and Leninism as interpreted by Togliatti provided sure guidelines for the activity of Communists. They were comforted in their beliefs by the regular reiteration of the commitment to the supercession of capitalism, the rejection of social democracy, the importance of the party and of complete dedication to the cause. Given that in many cases the PCI's ideology had been instilled in them in the 1940s, 1950s, or 1960s, it was only to be expected that the vision of Communist identity among the rank and file was fairly traditional. As Marzio Barbagli and Pier Giorgio Corbetta showed with a survey undertaken in Emilia-Romagna in 1977–78, identification with the Soviet model and belief in its superiority was still strong, and criticisms were absorbed only slowly and with difficulty.[19] As it is unlikely that this situation changed much over the next five years, it is fair to say that most of the PCI base entertained a basically conventional and revolutionary idea of the party, tempered only by acknowledgment of some of the Westernizing modifications that were formally incorporated into the theses presented at the fifteenth and sixteenth congresses in 1979 and 1982.

It is important to understand this because it was precisely the more conventional features of Communist identity that were challenged and undermined by the social and cultural trends of the 1980s. Even the most diehard of activists could not help but notice that society was changing, new concerns were taking the place of old ones, categories once sympathetic to the PCI were now diffident, old techniques of mobilization were less effective, and organizational procedures were subject to questioning. To be a Communist had perhaps never been easy, but in the 1980s the doubts and uncertainties, on the one hand, and the temptations of the existing society, on the other, both increased. As the political paradigm of previous years fell away and the level of interest in politics dropped to a point unprecedented since the 1950s,[20] familial and individual concerns took the place of collective ones while the impulses to protest that emerged did so in forms and along lines that were different from traditional ones. In a series of ways, therefore, the goals and customs of the PCI organization and those of Italian society diverged.

The question of cultural change is especially relevant in examining the great difficulties of the PCI not just in recruiting the under twenty-fives but in acquiring their votes. In 1975 eighteen to twenty-five year olds were overrepresented by 13.3 percent in the PCI's electorate with respect to the electorate as a whole. By 1987 they were underrepresented by 2.9 percent.[21] This, Renato Mannheimer has argued, was the largest single contributor to the PCI's declining fortunes in the 1980s.[22] However, not all of those who grew up at this time were integrated into the dominant value system. Various currents of opposition emerged that were pragmatic, loosely organized, and related to specific issues such as peace, environmentalism, or the campaign against drugs. These new forms of activism drew on the protest repertoire of the previous decade, but they were marked by a commitment to nonviolence and individual responsibility that was relatively new. The PCI was able to draw little comfort from these initiatives. For young grassroots activists, the party had little to say or to offer, as it was committed to a global ideological project and to a traditional type of political practice. At the same time it had become, or appeared to have become, a part of the political establishment, losing in the process its capacity to transmit radical values and ideals. To young people the PCI represented efficiency and honesty, but it was also perceived to be severe and intolerant,[23] a paternalistic force more concerned with quantitative questions than the qualitative ones that constituted an emerging agenda.

After the sudden death of Berlinguer in 1984, debates of a far freer and uninhibited character took place in the PCI. The future of the party was discussed openly, and the sense emerged clearly that many features of its theory and practice were outdated and inadequate in contemporary conditions. As discouragement set in, the practice of unanimity in crucial decisions fell by the wayside, and pressure for transparency and internal accountability increased. De facto factions took shape. The whole being of the party was subject to question. For the first time the need to embrace qualitative questions and to review the culture and the mentality of the party and its members won genuine acknowledgment at the top of the PCI.

From the late 1970s a series of large- and small-scale social developments contributed to a process of change in the mass parties that led to their losing the dominance they had long exercized over all aspects of the political process. By the same token their control over political communication and their central role in social organization was sharply undermined. The causes of this were numerous: the detachment from politics and the crisis of political commitment, the erosion of old political identities and the multiplication of attachments, the fragmentation of society, the growth of grassroots voluntary activity, and the incorporation of parties within the state. Two further causes will be given special attention in this section: the extension of the mass media and the growing importance of commercially organized leisure.

From the mid-1970s, and especially in the early 1980s, the media took on a dominant role in political communications, displacing informal and face-to-face encounters, the family, the community, and the workplace as sources of influence. The media became central in popular culture, in processes of socialization and in determining the framework of every type of social communication and collective action.[24] All political parties were affected by this development, but none more than the PCI. More systematically and completely than the DC or the smaller parties, it had built up its own network of communications consisting of organized activists, newspapers and magazines, publishing activities, rallies, festivals, wall newspapers, and leaflets. These circuits were counterposed to the dominant national and local media and were designed to promote the class and political consciousness of party members and sympathizers. Independent newspapers, the commercial press in all its forms, as well as much of radio, television, cinema, and sport, were seen as hostile or questionable means, purveyors of ideas and cultures typical of capitalist society and that therefore needed to be fought and overcome. The Communists never succeeded in displacing commercial culture even among dedicated members even in the divisive 1950s. But the fact that the party produced an autonomous culture of its own that was distributed through channels it controlled was very important in reinforcing its subculture, identity, and ideological cohesion.

This model basically survived through the 1960s and 1970s, but the developments of the latter decade raised questions about its continued viability and validity. The far left and the social movements broke down old barriers and pioneered more flexible and pragmatic forms of political communication. Moreover, the party acquired support in unprecedented quarters among people who were external to its apparatus and subculture and who therefore could not readily be influenced or directed by its parallel media. Both these factors served to undermine the PCI's perception of itself and render more complex its relationship to its electorate, to public opinion, to the mainstream media, and to its own followers. The problem was rendered even more intricate by the fragmentation of old class-based identities and the emergence of corporativist tendencies, the dissolution of stable urban communities and the emergence of new forms of social deprivation and marginalization, and the deregulation of broadcasting and the subsequent extension of the role of the mass media in all areas of life.

For the first time television and the press in the 1980s assumed a more central role than the parties in determining political themes and issues; galvanizing public opinion; shaping the rhythms, nature, and style of political conflict; and conveying information to the population.[25] In this context the old forms of communication and emphasis on separateness and distinctiveness that had characterized the PCI ceased to serve their purpose and became an obstacle to the effective construction of a strategy of communication that exploited the party's greater access to the media and ability to interact with public opinion at large. The election campaigns of 1979 and 1983 demonstrated this very well. Although the PCI continued to rely largely on leafleting, face-to-face contact, rallies, and its own press, all of which reached its conventional electorate but not beyond, other parties (first the creative Radicals but then the DC, the Socialists and the Republicans) utilized the program slots and advertising space of the private channels and networks to seek to convey an image and to respond quickly to the specific themes and issues of the election.[26] This is not to say that they adapted perfectly to a media logic and to media dynamics; indeed, sociologists of mass communications were united in concluding that this was far from the case.[27] But their high-profile tactics removed the PCI from the center of the campaign for the first time since 1948.

Faced with a challenging and unfamiliar situation, the Communists needed to learn how to influence and persuade opinion in the community at large, to acquire new techniques to enter into contact with the various segments of a volatile electorate, and to offer more specific and practical applications of Communist ideology. This in turn required the party to review and modify the strategies of communication of the mass party. As Giorgio Grossi argued, it needed to "stress information rather than propaganda and the importance of image over simple ideological identification, move toward dialectical pluralism instead of confirming the pedagogical style of leadership, open up to the role of mass culture and leisure in socialization at the expense of a rigid perpetuation of the culture of militancy."[28]

That this was a complex and problematic process is revealed by the persistence within the PCI of a theory and practice that dated back to the formative period of the mass party. Although the leadership was happy for Communists to occupy positions in RAI or work for mainstream newspapers, viewing these, like the cinema in the past, as areas in which party influence might usefully be extended, it profoundly objected to the way independent publications like *La Repubblica, L'Espresso,* and *Il Manifesto* began to intervene in and condition the internal and external circuits of communication of the apparatus. In the mid-1970s, when the bourgeois press had first set aside its ostracism of the PCI and published interviews with Enrico Berlinguer and others, leading Communists had reveled in the novelty. Indeed, the party secretary was in such demand between 1973 and 1979 that a press office was created in Via delle Botteghe Oscure and its chief, Tonino Tatò, became the most valued member of his personal staff. Communists regarded the mainstream press as a potential adjunct to the propaganda tools of the party, a channel for addressing external audiences while the party's organs served the needs of loyal supporters. What they did not realize was that, by reserving important communications for the independent press, they would render the latter more attractive than the Communist press to activists and left-wing opinion generally. While *L'Unità* provided dull, official accounts of PCI debates, and verbatim reports of central committee meetings and congresses, often passing over or burying clashes of opinion, *La Repubblica* offered brief synthetic reports, drawing on off-the-record comment, which frequently personalized and sensationalized disputes. Much to the chagrin of traditionalists, it was the latter, as a consequence, that became the bible of those who wanted to know what was really going on in the PCI. The problem was all the more grave because *La Repubblica,* like the right-wing *Il Giornale,* was a paper with an agenda of its own. By acquiring a readership among Communists it also acquired the possibility of influencing internal debates and shaping the opinions of PCI voters. This situation provoked anger and anguish, as the party had been used to determining what was news about itself and controlling the flow of information on its inside.[29]

Most senior Communists regarded these developments as a temporary setback. Their response was to urge measures to reinforce the party and to seek to restore the status quo ante. Activists were encouraged to put more energy into recruitment drives, into promoting Sunday sales of *L'Unità*, and into gaining subscriptions to the paper and to *Rinascita*. Slow to appreciate that qualitative changes had occurred and that the party no longer controlled a sufficiently compact and homogeneous subculture for it to play a countercultural role, they maintained a diffident, even hostile attitude toward *La Repubblica* and *Il Manifesto* and toward private radio and television, even though Communist-sponsored stations were set up in areas of traditional strength. A conventional idea of communication as propaganda, as something pedagogical geared to a project of transformation, persisted well into the 1980s.[30]

Yet there were also important innovations that went in the direction indicated by Grossi. Here the nature and sources of these will be analyzed and the debates that accompanied them illustrated. It should be stressed from the outset that an important catalyst of change in the Communist media, in the party's attitude toward mass culture and in its policies on the mass media system, was the generation gap that opened up from the 1960s between older cadres and younger Communists who had grown up during the years of the economic boom. In public, functionaries and activists in their thirties often endorsed and identified with the rather austere model of committed, progressive culture with which the PCI was associated. In a party in which promotion and advancement were determined from above by the rules of co-option, there were obvious advantages to conformity. Yet, in reality, adhesion to orthodoxy in culture and communication was weak among men and women who had lived their entire lives in the television age, who had invariably participated in student and social movements, and who had often also belonged to the groups of the far left. They brought into the party a baggage of experiences and attitudes that were external to it and that clashed with some features of its militant culture.

Some examples demonstrate this. Between the late 1960s and the early

1980s, when the decline of collective involvements and the appropriation of film culture by television provoked their demise, film clubs enjoyed enormous popularity among students and young educated people
in general. Many of these clubs began life as emanations of the PCI or at
least belonged to the alternative circuits serviced by ARCI. They aimed to
transmit the progressive cinema of the past to a new audience and to
show art and third-world films that were denied access to mainstream
circuits.[31] In some cases, such as that of La Cappella Underground in
Trieste or the Angelo Azzurro in Bologna, this cultural mission was
performed with much intellectual rigor. However, over time, many of the
conventions of the old-left film clubs were overcome. Debates became
less frequent, political filtering diminished, and there was a rediscovery
of cinema as a popular phenomenon to be enjoyed and celebrated for
itself. Film Studio 70, a Roman club founded in 1967, pioneered eclectic
programs in which Eisenstein rubbed shoulders with the classic Hollywood cinema of John Ford and Howard Hawks, and Bogart mixed with
Italian stars of the past like the comic Totò and the Italian Errol Flynn,
Amedeo Nazzari, who in their heydays had been criticized or ignored by
the left. The detachment from a critical orthodoxy, which continued to
regard the works of Roberto Rossellini, Luchino Visconti, and Vittorio
De Sica as the only worthwhile Italian cinema, proceeded with the revival of several of Totò's better films of the 1950s and the critical re-
habilitation of his work.[32] At the annual international festivals of "new
cinema" at Pesaro in the mid-1970s, neorealism as a cultural movement
was attacked with polemical vigor while the once despised "white telephone" films of the 1930s and the tearjerking melodramas of the 1950s
were admired and applauded.

This phenomenon was bound up with the decay of the rigorous culture
of commitment that the far-left vanguards had sustained and the attempt
to rethink cultural policies in a way that took account of the reality of
popular tastes. However, the elitism of the operation could be seen in the
way engagement only took place with the popular culture of the past,
whereas that of the present was deplored in much the same way the
critics of the 1950s had perceived Totò.

The revisionist fervor took place outside the PCI and in explicit polemic with the cultural positions and values it sustained. Yet, precisely
because the impulse behind it was more than anything else a generational
one, it was inevitable that it should find an echo among younger Commu-

Between Hollywood and Moscow

nists. The FGCI endeavored to influence and appropriate the youth coun-terculture of the 1970s, and several of its leaders in Rome, including Gianni Borgna, Walter Veltroni, and Ferdinando Adornato, promoted debates on the cultural and political identity of Italian youth in the 1960s. These ideas were carried over into *La città futura,* an FGCI paper pub-lished from 1977 that aimed to establish links between the Communist tradition and youth culture, renewing both. Systematic attention was dedicated to the myths and legends of American and Italian mass culture.

This small-scale initiative (the paper sold poorly and folded within two years) would be of little interest were it not for the fact that a great shift in Communist attitudes to mass culture occurred in the 1980s, and ten years later Borgna and Veltroni were mainly responsible for shaping the party's policies on cultural industries and mass communications. Even in the mid-1970s their views were significant because they were among the new category of Communist administrators (45 percent of whom were under age thirty) that came into being after the PCI's advances in local elections in 1975–76.[33] It was largely through the activities of left-wing city administrations in the cultural sphere that new techniques were pioneered, old positions and approaches were attacked and discredited, and the way was prepared for the adoption of more flexible and limited cultural policies.

The "Roman Summers" and the Reinvention of Cultural Policy

The most innovative policies were pursued by the Communist-led ad-ministration in Rome, which provided a model that was rapidly adopted in other cities. Lacking an organized and supportive civil society and any tradition of left-wing government in the city, the coalition used film, dance, and music to promote a mass leisure culture that drew in citizens from all parts of the city. There was a carnival-style usage of historic public spaces during summer months in which cinema and the-aters were closed; in and around ancient monuments were staged film shows, dances, poetry readings, and musical events, with admission prices being held to a minimum. Culture and entertainment were not seen as a special sector but as resources to be used in governing the society.

The mastermind behind the "Roman Summers" was Renato Nicolini, a thirty-four-year-old architect who became chief of the newly created culture department in the administration that was headed first by the left independent art critic Giulio Carlo Argan and successively by the leader of the Communist group in the city council, Luigi Petroselli.[34] Although he had been a member of the PCI since 1962, Nicolini was an unorthodox and inexperienced figure who had not been immersed in party politics. He was familiar, however, with the archipelago of experimental theaters, independent cinemas, free radios, and film clubs like Film Studio 70 that constituted a sort of counterculture in Rome.[35] He was fascinated by and approved their rejection of conventional barriers between high and low culture and experimentation with primitive forms of expression and high technology.

Nicolini was determined to effect a sharp break with the policies of previous Christian Democrat administrations. At the 1976 congress of ARCI-UISP, he indicated that the first task was to do away with an old type of practice that consisted of "periodically exhibiting a sculpture or painting by this or that usually unknown personality, with posters, receptions, and little cocktails paid for by the administration." If the left was to give an overall meaning to its policies on culture and the arts, it had to make contact with "a new audience and a new type of demand." This could only occur if there was "a new, different way of managing public spending, to activate permanent channels of democracy and give this new audience the chance to become the subject and express itself." Concomitant with this was "a completely different way of running the city in which culture cannot be seen as a separate fact or merely as a rhetorical moment."[36] However, Nicolini was no less concerned to move beyond the conception of the PCI as an omnipresent hegemonic force that aimed to establish a pedagogical relationship with supporters and citizens in general. He had little time for the ideological conventions and party orientation of much of what was considered to be progressive, committed culture, and he also distanced himself from ARCI and its institutional scheme for extending the cultural power of the labor movement in conjunction with local and regional government. He recognized that much of what passed for progressive culture was not genuinely popular and that the values and goals that underpinned it were being questioned. Although the left preferred not to acknowledge the fact, the culture of workers, housewives, families, and young people consisted

Between Hollywood and Moscow

ever more of commercial popular music, television quiz shows, American soap operas, and spectator sports.

In 1977 Nicolini launched a program of summer activities that, with developments and modifications, would become an annual event for seven years. The centerpiece was outdoor all-night film shows that in the first year were held in the Basilica of Maxentius and successively in the Forum, by the Coliseum, and at the Circus Maximus. There were a number of screens in these extraordinary settings that mixed diverse films: classic Italian films, Hollywood greats, French thrillers, and silent comedies. Sideshows and other amenities meant large audiences could move around easily, seek refreshment, and find new diversions. The whole of central Rome was revitalized with evening events including open-air theatrical performances, dance areas, rock concerts, and even large-screen television showings. With historic monuments and public squares being used for shows and entertainments a joyous atmosphere emerged that some saw as the possible basis of a new civic spirit. In contrast to the *feste dell'Unità,* which were wholly party affairs held usually on special sites well away from city centers, the "Summers" involved taking possession of the existing city and making its sacred places into gathering points for all inhabitants, including those from slumlike peripheral estates. The events, moreover, were not staged directly by the commune but were organized in conjunction with cooperatives and clubs from the alternative arts sector.[37]

Nicolini's high-profile programs were interpreted in various ways. Given that a good part of the public of the Roman Summers was drawn from among those who had been engaged in the social movements and the counterculture, some saw these activities as an institutionalized prolongation of the joie de vivre and passion for noncommercial collective entertainments that marked youth culture in the 1970s. Less charitably, others saw them as a case of the PCI desperately offering bread and circuses to a section of the population it had won in 1975–76 and was now deeply alienated from its national policies. By others still it was described as an aspect of the *riflusso* in public involvements, a channel through which former activists passed before withdrawing into the private sphere. To make sense of these interpretations it is important to distinguish between intentions and results. The first interpretation comes closest to capturing the original content and purposes of the "Summers."

The second is perhaps a truer reflection of what happened when the idea was taken up by Communist-led administrations in Naples, Florence, Bologna, Perugia, and other cities, and it in effect became a national aspect of local government policy. Although the culture assessors were often similar sorts of figures to Nicolini, unorthodox individuals who happily cast themselves in the part of jester at the court of the left, they rarely had the background or geniality of their model. They were appointed after the Roman experience demonstrated the rewards that could be reaped in terms of popular consensus from cultural programs (even the 1979 Communist vote in Rome increased by 0.4 percent in 1981, when personal preference votes for Nicolini increased from four thousand to thirty-six thousand).[38] The third interpretation will be assessed in a moment. First, it is necessary to draw out the new ideas in the Roman policies, ideas that were the product of an attempt to rethink critically the role of the left in relation to the culture of a capitalist society.

First, there was a recognition that there were important relationships at play in the consumption of culture, which was no longer seen as a passive activity, something to be combated or improved. The aim was to liberate the imagination by creating possibilities for new forms of consumption through special events. Second, the aim was to combat the loss of a civic culture in a vast city marked by the phenomenon of social deprivation and private isolation. Most events were focused on the historic center, but there was also an attempt to utilize neglected spaces on the outskirts. Third, there was an abandonment of any notion of cultural hierarchy in favor of a mixture of styles, languages, and forms. Fourth, although not improvised, events and programs were created and staged in a short time and enjoyed some of the advantages of spontaneity. Fifth, in promoting events in collaboration with the private sector, administrators and politicians were compelled to confront the reality of popular demand and taste and work with it. Sixth, there was a desire, through public intervention, to widen choice and counteract a market tendency to raise constantly cinema and theater entry prices to combat falling audiences. Finally, the aim was to find new means to maintain a participatory public sphere and tackle the atomization and privatization fostered by the development of commercial television. The point of the Roman Summers, Nicolini stated in a newspaper interview, was that when they were inserted in a "mass cultural initiative," fun, games, and popular pastimes assumed a new significance. "Dancing can be very nice if it is set in this framework," he said, "but if it just becomes an end in itself then it is a load of crap."[39]

The last point should make it clear that one intention was to impede the demobilization of the late 1970s, to overcome the fracture between the political forces and parts of civil society that occurred in 1977 and that grew worse during and after the kidnapping and assassination of Aldo Moro. But if, in terms of form, the Roman Summers were conceived in opposition to the disillusion and violence that accompanied the end of the protest cycle, in their content they were intimately bound up with the *riflusso*. Everything that had been rejected by the student activists of 1968 was accepted and celebrated, including American culture, popular Italian culture, dancing, the mass media, and uncomplicated enjoyment. There is no evidence to suggest that the left-wing, educated young constituted more than a segment of the public, but for them, as for Nicolini and his colleagues, the events were a way to discover cultural phenomena that had nothing to do with the traditional left. They were the vehicle through which a collective liberation from the engaged occurred and a reconciliation took place with mass culture and its myths. In this sense the phenomenon cannot but be seen as an aspect of the crisis of Marxism and the decline of the conventional cultural project of the left.[40]

Nicolini's cultural policies provoked much controversy. Concerned commentators, political adversaries, and cultural snobs were at one in expressing disapproval of policies that involved public institutions engaging with and promoting the games and languages of commercial lowbrow culture instead of seeking to raise the level of the public. Nicolini was accused of wasting vast amounts of money on what became widely known as "the ephemeral" at the expense of investment in permanent structures such as libraries and museums. He and his peers in other cities were charged also with instrumentalizing cultural policy for political ends and misusing historic monuments.[41]

This concern was sometimes overstated, but not perhaps unfounded. In some respects it could be said that Nicolini's approach, and that of other PCI culture assessors, merged a rather static view of popular mobilization recurrent in the Communist tradition with an "integrated" cultural outlook. The important thing seemed to be to get people to participate in droves in this or that event, and more or less any means was justified to achieve this. Whereas Communists had once all but ignored the organization of culture and concentrated on ideological criticism of single films or television shows, the reverse arguably now seemed to be the case. The structural aspects of cultural production and consumption were managed and manipulated with great sophistication, but attention to the contents seemed to be reduced practically to zero.

In their defense the culture assessors and their allies argued that precisely the undifferentiated flow of films and performances that others saw as undermining the critical faculties of the public in fact represented a possible challenge to bourgeois hegemony. It was argued that, far from "leaving nothing behind," the summer events left cultural models by seeking to create new social relations through the stimulation of the imagination and the construction of new collective contexts of consumption.[42] However, this view was never developed with the necessary clarity and rigor even by the most articulate and forceful theorist of the ephemeral, the media sociologist Alberto Abruzzese. As the chief inspirer of the nonstop film shows at the Basilica of Maxentius and the leading promoter of the new generation of Communist cultural operatives that had emerged and achieved power in local government, he repeatedly attacked the PCI leadership and Italian intellectuals in general for being slow to understand the mass media and acknowledge their dominant position. Nicolini was a convenient symbol, because he helped the party project externally an image of vitality and modernity and maintain contact with youth, but, Abruzzese argued, his views were merely tolerated and not absorbed.

Borgna, Abruzzese, and others championed a new, more limited, and flexible model of cultural policy than that which the PCI had sustained in the past. They accepted pluralism, the market, consumption, the modern metropolis, and the mass media as intrinsic features of contemporary society and aimed to promote alternatives within a context that was designed by them. "When in an advanced capitalist country mass communications begin to assert their effective dominance it is impossible to get round them by means of pretechnological practices, such as the education of the public according to the classical techniques of associationalism," the latter insisted.[43] It was only possible to intervene at an appropriate technological level, to seek to shape and enrich consumption by connecting it to other social relations. For this reason many of those involved in or supportive of local cultural policies saw as one of the chief merits of these the fact that they transgressed the codes of the old Communist culture. Provocation, the flouting of taboos, the celebration of the

Between Hollywood and Moscow

long deplored and the ridicule of established left-wing legends were all part of the struggle to clear the ground for a new approach and force the party hierarchy to set aside old preconceptions. As the utter opposite of the gloomy culture of sacrifices with its strong emphasis on the achievement of hegemony through pedagogy, the "ephemeral" contradicted Berlinguer's project for austerity and contributed to its demise.

The Crumbling of an Old Cultural Model

The battle within the PCI between the old and the new continued into the second half of the 1980s. The troika of young Roman Communists all published books and articles, whose iconoclasm contributed to their rise to cultural power. Gianni Borgna published a study of the San Remo song festival that celebrated it as a popular phenomenon and site of collective passion. In February 1986 he even hailed the opening of the festival in a front-page article in *L'Unità*. Walter Veltroni edited works on football and on the 1960s; Ferdinando Adornato edited *Eroi del nostro tempo* (Heroes of our times), a volume subjecting such figures of contemporary mass culture as J. R. Ewing, Rocky, and Clint Eastwood to sympathetic investigation.[44] All these initiatives had a slightly daring quality about them. They were intended to confront an idea still strong in the PCI according to which only that which was engaged and progressive could be popular. The aim was to redefine the Communist conception of culture to include light music, pop and rock, popular television programs, mass-produced literature, and sport, as well as the industries that furnished them and the market channels through which they were distributed. Abruzzese also kept up his attack, widening progressively the range of his targets. In a polemical pamphlet published in 1982 he claimed to speak for a whole generation that was deeply dissatisfied with the lack of new blood at the top of the PCI, the sloth with which the party accepted new ideas, its attachment to outdated class approaches, its puritanism, its hostility to diversity and pluralism in society, and its distrust of the contemporary and the immediate.[45]

That there was resistance within the PCI to ideas that to older cadres seemed to threaten fundamentally the identity and cohesion of the party is undeniable. Although those chiefly responsible for cultural policy, Aldo Tortorella and Giuseppe Chiarante, were tolerant, capable men, they were also profoundly attached to the PCI's traditions and historic goals. Much to the astonishment of outside observers, none of the culture assessors or supporters of "the ephemeral" was invited to the central committee session dedicated to culture in 1981. In many less visible ways old conceptions persisted and new schemes were kept at arm's length. Yet by any comparative standard the PCI was not slow to modify its approaches to mass culture and mass communication. In 1981 a consultative assembly on mass culture was established that did include Nicolini and that external intellectuals and media professionals were invited to join. The proceedings of the first meeting of this assembly demonstrated that to some degree mass culture was accepted by all.[46] Cinema and television were not seen to be separate from but rather part of popular culture and important factors in determining collective orientations and desires. That positions were shifting within the PCI itself was clear in the mid-1980s when there was a significant shift toward acceptance of both public and private initiatives in cultural activities. Whereas in the early part of the decade the party had watched with horror the development of a large private television sector and the subsequent concentration of national commercial networks, it now largely accepted the existence of a mixed system in which RAI competed with commercial television. Of course, Communists did not approve of Berlusconi's monopoly, which they opposed vigorously and sought to dismantle by promoting antitrust legislation, but they did not champion a return to the pre-1976 public service monopoly. In other areas, too, there was recognition that the state could best play a role not by displacing the market but by intervening to create spaces, widen choice, permit new enterprises to emerge, and ensure that national products were defended and cultivated. As Forgacs notes, all this was proof that an old cultural design had been eroded and that a new one had started to replace it.[47] In the new scheme there was no attempt to take a stance on the contents of cultural activity or to conceive of intervention primarily in party terms. Rather, a strictly party approach was superseded by an attempt to frame public policies that could command wide support in national cultural industries and among their audiences. Among the architects of the new model were Borgna and Veltroni, who at this time assumed the chief responsibility for formulating policy in these sectors. The shift was of general application, though. In all its dealings with the mass media the PCI became more relaxed and less suspicious. Berlinguer's successor Alessandro Natta

Between Hollywood and Moscow

appeared on television entertainment shows such as Raffaella Carrà's *Buonasera Raffaella,* and other senior Communists showed up on chat shows. Election programs were handled with skill, and there was an effort at local and national levels to utilize, sometimes to the point of fielding them as candidates for election, some of the personalities from the entertainment world who belonged to or, more frequently, were sympathetic to the party. In terms of campaign techniques, traditional forms of activism were supplemented but not replaced by spot announcements, paid advertisements in the independent press, thematic highlighting, the wider use of prestigious independent candidates, telephone canvassing and opinion polling, and the attempt to construct a pragmatic profile of wide appeal.[48] The PCI did not completely embrace media politics; indeed, it remained deeply skeptical of many aspects of the show-business razzmatazz that other parties so eagerly embraced, but it learned to move with greater agility in contexts that were not congenial to it.

In a situation in which the PCI was beginning to alter fundamentally its cultural policies and renew its model of communication to account for the loosening of subcultural ties and other social changes, it remains to be considered whether the party's traditional tools of ideological mobilization could continue to be of use or whether they were not merely relics of a bygone era. Certainly, there were some who thought there was no need for the party to continue to subsidize a vast array of press and publishing activities or to maintain a network of flanking organizations, just as there were some who questioned the need to preserve the mass party. But the view of the overwhelming majority of the party and the apparatus was that these tools were vital to both a capillary Communist presence in society and to effective political communication. The task was not to abolish old instruments, but renew them.

In the 1960s many of the local newspapers published or sponsored by the PCI closed. By the early 1980s only a handful remained, including *Paese sera* in Rome and *L'Ora* in Palermo, both of which accumulated fearful debts. The situation of *L'Unità* and the weekly *Rinascita* was scarcely better. After years of steady decline, they recovered ground in the 1970s and took on extra staff, only to be compelled to face possible extinction when organizational decline resumed sharply. The financial circumstances of *L'Unità* were disastrous, even though it was the only party political newspaper in Italy to enjoy sales similar to those of some of the leading independent newspapers.[49] In 1984 formal measures were adopted to reduce the debts and relaunch the paper. To find an audience not only among activists who were themselves becoming more demanding but among a wider and less controllable audience of sympathizers, *L'Unità* was bound to reduce its characteristics as a party organ and expand those that would make it an adequate alternative to an independent paper. To some degree this was achieved by dedicating the first few pages to major national and international stories, the abolition of the traditional cultural "third page" and its replacement with a more contemporary rubric dedicated to culture and entertainments, more interviews and inquiries, debates, and local supplements in regions in which sales were concentrated. Despite strong resistance within the PCI leadership and among a section of the membership, the paper also took a more independent line and began to write up party events in the personalized manner of *La Repubblica*. A moderate critical success was achieved; however, although the debt problem gradually improved, sales only increased by a small margin, and the doubt about the paper's long-term future was never entirely overcome.

The fate of the *L'Unità* festivals was a separate but related issue. In chapter 5 it was noted that these changed in the 1970s. They ceased to be structures that served a purpose purely within the PCI's subculture and became key instruments in the party's attempt to communicate political messages to the wider population. There can be no doubt that the larger festivals, that is to say those held at the provincial or national level, performed this task very well. Even the smaller ones made a contribution. With fifteen million visitors in 1986 and gross earnings of 300–500 billion lire, the festivals as a whole brought the party into direct contact with more Italians than could be reached by any other form of communication.[50] Thanks to press and television coverage of the many debates and face-to-face confrontations, they became a fixed item in the national political calendar. Yet there were problems. Although the vast earnings were vital to the PCI, there were questions about how far the festivals actually served to win support for the party and whether they would be sustained in circumstances marked by a decline of activism. From the 1970s critics regularly suggested that the festivals had become neutral containers like a supermarket or the Sunday afternoon TV variety show *Domenica in*. Families came to eat, shop, admire the displays of new cars, look at the exhibitions, and then departed without encountering politics. Similarly, young people flocked to see the Italian pop stars and international rock groups who often based their national tours on the larger festivals but failed to perceive in the structure of these any alternative way of conceiving social life. Observers noted that among visitors it was more common to hear the formal *Lei* mode of address than the familar *tu* that was the norm among comrades. To some degree these criticisms were informed by nostalgia for the days when the festivals were largely internal, subcultural affairs marked by warmth and comradeship. But almost identical views were advanced by those who saw them as holdovers from the days when the party could readily marshal an army of volunteers willing to give up their summer holidays to construct stalls, serve in restaurants, and so on. In the 1980s fewer and fewer people were willing to do this, with the result that it became necessary for several sections to pool their resources and organize shared festivals.[51] The number of small festivals declined markedly.

In 1976 ARCI reached a hiatus. Buoyed by recent expansion and the conquest of legitimation, it articulated, in parallel with the PCI's ostensible advance to power, a project for the overall transformation of the Italian social and cultural system, reserving a preeminent place for organized recreational associations. When this project failed, and culture assessors successively bypassed the association and what remained of the once vital network of Case del popolo, it would not have been surprising if ARCI-UISP had entered a phase of terminal decline. In fact, this did not occur. Under new leadership the association acknowledged that in the 1970s mistakes had been made. Too much effort had gone into formulating excessively grandiose schemes, which then became bogged down in the bureaucratic inertia of local government where they encountered resistance and where in any case, owing to the premium placed on collaboration with the DC at all levels, structural innovations such as democratic decentralization failed to materialize. It was recognized that ARCI had also passed too quickly from an "alternative" approach to a hegemonic one, against the wishes of a part of the association. In so doing it had counted heavily on grassroots structures that were in fact quite fragile or, where they had been established much earlier, were in decline.[52]

ARCI thus needed to try to find a new vision of its cultural role in circumstances that were anything but propitious. It needed to comprehend new social dynamics and find ways to promote grassroots democracy and participation. Like the FGCI, ARCI opted to modify its organizational structure to permit greater specialization and capture sectoral interests and themes. *Arci Kids, Arci ragazzi,* and *Arci comics* ensured it was inserted in the group pattern of youth culture; *Arci pesca* (fishing), *Arci caccia* (hunting), and the *Unione giochi* (games) provided for popular leisure pursuits; *Arci gay* and the Environmental League campaigned on specific issues; and *Arci media* acted as an observatory on broadcasting trends. According to the ARCI president, Rino Serri, diversity and subjectivity was in this way recognized and encouraged. In 1987 the transformation was completed when the organization adopted a confederal statute that accorded a large measure of autonomy to its single components.[53]

Inevitably, it proved difficult to keep some of these leagues in a single umbrella association. The Environmental League's opposition to blood sports brought it into bitter conflict with the hunters. Overall, however, the tensions bore witness to the success with which ARCI reinserted itself in the articulations of civil society. It was well placed to draw advantage from the growth in the demand for leisure in Italy's more prosperous regions. After declining in the late 1970s, membership increased steadily throughout the 1980s, reaching 1.2 million in 1986. This revival, although it showed the potential vitality of subcultural activities that, according to some accounts, should have found even less space available to them in the 1980s, cannot be seen simply as an advantage for the PCI. Rather, it went in tandem with a certain depoliticization of the association and an increasing distance between it and the party.

This trend was matched in all areas. To succeed as a social and cultural force the PCI had to shed a good part of its heritage, lose its distinctiveness, open up to cultures that were extraneous to it, reinvent its strategies of communication, and abandon much of its ideological baggage. It was a tribute to the mass vocation of the party that it was able to overcome opposition and move in this direction. Young cadres and enterprising members of the 1970s generation were able to exploit the opportunities offered by a new role in local government, disorientation in many areas of the party, gaps in policy, and the desire to recover and reassert after a defeat, to avoid decline, and to embrace novelty. The high visibility and success of some of the cultural departures, however, should not conceal the fact that an old cultural model, that which the PCI had sustained for most of its existence, was definitively defeated. This was a historic passage of considerable moment. The new model that emerged was very

Between Hollywood and Moscow

different from the old, even if some of the tools and means bore the same names and labels. It was less ideological, more respectful of diversity, more realistic, and less ambitious. It was a niche within the existing order rather than an opposition to it. More suited certainly to the circumstances of the time, and the only viable option, it amounted to very much less than the revolutionary cultural project of the 1940s. Modern in their outlook and at home with the cultures of the rest of society, younger Communist cadres were willing to sell their souls and risk losing the historic Communist identity of the party in order to innovate.

7

The Last Tango

The Collapse of Communism and

the Dissolution of the PCI

In the 1987 election the Communist share of the vote fell for the third time running, to 26.6 percent. For a party that had advanced markedly in the 1970s, it was a major shock to return to the level of support it had commanded in 1968. The defeat showed that the idea that there was a rock-solid PCI vote of 30 percent, which had complacently been theorized in 1983, was false. The crisis of the PCI vote was undeniable, and the specter of long-term historic decline cast a menacing shadow. In these circumstances much changed in the party: anguished, divisive debate took the place of composed unanimity, signs of anger and frustration permeated the grass roots, young intermediate cadres grew impatient for the removal of the older men who dominated the leadership, and once-hallowed rituals and totems were subjected to ridicule and attack.

After replacing the ailing Alessandro Natta as secretary in June 1988, Achille Occhetto engaged in a vigorous campaign to revive the PCI and show that its demise was not inevitable. These moves restored a measure of dynamism to the PCI and helped slow down the decline in its electoral standing. But they did not reverse the negative trend that dated back to 1977 and that continued in elections held in summer and autumn 1989. There were several reasons for this. First of all, the crisis of the PCI was not a conjunctural one owing to relatively superficial factors. Poor leadership and lack of initiative compounded the sense of disorientation that marked the party in the mid-1980s, but, at bottom, the erosion it suffered was due to the decline of the industrial working class, the breakup of what had been taken to be a relatively compact social bloc, the disarticulation and decline of the left-wing subculture, and the loss of the youth vote. None of these historic factors could be counteracted as long as the structures, identity, and values of the party were primarily geared to an old model of politics that was no longer entirely relevant. Yet the basic features and identity of the party could not easily be changed, for they were the object of deep loyalty on the part of cadres and members.

In a desperate and unplanned move to save the specific and original experience of Italian Communism from being dragged down with parties and regimes that PCI leaders had long criticized but never wholly condemned, Occhetto seized the opportunity offered by the fall of the Berlin Wall in November 1989 to proclaim his intention to seek the termination of the PCI and the formation of a new reformist political party that would draw in not only Communists but also other left-wing and progressive forces. The declaration provoked an extended, anguished debate that involved ordinary Communists up and down the country and had a wide impact on public opinion. The argument over what Communist identity was or could possibly continue to be in a contemporary context ceased to be a matter of political reflection and became a social and cultural event whose dimensions bore witness to the deep roots and important role of the PCI in Italian society.

A Party in Crisis

After the electoral defeat of 1987, it was widely felt that the party's political culture and very identity were in crisis. Partial adaptation to capitalist society, on the one hand, and the great cultural offensive that had been launched against the left in the 1980s, on the other, had eroded the very sense of what it meant to be a Communist. "Our identity has faded," "We have become a lay party but without a political identity" were examples of a recurrent complaint.[1] Because a version of modernity that the left had resisted had won out, Gavino Angius lamented, the PCI found itself deprived of a connecting texture of new ideas and values that bring about "a sort of 'basic program' of renewal of society and the state."[2] This was not an abstract problem but a very concrete one, because it meant that all sense of inspiration and purpose was obfuscated.

Because Communists at all levels shared a sense of disorientation, the impulse to redefine, rethink, or at the very least restate the basic premises of the party's identity as part of a general reelaboration of its goals and methods was strong. Disagreements of a fundamental kind arose, however, over how this should be achieved. The nub of the question concerned the continuing validity and relevance or otherwise of Communism. Although Napolitano argued that the time had come to "move decisively beyond the confines of tradition and of the Communist movement" and CGIL leader Luciano Lama, in a press interview, even advanced the notion that the PCI should seek membership of the Socialist International, left-wingers took the view that too many concessions had already been made to "ideas, conceptions, values, and models of society distant from those of the workers and democratic movement."[3] For his part Armando Cossutta threatened to set up a separate Communist force should the party cast off from its historic moorings.[4]

Occhetto sought to introduce new energy to the PCI. He also aimed to provide the PCI's reformism with a proper foundation in terms of political culture, policies, and strategic goals. To this end he called for a "new course" and a "new party," two terms that Togliatti had employed when he set about reestablishing the PCI on new bases in the closing years of the war. Communication was crucial to the new course. One central task, as Occhetto and his associates saw it, was to put the PCI back in the headlines after several years in which it had ceased to dominate the news. The intention was also to lend the PCI a more modern, less austere, and remote image. To achieve this, closer attention than ever before was paid to the rhythms and requirements of the mass media. Professional assistance was sought from advertisers in preparing election and campaign materials, and the personal qualities and image of the party leader and Communist mayors were highlighted in stark contrast with the rigorous depersonalization of earlier times. Party spokesmen avoided the complex, jargon-ridden language that leading Communists and other politicians customarily employed and opted instead for pithy remarks and sound bites. Occhetto himself became a highly public and even fashionable figure who regularly appeared in the press and on television. Quite deliberately he cultivated a different, more human image to the aloof model of previous Communist leaders. This culminated in the controversial publication of a series of color photographs in the weekend supplement to *La Repubblica,* which depicted him fondly kissing his third wife, the PCI senator Aureliana Alberici. It is significant that this stunt, which was greeted with horror by traditionally minded Communists, was seen as a symbol of the end of Communist "anthropological diversity." When Occhetto shed tears at the PCI's final two congresses, the residual stereotypical image of the tough, emotionless Communist was definitively buried.[5]

By the mid-1980s men and women in their thirties and forties, recruited in the aftermath of 1968, made up the bulk of the active membership and filled most executive positions in the party at local level. They were different from older Communists in a variety of ways. They were better educated, more vocal, and less inclined to be deferential toward the leadership. They were also not as fully integrated into the culture of the party as older members. Although they were strongly motivated, especially in an ethical sense, they were less attached to given rituals and procedures. The first political experiences of many had been outside the PCI, and they sustained friendship networks and leisure and cultural interests that went well beyond a party environment. Their antisystem outlook, Piero Ignazi found, was not bound up with either economic hardship or personal frustrations but was the result of formative experiences and intellectual reflection.[6] Precisely for this reason, this was the category that was most directly affected by the crisis of Communist ideology. Because they were at once members of the party and fully inserted into a society that was rapidly evolving in unforeseen directions, these people could not be insensitive to the collapse of an old idea of the party as a monolithic, controlling entity. This development provoked in them at once nostalgia and impatience. They grew intolerant of the persistence of outdated rituals and assumptions about who the Communists were and what they wanted, and yearned for a more effective response to the crisis on the part of a leadership that with each new defeat lost more of their respect. Perhaps this process of detachment may best be examined in terms of the cultural conflicts that took place in the PCI and that expressed the changing attitudes and disorientation in the body of the party.

The symbol of the new type of activist was Bobo, the cartoon character who was also the self-portrait of his creator, Sergio Staino. Bobo first appeared in the comics monthly *Linus* in 1979 before spreading to *Il Messaggero* and the "Satyricon" supplement of *La Repubblica,* and finally becoming a regular fixture of *L'Unità* from 1985. On paper the idea of a strip cartoon whose hero was a bearded, middle-aged Communist was somewhat improbable. If it became a success (so much so that it was turned into a television sitcom and was also taken up by the million-selling TV listings magazine *Sorrisi e canzoni TV*), this was largely due to the artistry with which Staino turned his personal itinerary into the collective biography of a generation. A former Maoist who moved toward the PCI at the end of the 1970s, Staino drew on the narrative formulas and language of the best American comic strips to create the saga of a generous, romantic ex-'68er whose high hopes are consistently deflated by the cruel course taken by political events. Overweight, bespectacled, and perennially scruffy, Bobo was continually tested in his views by a feminist wife, a hard-line comrade nicknamed Molotov, and two annoying and inquiring children. Two additional factors facilitated identification with, or recognition of, the sentiments and psychodramas of the character even among non-Communists: the fact that his hobbies, desires, holidays, and cultural tastes were simply those of an average person (this in itself had an air of transgression for Communists); and the fact that the strip and the character were quite strictly linked to current events. So Bobo not only aired his idiosyncratic views on every political issue from the divisions in the leadership of the PCI to Craxi's relationship with the DC, he could also "go serious" if the occasion demanded it and participate in the joys and tragedies of ordinary Communists. With his head bowed and in tears he appeared on the front page of *L'Unità* on the day of Berlinguer's funeral; he exalted a few days later when the PCI won the largest share of the vote in the 1984 European elections, and in 1989 he displayed his horror at the bloody events in Tiananmen Square.

From the start Bobo was a controversial presence in *L'Unità*.[7] The cartoon was a challenge, a break with the official, formal character of the paper. It was a moment of light relief, a free space, which senior Communists and some militants either disapproved of or failed to understand. By offering an apparently realistic or at any rate non-rose-colored picture of the life of a rank-and-file Communist, complete with his contradictions and delusions, Staino opened a far-reaching debate involving party members, leaders, sympathizers, intellectuals, and outside commentators that touched and provoked the erosion of outdated judgments, assumptions, and viewpoints.[8]

This debate entered a new and more turbulent phase from March 1986 when *Tango,* a satirical supplement edited by Staino, was published free with *L'Unità* every Monday. Proposed by Staino and accepted by a PCI leadership keen to find ways to raise the sales of its ailing newspaper, *Tango* counted among its contributors many of the best progressive political cartoonists and humorists in the country.[9] The aim, as its creator conceived it, was to give rise to a full-fledged satirical newspaper with elements of nonsense, surrealism, passion, and invective. The targets of *Tango* included Craxi (a frequent and popular one), President Cossiga, self-important journalists, and the rituals of contemporary Italian life. However, it was the articles and drawings that lampooned the PCI itself and its leaders that caused the most controversy and that constituted the supplement's distinctive feature.

In the eyes of its critics and opponents the *Tango* phenomenon (sales of *L'Unità* on Mondays increased by up to fifty thousand in 1986–88) was a dramatic sign not that the PCI had changed and fully absorbed a culture of tolerance and free expression but rather that it no longer had confidence or pride in its own leaders, purposes, culture, and vision of the world. The juvenile humor of the supplement was read as a sign of the ideological and existential crisis of a party that could no longer develop its own idea of modernity and was therefore compelled to adapt to the existing society and the existing culture by ridiculing its own diversity and spectacularizing its own lack of direction.

Cultures of Disintegration

Unquestionably, the second half of the 1980s was a period of cultural crisis in the PCI. Even though the party leadership cautiously began a process of transition, the gap between the party and society widened alarmingly. With the benefit of hindsight this can be described as the period of final crisis of the PCI and of the historically constituted project of Communism in Italy. Because Communism was not a minority phenomenon but a political movement with vast support that had exercised a significant cultural influence in postwar Italy, this crisis was not a matter of minimal interest. It was a highly public phenomenon that found a variety of interpreters in the cultural sphere, especially when the fall of the Berlin Wall and Occhetto's shock announcement made it clear that the PCI, so long a fixed continent on the political mental map of every Italian, would cease to exist. One of the most memorable products of this cultural current was *Palombella rossa* (Red lob), a film by Nanni Moretti released in September 1989 in which the director played a Communist functionary and water polo enthusiast whose existential crisis explodes during a crucial match that becomes a metaphor of his party's political trajectory. The running phrase of the film, "Siamo diversi? Siamo uguali?" (Are we different? Are we like everybody else?), with its evident nostalgia for Berlinguer and his concept of diversity, seemed perfectly to capture the state of uncertainty and crisis in which Communists found themselves.

It is interesting to consider attitudes toward the memory of Berlinguer. Although numerous homages were accorded the former party secretary on the occasion of anniversaries and so forth, his memory became something of an embarrassment to a leadership that was aiming to end the "hyperidentity" of the party and turn it into a basically reformist force that accepted bourgeois democracy and the market economy. For all his apparent moderation, Berlinguer had been a great cultivator of the specificity of Communist identity and had resisted calls to the PCI to abandon its ideological heritage. For precisely this reason he was adored by rank-and-file Communists whom he had taught to be proud of their political vocation and whom he had led to tremendous electoral success. Many conserved in their homes copies of *L'Unità* announcing the successes of 1975 and 1976 and sometimes even photographs of the only PCI leader to be known to Communists by his first name. His tragic, sudden death and mass, televised funeral consecrated the myth. For the base, then, Berlinguer was a symbol of nonintegration, of a refusal to surrender and of a persistent opposition of principle. In Trieste the head of the party's propaganda department, Tullio Margutti, told Mino Fucillo "I am for utopia, for the party of Berlinguer that wanted a new man with new values."[10]

The former leader was a unifying symbol of some importance for all generations of Communists, since his memory was bound up with the two core elements of his politics: an identification with the working class and an absolute belief in the higher morality and purposes of the Communists. It was no accident that his ascendancy as a symbol coincided with the questioning of these two beliefs. There were, however, differences in the form admiration for Berlinguer took. Older activists, workers, and sympathizers associated him with the party as an institution and its past successes. This was important to younger activists in their thirties, too, but their view was generally less party-centered: it was Berlinguer's stern critiques of capitalist modernity and confident articulation of left-wing values that figured most prominently in their admiration.

For this reason it would be wrong to see *Tango* simply as a manifestation of this crisis, a parasite. Although Staino's sole aim in launching the supplement was to scandalize and amuse, other members of his team wished to pursue more ambitious ends. For the journalist and humorist Michele Serra and the acerbic cartoonist Elle Kappa (Laura Pellegrini) — both of whom, unlike some other members of the team, were paid-up party members — *Tango* became almost what its enemies always thought it was: a factor in the generational struggle between the old leadership group of the PCI and the impatient forty-year-olds who ran the party in the provinces. The latter did not view the party as a sacred object; they regarded renewal almost on any terms as preferable to conservation of a historically sedimented but burdensome and decaying identity.

The "blasphemies" of *Tango,* Serra has written, did not have a depressing effect,

> rather they functioned as a catalyst to the point that, contrary to all forecasts, they became a new "commonplace" through which many left-wing readers rediscovered an *identity.* . . . The deep crisis of hierarchies and dogmas, of parameters and rites, did not signify the end of the physical persons who had lived the Communist experience and, in a wider sense, a left-wing experience. By calling together a large number of heretics, *Tango* on the one hand invited [its readers] to mourn the death of ideology — above all with the saga of Bobo — and on the other to recognize each other in a secular manner not as survivors but as lively people who managed to snigger at the funereal and self-pitying aspects of the crisis (they blasphemed in fact even in the presence of the excellent corpse of Renato Guttuso) and to rediscover intact in a new setting the motives of anger, contempt, commotion, and "overwhelming passion." [11]

The positive dimension of *Tango* found expression in the hugely successful annual festivals organized at Montecchio in the "red" province of Reggio Emilia and in the almost intimate dialogue that was developed with readers in the pages of the supplement. It was clear that for many orphans of ideology, the supplement was indeed, as Serra claimed, not merely a debunker of the party but a new tool of social and political criticism. Thus when an exhausted Staino suddenly decided in October

1989 to close *Tango,* it was Serra who picked up the torch and founded a new supplement, *Cuore,* that was more expressly political and antagonistic than its predecessor. Satire was not directed inward to the same extent but rather against "luxury consumer goods, the so-called VIPs, the vulgar misery of Western wealth, its obese self-satisfaction, and its cholesterol."[12]

The differences between *Tango* and *Cuore* were expressions of the different standpoints of their editors. Staino was fundamentally a purveyor of irony who reveled in the anarchic mix of scandals, ideas, provocations, and practical jokes that his supplement provided. He was an artist more than a political militant in temperament, and he had few constructive ideas to offer. Serra, by contrast, was more strictly a practitioner of satire because his outlook was underpinned by strongly held values and beliefs. He was not a perpetrator of chaos so much as a purveyor of a credo in which a Manichaean vision of good and evil was applied to society, culture, and politics. For this reason he was often compared to Mario Melloni, the former Christian Democrat who, under the pseudonym of Fortebraccio, wrote caustic pieces satirizing the PCI's adversaries for *L'Unità* between 1967 and 1982.[13] Yet whereas the party and the metal workers were fixed points, the pure embodiment of good, in Fortebraccio's world, neither could be in Serra's, for the party was no longer sacred and the working class was in decline. For him good was defined largely as the opposite of what was bad, and bad was more or less synonymous with everything "modern."

In Serra's outlook, the 1970s had been an inspiring period, whereas the 1980s had witnessed the negative diffusion of a vulgar and crassly commercial idea of modernity that could only be totally repudiated. His symbolic enemy was not the capitalist class in general ("lor signori" in Fortebraccio's vocabulary) but Berlusconi. In his articles and thumbnail sketches, Serra ridiculed the jargons, the fashions, the fads, and the personality types that the boom of the 1980s had spawned in the name of a purer, simpler, and less wasteful idea of civilization that clearly owed much to Berlinguer's concept of austerity.[14] Precisely the schematic, moralistic, and uncompromising qualities that had made Berlinguer's vision unappealing as politics to the young in the 1970s lent it a special appeal as postmaterialist cultural criticism in the late 1980s. Certainly, it was a paradox that some of those who had been skeptical of the politics of austerity should now articulate similar values; but in fact, the difference of form and context was crucial.

The position of *Cuore* and of its dedicated readers was full of contradictions. They reveled in the schematic jibes and humorous barbs that were leveled at the media, yet Serra (not to mention other members of the *Cuore* team) was in fact something of a media personality who wrote for the illustrated weeklies and appeared from time to time on the Communist-dominated television channel, RAI-3, whose innovative low-budget programs made a virtue of necessity. Inevitably, most *Cuore* followers were inserted in practice into the contemporary world and in their daily lives accepted most of its rituals even if they preferred sometimes not to admit this to themselves. The revival of the rhetorical figures of the Communist tradition was significant and often humorous, but it did not prevent or even disguise the total integration of most Communists into the average customs and tastes of contemporary Italy.[15]

This, however, did not mean that there was no further cultural role for Communists to play. RAI-3 represented a striking example of how a Communist culture could offer a stimulus to, and constitute a lively spark in, a repetitive and conformist media scene even at the time Communism was collapsing. Even though the ideology was crumbling, the people of the left still existed and were still ready to do battle. Initially intended to be the regional channel, RAI-3 constituted so minoritarian a presence for the first few years of its existence as to be invisible. But under the direction of Angelo Guglielmi, a literary critic and former member of the Group of 63, it acquired respectable audiences and at times challenged the leading RAI and Fininvest channels. In contrast to RAI-I and RAI-2, which sponsored a traditional entertainment largely closed to societal impulses, RAI-3 broadcast satire and pioneered the screening of the proceedings of magistrates' courts (*Un giorno in pretura*), facilitated the search for missing persons (*Chi l'ha visto?*) and coproduced some of the most stimulating feature films of the period. In the mesmerizing *Prove tecniche di trasmissione* and in *Blob,* a cult program broadcast each day after the evening news in which clips of the worst moments on all public and private channels from the previous day were shown assembled in a mind-boggling carousel, a new form of social criticism was invented that was internal to what Umberto Eco defined as "neotelevision."[16]

Overall, it may be said that the cultural and social transformations of the 1980s created the conditions for the emergence from the ruins of the conventional Communist subculture of a new form of apocalyptical cultural critique that offered little in the way of prescriptive choices but that provided a way in which the critique of the existing could persist. At the root of all of this was a desire to keep faith with the basic principles of the left and breathe cultural force into political opposition, ensuring that it made a contribution to the shaping of modernity in Italy.

The protagonists of *Tango* and *Cuore* viewed Occhetto with some ambivalence. On the one hand, he was one of them, a member in political terms of the younger generation. On at least two occasions he visited the *Tango* festivals at Montecchio and submitted himself to the gentle lampoons of his hosts. He was also strongly backed in the attempts he made between 1988 and 1989 to revamp the PCI, to renew it by replacing a strong but decaying ideology with purposeful reformism. But there was a fear of integration and a mistrust of Occhetto's predilection for the media and the sensational. There was an awareness that he was no Berlinguer and that in the end he would be bound to disappoint. In the Bobo strip, he appeared as a love-hate figure. However, although Serra and company were sectarian and Manichaean in many respects and were strongly bound to the basic principles inspiring the PCI, they were not blind to the crisis. Although it was widely expected that they would sternly oppose Occhetto's attempt to cut off all links with the Communist movement, in fact Serra provided him with a pained but firm endorsement. This was valuable backing that assisted Occhetto in winning a majority for his plan in difficult circumstances.

The Drama of 1989–91

Within days of the fall of the Berlin Wall, Occhetto appeared one Sunday morning at a gathering of former partisans in the Bolognina quarter of Bologna, long the PCI's greatest stronghold. To this audience, and without previously consulting other senior officials, he announced his intention to seek the dissolution of the PCI and the creation of a new, broadly based force that would be reformist in inspiration. This desperate move was dictated largely by the failure of the "new course" to improve significantly the fortunes of the PCI. The party leader assumed that he would be able to carry party officials and rank-and-file officers in their thirties and forties with him and hoped he could count on the vast numbers of older members who usually went along with the leadership out of loyalty and tradition. Some opposition from the hard-liner Cossutta must have been allowed for, but otherwise he appears to have been convinced that the main body of the party would accept as desirable the prospect he offered of a new alignment to bring about alternation in government.

This calculation proved to be wildly wrong. Although the secretary sought to highlight the positive aspects of his plan, many members and supporters viewed it as a shocking and inexplicable attempt to liquidate the PCI. Even many of those who accepted the reasoning of the party leader were moved by the probable disappearance from the political scene of a party that had been an important focus of their lives. Rank-and-file Communists filled up sections and jammed the switchboards of federation offices with calls. For several weeks the party was plunged into a phase of collective self-examination that was amply covered in the press and formed the subject of a remarkable documentary film by Nanni Moretti, *La Cosa* (The thing). Tens, if not hundreds, of letters were published in *L'Unità*.

Occhetto knew that the Communist base continued to share a strong sense of identification with the party and its institutions. The party's symbolic system and rituals constituted a source of social and politcal identity uniting what the press referred to as *il popolo comunista*. In the "red" central areas of the country, family and community traditions continued to act as a bulwark against any process of disintegration. On a political level party members were not on the whole very receptive to novelty. New ideas, whether they were liberal or ecological, were reluctantly accepted as a necessity if the PCI was to overcome its impasse and attract support once more from young people. They were seen, though, as grafts or additions, not as replacements for more conventional ideological positions. However, the rank and file did not view kindly any attempt to modify established symbols or traditions. Both ideology and community were symbolized by the red flag, the hammer and sickle, and the association with the Soviet Union.

Although both supporters and opponents of the proposed change in the PCI accepted that the party had been in decline, that its old structures and political methods had in part ceased to function, and that a real breakdown of communication with young people had occurred, the situation was not grave enough to convince all that a new type of party was

The Last Tango

necessary. One reason for the trauma was that Occhetto simply failed to address the main concerns of the rank and file. At no point did he indicate whether the subculture and community bonds of the PCI would survive in the new political formation or what would happen to the party's rich symbolic system. On this crucial plane, David Kertzer has argued, Occhetto's plans and strategy were woefully inadequate.[17]

This terrain required special attention and extremely sensitive handling regardless of whether the intention was to perpetuate the subculture and some of the symbols or allow them to wither. However, Kertzer's suggestion that Occhetto should have pursued a "ritual strategy" is inappropriate, for, by the 1980s, the PCI was a much secularized organization, and, in any case, one of the leader's central purposes was to break with the liturgy of the party and embrace a more pragmatic politics. But it is worth considering why, after the symbolic choice of a gathering of former partisans as a setting for the announcement of the *svolta,* so little was said on these crucial issues. It may be suggested that Occhetto, like every PCI leader before him, held an ambivalent view of the left's subculture and folklore. He saw them not only as a source of strength but also as a limiting factor, an impediment to the full realization of the party's potential appeal to lay and centrist voters. Although other party officials, such as Pietro Secchia and Giancarlo Pajetta in the past, had tended the faithful, Togliatti, Berlinguer, and Occhetto addressed themselves to a broader audience and sought to resolve national questions. It was thus to the power of rational argument rather than symbols that, for better or worse, Occhetto made recourse. He hoped that the practical arguments he deployed would be persuasive, that it would be widely accepted that the old party model had been losing validity for some time and that the disintegration of Communism left the PCI with no choice but to transform itself thoroughly.

The party's left-wing was not opposed on the whole to renewal, but it rejected the equation of the PCI with the East and the focus on the party's name. It was fearful that a transformation along the lines outlined by Occhetto would not "unblock" the political system but rather lead to a diminished link to the working class and the emergence of a party that would be no more than a satellite of the PSI. On many matters Occhetto compromised to preserve internal unity. The period between the PCI's nineteenth congress in March 1990 and its twentieth and final congress in late January and early February 1991 therefore was marked more by conflict and uncertainty than by the purposeful definition of the characteristics of the new formation. Between November 1989 and October 1990, the unnamed new force was known simply but brutally as *La Cosa*.

Nevertheless, a critical review was undertaken of the PCI's past relations with Soviet Communism, and men who in past decades had been expelled or punished for criticizing Stalinism were honored in the party press and at conferences. Because of his association with Stalinism, Togliatti was consigned rather unceremoniously to the history books, but all sections of the party were keen to retain Gramsci as a symbol. As the PCI's "man for all seasons," the symbol of its peculiar and original history, Gramsci had been presented in a variety of guises since his tragic death. Always he was depicted as a great Italian, but politically he had been linked first to Stalinism in the late 1930s and late 1940s and then to Leninism from the late 1950s. In the 1970s Communist ideologists rediscovered him as a post-Leninist. With no less manipulation, he was described in January 1991 as the first post-Communist on the basis of his sharp dissent from the policies of the Communist International from 1926. If in the past Gramsci's isolation from the PCI and the mainstream Communist movement during his years in prison had been a source of embarrassment and had been wholly obscured in party mythologies and iconography, now it became a rich source of legitimation for the new party that was to be created.[18]

The launch of the Democratic Party of the Left (PDS) in February 1991 was not a triumphant moment. Rather, it was the end point of a protracted and highly divisive debate. Moreover, the delays and retreats, although they compromised the new, were insufficient to prevent a damaging schism. In autumn 1990 Cossutta and the trade unionist Sergio Garavini announced their intention to ensure the continued existence of an "autonomous Communist force" if the PCI's transformation was to be completed. They fulfilled their promise by walking out of the Rimini congress with their followers and setting in motion the process that would lead in May 1991 to the establishment of Rifondazione Comunista (Communist refoundation). The split was not a minor one. Leaders of the PDS tried to depict Rifondazione as a tiny band of diehard Stalinists. Yet within weeks of the Rimini congress it claimed over 100,000 adherents, and by the end of the year this figure was said to have risen to 150,000. Most of these came from areas like Tuscany, where motions opposing the change had done well.[19] An acrimonious struggle ensued during which former comrades disputed the rights to the property, funds, and the legacy of the PCI.

At the base of both the PDS and Rifondazione there was much yearning for a simple continuity with the PCI. There was a desire to perpetuate the communitarian model, its rituals and bonds of fraternity, and at least some of the symbolic system that for fifty years had been such a source of strength. This had all provided a common texture of meaning, despite political and ideological differences, and a source of identity. Those who attached more importance to the name and to the hammer and sickle joined Rifondazione, those who trusted the leadership to navigate the community through the storm joined the PDS. But it may be argued that during the crisis of 1989–91 a series of devastating blows were struck at the symbols, rituals, organizational norms, solidarities, and values that had made the PCI what it was. The result was the final disintegration of the left-wing subculture.

It has been argued in previous chapters and earlier sections of the present chapter that economic, social, cultural, and political changes all undermined the identity and community bonds the PCI had constructed. By the 1980s the interests that had bound people to the party were more diversified, the structures of the subculture were more fragile, and the tradition was less forceful. The defeats of 1985–87 threw these developments into sharp relief. Further secular decline would undoubtedly have ensued, but the crisis of 1989–91 rapidly accelerated the process. The *svolta* itself entailed three factors that specifically contributed to this. First, the doctrine of unity was broken. Second, the symbolic system and the tradition were dramatically undermined. Third, the PCI ceased to exist. The principal object of loyalty that for nearly half a century had been a central pillar of civil society and a part of private as well as public life was removed from the scene, leaving much bitterness in its wake.

The final devastating blow to the left-wing subculture was the collapse of the USSR and the dissolution of the CPSU following the failed Moscow coup of August 1991. For the PDS majority, the short-lived coup by Gorbachev's enemies in the Soviet old guard provided the occasion for a full and final condemnation of the historical experience of Communism. However, at the base of both the PDS and Rifondazione there was bewilderment and disbelief. For over seventy years the existence of the USSR had been a symbol, a source of strength and purpose. It offered proof that it was possible to construct a wholly new society and therefore that it was worthwhile investing one's life in the political struggle against capitalism. Whether it was criticized or admired without reservation, it constituted a fixed point in the global outlook of every Communist. Positive representations of the Soviet model were deeply entrenched within Communist culture and continued to constitute a part of the world-view of a large proportion of the rank and file.[20] No matter how reluctant anyone had previously been to alter the convictions of a lifetime, the liquidation of Communism in the land of the October Revolution forced a reassessment of everything that had been thought certain. It was the final straw, the final blow to a subculture whose old roots had already been eroded by socioeconomic and cultural change and whose structures had become fragile.

The electoral result of the PDS in the 1992 election was a source of great disappointment. Although Rifondazione gained an impressive 5.6 percent, Occhetto's party managed a mere 16.1 percent. Inevitably, questions were raised about whether the transformation of the PCI had been worthwhile. In fact, the historic links with Soviet Communism, on the one hand, and the repeated efforts of the PCI since the mid-1970s to develop more of a Western European profile, on the other, meant that change was unavoidable. In response to a clearly negative organizational and electoral trend, it had been recognized that the mass cadre party, with its basically authoritarian structures, was no longer an appropriate political vehicle, that Marxist-Leninism was at best a blunt instrument for analyzing reality, and that fundamental change was required to avoid irreversible historic decline. Already in 1989 Occhetto had taken renewal within Communism to its outer limit.

Given these factors, the *svolta* was a logical development if not the only possible one. It would undoubtedly have been better if it had occurred earlier. This could have saved the party from appearing to be forced by external pressures to repudiate part of its heritage. But the resistance that there was even as historical Communism entered a final crisis shows that it simply could not have been achieved before. And at least the transformation of the PCI meant that it survived the collapse of Communism in better condition than any other Communist party. Like the PCI before it, the PDS was unable to present itself alone as a credible force of government. But, unlike the former, the PDS could form alliances with Catholics and with the secular center. It was thus well positioned to emerge in the medium term as a key player in a political system that, following mounting protest, the devastating corruption inquiries of 1992–93, the demise of the established parties of government, and the replacement of proportional representation with a mainly majoritarian electoral system, was evolving in new and unforeseen directions. The PDS could not aspire to be a cultural force or to transform the whole of society, but it could more realistically aim at achieving political power.

Conclusion

Throughout the twentieth century, the left acted as a catalyst of change. By constantly challenging capitalism, exposing its inadequacies and injustices, Socialists and Communists forced it to adapt and alter. Over a long period of time, extending even into the 1970s in Mediterranean Europe, they were at the forefront of the battle to assert and guarantee the full political and social citizenship of excluded groups. Whether in government or outside it, left-wing parties and movements brought pressure to bear that resulted in the achievement of material gains as well as benefits in terms of welfare, education, and social policy for the lower classes. For this reason it would not be correct to describe the post-1945 years as a period of defeat for the left. Inscribed within the bedrock of values and norms accepted with greater or lesser conviction by all major parties and social forces are notions and ideas that form part of the legacy of socialism.

Parts of the left-wing credo, however, became less relevant over time or were bypassed by events. For all its commitment to innovation and change, the left remained to some degree suspicious of, or hostile toward, phenomena that became central to the organization of contemporary societies. To the ethical individualism of capitalism, it counterposed an emphasis on community that, quite apart from the theoretical and practical objections this mode of perceiving the social order may give rise to, contradicted the fundamental trend of the postwar years toward privatization and the demobilization of collective identities. Over a long period, moreover, socialist parties and intellectuals sought to resist consumerism and commercial entertainment. Consequently, the left often found itself at a loss to understand new sensibilities and values or know how to respond to the patterns of behavior that sprang from them. The result, as became clear in the 1980s, was a serious erosion of socialists' ability to present a coherent, appealing, and practical vision of the goals of socialist politics.[1]

The causes of the left's inability to grasp contemporary economic, social, and cultural change are largely rooted in the way socialism developed as an idea and as a historical practice. Some blame must be attributed the the theoretical heritage of Marxism, for the simplified, vulgar version that gained currency in the Second and Third Internationals provided socialists with keys for interpreting reality that were reductive or defective or both. Economics was perhaps given disproportionate weight (although the teleological element predominated over analysis), and the importance of other spheres was not grasped. Marxism also provided an important justification for the belief that Socialists and Communists themselves, as the political representatives of the industrial working class, stood at the forefront of historical development. Consequently, within the practical universe of socialism a dominant and possibly excessive emphasis is placed on the political as the determinant sphere of society. The party or parties of the left are viewed as the main agents of social cohesion, the forces whose task it is to embrace as much of society as possible and promote and provide channels for participation. The inevitability of socialism's triumph produced a dismissive attitude toward temporary obstacles and a lack of attention toward changes in the surrounding society.[2]

Labor and in particular productive manual labor constituted the center of social identity for most left-wing movements. The worker was, of course, a key reference point here, but so too was the conception of socialism above all as a system in which the forces of production would finally be able to develop to their full capacity. In consequence, the interests of nonproductive strata and their cultures were not taken fully into account. In addition, relations of consumption were often ignored or deemed to be of little significance. But there are other factors. In Leonardo Paggi's words, it was the "mythical projection of the producer, as the expression of a higher form of economic rationality," that inevitably led men of the left "to ignore the irreversible reality of an economic development in which private consumption had definitively established itself as the regulator of investment."[3] It might also be added that, for many socialists, even long after it became widespread, consuming was simply not an important activity. It was trivial, confined to the private sphere, and possibly corrupt.

From the beginning, socialism was identified with a collective, communitarian vision of human activity. In socialist thinking, the community is the site not only of the realization of individual potentials but a good in itself whose furtherance and preservation is deemed more important and worthy than the transitory claims and desires of individuals. This is a theoretical standpoint, one with noble antecedents, but it is also a belief derived from the experience of solidarity among the oppressed and the excluded. Moreover, because of the way socialism developed as a historical movement, certain values and norms of behavior became associated with it that provided rigid and in some respects inappropriate standards by which to judge evolving patterns of collective and individual behavior. In particular, the emphasis on decorum and self-sacrifice identified with the early working-class movement lost force as more individualistic and "permissive" norms became widespread. This emphasis was connected to a certain historically and socially grounded psychological outlook. Socialists of almost all types have conventionally favored rational, logical argument over appeals to the emotions or to hidden areas of the psyche. This preference for the cerebral influenced the taste for words over images and for realism over abstract expression in art and propaganda (where the two were actually separate). This contrasted with the experience of ordinary people living in urban environments shaped by speed, rapid communication, fantasy, and emotion.

In addition to these subjective factors, socialism's capacity to offer an appealing alternative to capitalism was profoundly affected by the objective successes of capitalism in creating a universe in which the material and even cultural needs of a majority of populations of the advanced industrial world could to a considerable degree be met. In Western Europe this occurred after 1945, as indigenous patterns of modernization underwent mutation under pressure from America's phenomenal productive power and expanded political and material presence abroad. Following the American example of the 1920s, consumption became central to the productive system and to social organization. Patriarchal relations were undermined as a result, and contractual negotiation between interest groups replaced the all-out conflict of the prewar years. Social democratic parties actually derived prestige and legitimacy, often for the first time, as forces of government, as a consequence of these changes and the raised expectations to which they gave rise. But as a result they gradually lost their class-centered, mass-based characteristics. As Michael Mann has written, "by the mid '50s the battle was over: a cross between Marshallian citizenship and American liberalism dominated the West, less through its internal evolution than through the fortunes of war."[4]

Had Americanism been proposed only at government level, socialist goals might have been reached more easily, but enterprises, trade unions, and opinion leaders were also involved. Moreover, the American idea of prosperity was conveyed directly to the people through propaganda, entertainments, and consumer goods.[5] It transcended economic policy to invest social models, patterns of behavior, and ideologies. Even where governments controlled advertising, regulated film imports, and blocked commercial television, glossy magazines and Hollywood films conveyed images of wealth and social mobility that were extremely attractive, especially after the privations of the war. Long before the full implications of the American recipe for stability and growth were grasped by societal and political elites, the notion of individual consumption as a force for economic development and progress had become rooted in popular common sense.

The expectation that the processes of development could be directed through planning and made to favor collectivist goals was undermined in the 1950s and 1960s, as the new order founded on consumption was consolidated and social values began to change. As the social democrats who sought to implement a version of the planned economy in the Western sphere of influence after the Second World War discovered, neither the ethic nor the practice of collective solidarity could be combined in the long term with mass consumerism. The consequences were significant for the parties of the left, since the separateness and identity of the working class, which since before the turn of the century had been expressed in distinctive rituals and values, began to crumble.

Did this mean that America won out, as both Paggi and Mann have suggested? In fact, things were not so straightforward. Although the United States embraced decolonization as a key plank of its bid for a new world order, communism advanced in the third world in the 1960s and 1970s, and, even in certain areas of the advanced capitalist world, parties of the Marxist left continued to enjoy mass support. This occurred where dominant groups failed to co-opt the lower classes or carry through the promise of widespread prosperity. In these contexts it is quite conceivable that Americanism actually aided the radical left, since the possibility of improvements was raised without expectations being fulfilled.

In addition, the explosion of protest in 1968 indicated that consumerism alone could not guarantee long-term stability. On the contrary, it produced values and expectations and generated models of behavior that conflicted with societal and institutional norms, leading to political unrest. Once their primary material needs had been satisfied, men and women demanded more space for participation, self-fulfillment, cultural diversity, and individual expression — objectives for which material solutions could be found only to a limited degree and which, for several years at least, were often cast in an explicit anticapitalist mold.[6] The decline of neocapitalism and American hegemony appeared to be confirmed by the events of 1968–75, which saw the breakup of the Bretton Woods international monetary system, American defeat in Vietnam, and the oil crisis.

Despite these observations, the United States clearly remained a reference point for the industrial world. The oppositional cultures of the 1960s and 1970s drew much of their inspiration from the countercultural movements of the United States, and, although the left in Europe was temporarily buoyed by the influx of new blood, new demands were posed and issues raised that for historical, cultural, and organizational reasons it was poorly equipped to deal with. As the United States once again led the way in restructuring relationships within the world economy in the 1980s, the left was finally compelled to come to terms with the erosion of many of its most cherished values and beliefs.

The crisis was not purely that of the Communist left, although Communists faced specific problems, but rather of the class-based left as a whole. The collapse of the Soviet system first in Eastern Europe and then in the USSR itself came well after the identity crisis of the European left had begun and underlined its dramatic, historic character. It highlighted the failure of a type of socialism in which the state was seen as the primary instrument of a total revolution in social and economic relations within the confines of a single country. So spectacular were the events of 1989–91 that there were genuine fears that the whole historical experience of the left would be dragged down and discredited. These were confirmed by the gleeful reactions of conservatives, the conversion of some leftists, especially in Eastern Europe but also Italy and France, to right-wing ideologies, and the frontal attack that throughout the West was launched on the traditions of the left.

In fact, the left did not disappear. But the left parties that emerged as strong contenders in the 1990s were those that either had never been subcultural parties, like the British Labour Party and the French Socialists, or had undergone the most thorough review of old traditions and procedures, or both.

It is incumbent to ask, in conclusion, if in the reconstructed left there can be a place for a cultural policy. There is a tendency to associate the very idea of a cultural policy with the past, to assume that, following the demise of the cultural project to which the left gave rise in the 1880s and which the PCI championed from the 1940s to the 1970s, that no such thing could exist again. This is understandable because there are certainly aspects of left-wing cultural policy that are no longer applicable. The assumption, for example, that the working class would establish its cultural leadership through the party under socialism has been cast aside with the critique of class, party, and the idea of global change. Yet, although the idea of cultural direction is no longer regarded as acceptable, the need for cultural policies remains. Most successful left parties have learned to use and to manipulate the mass media, not their own but commercial and state ones. They do not seek to change the way people live or build hegemony but rather to interpret the wishes and desires of mass society. They seek not to advance their own idea of modernity but to govern a complex modernity that they have proved that they accept and that they are in tune with. To borrow Umberto Eco's terms, they are "integrated" and not "apocalyptical."

In this context new possibilities are opened up. No political party that seeks to win or maintain power today can ignore popular culture or mass communications. Furthermore, in a society in which more time is spent on leisure and in which that leisure is increasingly consumed rather than made, action is needed to ensure choice, diversity, and opportunity. In particular, in mass media–dominated societies there is a risk that the whole idea of active citizenship will be undermined and most especially in the field of leisure. Already the poor spend more time at home watching television than anyone else, and the risk of excluding the less educated, the less well-off, the old and the ill from forms of personal growth and enrichment as well as participation is present. In a number of local government experiences in Britain and Italy in the eighties, a concept of public policy was developed that accepted popular tastes and contemporary culture but that sought to widen the range of possibilities by creating spaces for voluntary and noncommercial forms of expression, facilitating access and offering opportunities for educational and cultural development where these were desired. Forgotten or overlooked by so much of the left, policies for leisure and culture constitute yet the area in which it can most add to the qualitative enhancement of advanced industrial societies.

Notes

Unless otherwise indicated, all translations of excerpts in other languages are my own.

Introduction

1 Perry Anderson, *Considerations on Western Marxism* (London: New Left Books, 1976); Martin Jay, *The Dialectical Imagination: A History of the Frankfurt School and the Institute of Social Research, 1923–50* (London: Heinemann, 1973).

2 Ernest Mandel, *Late Capitalism* (London: Verso, 1978), 393. Compare Alan Ware, *Citizens, Parties, and the State* (Cambridge: Polity Press, 1987), 161.

3 Richard Hoggart, *The Uses of Literacy* (Harmondsworth: Penguin, 1959), chap. 7.

4 Otto Kirchheimer, *Politics, Law, and Social Change* (New York: Columbia University Press, 1969). See "The Vanishing Opposition" (1966), 336.

5 Guenther Roth, *The Social Democrats in Imperial Germany* (Totowa, N.J.: Bedminster Press, 1963); Roberta Ascarelli, "Comunicazione di massa e movimento operaio: le origini," *Critica marxista* 19.1 (1981): 69–99; Ascarelli, "Gli spettacoli di potere: ragioni teatrali ed emozioni cinematografiche nella socialdemocrazia tedesca," *Movimento operaio e socialista* 11.3 (1988): 443–52; Kurt Shell, *The Transformation of Austrian Socialism* (Binghamton: State University of New York Press, 1962); Helmut Gruber, *Red Vienna: Experiment in Working-Class Culture, 1919–1934* (New York: Oxford University Press, 1991).

6 It is regrettable that Donald Sassoon, in his otherwise masterly *One Hundred Years of Socialism: The West European Left in the Twentieth Century* (London: I. B. Tauris, 1996), gives no consideration to culture or cultural policy.

7 On Italy since the war see Paul Ginsborg, *A History of Contemporary Italy: Society and Politics, 1943–1988* (Harmondsworth: Penguin, 1990). On the politics and organization of the PCI see Donald Sassoon, *The*

Strategy of the Italian Communist Party (London: Pinter, 1981); Joan Barth Urban, *Moscow and the Italian Communist Party* (London: I. B. Tauris, 1986); and Stephen Hellman, *Italian Communism in Transition: The Rise and Fall of the Historic Compromise in Turin, 1975–1980* (New York: Oxford University Press, 1988). See Robert Lumley, *States of Emergency: Cultures of Revolt in Italy from 1968 to 1978* (London: Verso, 1990) for the best treatment of the protest movements of the 1960s and 1970s; see Patrick McCarthy, *The Crisis of the Italian State: From the Origins of the Cold War to the Fall of Berlusconi* (New York: St. Martin's Press, 1995) for an analysis of political developments in light of the crisis of the political system in the early 1990s.

1. The Pen and the Sword: Politics, Culture, and Society after the Fall of Fascism

1 The two principal studies of the PCI's policies toward the intellectuals are Nello Ajello, *Intellettuali e PCI, 1944–1958* (Bari: Laterza, 1979); and Albertina Vittoria, *Togliatti e gli intellettuali: storia dell'Istituto Gramsci negli anni cinquanta e sessanta* (Rome: Editori Riuniti, 1992).

2 On the cultural implications of Thorez's overtures to the intellectuals see Evelyne Ritaine, *Les stratèges de la culture* (Paris: Presses de la Fondation Nationale des Sciences Politiques, 1983), 46–48.

3 Palmiro Togliatti, "Gli intellettuali e il Fronte nazionale" (5 July 1943), in *Da Radio Milano Libertà* (Rome: Editori Riuniti–Rinascita, 1974).

4 Palmiro Togliatti, "Discorso su Gramsci nei giorni della Liberazione" (1945), in *Gramsci,* by Palmiro Togliatti, ed. Ernesto Ragionieri (Rome: Editori Riuniti, 1972), 45.

5 The importance of the alliance policy of the seventh Comintern congress to Togliatti's postwar thinking is particularly stressed in Donald Sassoon, *The Strategy of the Italian Communist Party* (London: Pinter, 1981), chap. 1.

6 As Maria Antonietta Macciocchi put it, "in the Resistance his name was almost unknown to us youngsters" (*Per Gramsci* [Bologna: Il Mulino, 1974], 36). Pietro Ingrao makes the same point in *Le cose impossibili: un'autobiografia raccontata e discussa con Nicola Tranfaglia* (Rome: Editori Riuniti, 1990), 22. More generally, see Paolo Spriano, *Storia del partito comunista italiano,* vol. 5, *La Resistenza, Togliatti e il partito nuovo* (Turin: Einaudi, 1975), 406–9; and Luigi Cortesi, "Palmiro Togliatti, la 'svolta di Salerno' e l'eredità gramsciana," *Belfagor* 30.1 (1975): 1–44.

7 Joan Barth Urban, *Moscow and the Italian Communist Party* (London: I. B. Tauris, 1986), 55–56; Umberto Terracini, *Intervista sul comunismo difficile,* ed. Arturo Gismondi (Bari: Laterza, 1978), 141–47. The differences between the PCI and PCF are explored in detail in Marc Lazar,

Maisons rouges: Les Partis communistes français et italien de la Libera-tion à nos jours (Paris: Aubier, 1992).

8   Togliatti's major speeches and political writings of this period are con-tained in the volume *La politica di Salerno: aprile–dicembre 1944* (Rome: Editori Riuniti, 1969).

9   Sergio Bertelli, *Il gruppo: la formazione del gruppo dirigente del PCI, 1936–1948* (Milan: Rizzoli, 1980), 216.

10 Ibid., 232–33.

11 His only rival in this field was the historian Emilio Sereni, who from 1945 played an important role in forging links with the intellectuals.

12 Palmiro Togliatti, "La politica di unità nazionale dei comunisti," in *La politica di Salerno,* 7.

13 Togliatti, "Discorso su Gramsci nei giorni della Liberazione," 38.

14 Ibid.

15 "He appeared to be — and perhaps really was — detached from everything. We have no evidence of any attempt to re-establish contact with Togliatti, or other leaders or Party functionaries. At the Quisisana he was left rela-tively free, although an external watch was kept on the building. Had he wished, he could certainly have contacted the Party through the friends and relations who visited him, if only with a note, a few lines of greeting to be handed on. But there is no trace of any such step" (Giuseppe Fiori, *Antonio Gramsci: Life of a Revolutionary* [New York: Schocken Books, 1970], 289).

16 A stern recourse to democratic centralism was required to halt discussion of the *svolta* in Rome after the decision of the national council to back Togliatti. See Giorgio Amendola, *Lettere a Milano: ricordi e documenti, 1939–1945* (Rome: Editori Riuniti, 1973). Giacomo Calandrone reveals that there was also considerable unease in Sicily, where it was thought the republic was being abandoned (*Un comunista in Sicilia, 1946–1951* [Rome: Editori Riuniti, 1972], 41).

17 In *Gramsci, Togliatti, Stalin* (Bari: Laterza, 1991) Giuseppe Fiori exam-ines in detail the relationship between the two Italians in light of new research and on the basis of documents not available in 1966. He con-cludes that, whereas Gramsci broke with Togliatti even before the former's arrest, the latter struggled via intermediaries to maintain a link with his former comrade. Although Togliatti created a false image of Gramsci as a loyal Stalinist in the 1930s, he did so mainly in order to thwart pressures inside and outside the party to repudiate him.

18 See, for example, Eugenio Curiel, "Due tappe nella storia del proletari-ato," in *Scritti, 1935–1945,* ed. Filippo Frassati (Rome: Editori Riuniti, 1973), 2:74.

19 Palmiro Togliatti, "Programma" (1944), in *La politica culturale,* by Pal-miro Togliatti, ed. Luciano Gruppi (Rome: Editori Riuniti, 1974), 64.

20 Ibid.

21 Palmiro Togliatti, "Croce e il comunismo," in *I corsivi di Roderigo: interventi politico-culturali dal 1944 al 1964,* ed. Ottavio Cecchi, Giovanni Leone, and Giuseppe Vacca (Bari: De Donato, 1976).

22 See Alberto Asor Rosa, "Lo Stato democratico e i partiti politici," in *Letteratura italiana,* vol. 1, *Il Letterato e le istituzioni,* ed. Alberto Asor Rosa (Turin: Einaudi, 1982), 563–65. Particularly useful on the background to the passage of a group of young intellectuals in Rome to the PCI is Albertina Vittoria, *Intellettuali e politica alla fine degli anni trenta: Antonio Amendola e la formazione del gruppo comunista romano* (Milan: Franco Angeli, 1985).

23 See Vittorio Gorresio, *I carissimi nemici* (1949; rpt., Milan: Bompiani, 1977), esp. chap. 2.

24 Antonio Gramsci, *Quaderni del carcere,* ed. Valentino Gerratana (Turin: Einaudi, 1975), 3:1591.

25 In *Due inverni, un'estate e la rossa primavera: le brigate Garibaldi a Milano e Provincia* (Milan: Franco Angeli, 1985) Luigi Borgomaneri writes of 25 April in Milan: "No tremendous conflicts, no furious battles, no assaults among the smoke of the grenades and the sparks of machine-guns. These images will be born later, with the entirely hagiographic need to build up an epic image of partisan courage" (253).

26 Celso Ghini, "Gli iscritti al partito e alla FGCI, 1943–1979," in *Il Partito comunista italiano: struttura e storia dell'organizzazione 1921–1979,* ed. Massimo Ilardi and Aris Accornero (Milan: Feltrinelli, 1982), 246.

27 Ibid., 279–86.

28 D. J. Travis, "Communism in Modena: The Provincial Origins of the Partito Comunista Italiano (1943–1945)," *Historical Journal* 29.4 (1986): 889–91.

29 Elio Vittorini, "Politica e cultura: Lettera a Togliatti," *Il Politecnico* 3.25 (1947): 2–5, 105–6, 4.

30 Gabriele De Rosa, "Verso la creazione di una 'Unione degli intellettuali,' " *Voce Operaia,* 3 December 1945; cited in Bertelli, *Il gruppo,* 299.

31 Rossana Rossanda, "Unità politica e scelte culturali," *Rinascita* 34 (28 August 1965): 19–23.

32 Togliatti, "Discorso su Gramsci nei giorni della Liberazione," 40.

33 The most celebrated attack on the left-wing populism of the postwar years is Alberto Asor Rosa, *Scrittori e popolo* (Rome: Samonà and Savelli, 1972). Also relevant is Romano Luperini, *Gli intellettuali di sinistra e l'ideologia della ricostruzione nel dopoguerra* (Rome: Edizioni di "Ideologie," 1971); and Luperini, *Il neorealismo cinematografico italiano,* ed. Lino Miccichè (Venice: Marsilio, 1975). Of particular interest in this volume is the essay by Alberto Abruzzese, "Per una nuova definizione del rapporto politica-cultura."

34 See "L'associazione culturale cinematografica italiana" (1944) and "Il

cinema e l'uomo moderno" (1949), in *Neorealismo ecc.,* by Cesare Zavattini, ed. Mino Argentieri (Milan: Bompiani, 1979).

35 Interview with Togliatti, *L'Unità,* 11 December 1945, 1.

36 Mario Alicata, "La corrente 'Politecnico,' " *Rinascita* 3.5–6 (1946): 116. Brief accounts of the pressure that was put on Vittorini in formal party meetings in Milan are contained in Fidia Gambetti, *La grande illusione, 1945–1953* (Milan: Mursia, 1976); and Davide Lajolo, *Ventiquattro anni* (Milan: Rizzoli, 1981), 74–76. In 1976 Giorgio Amendola revealed that he and Alicata had "a relationship based on a moral break with Vittorini" because the latter had "stayed in hiding during the partisan war" and then "dared to present a novel . . . *Uomini e no,* that provided a false and rhetorical picture of the Urban Resistance (GAP)" ("Mario Alicata, partito nuovo e Mezzogiorno," in *Mario Alicata intellettuale e dirigente politico,* by C. Salinari et al. [Rome: Editori Riuniti, 1976], 103–4).

37 Palmiro Togliatti, "Politica e cultura: una lettera di Palmiro Togliatti," *Il Politecnico* 2.33–34 (1946): 3–4.

38 Vittorini, "Lettera a Togliatti," 3.

39 Felice Platone, "La politica comunista e i problemi della cultura," *Rinascita* 4.7 (1947): 188.

40 Vittorini, "Lettera a Togliatti," 105.

41 See Cesare Pavese, *La letteratura americana e altri saggi* (Turin: Einaudi, 1962). Essays written in the immediate postwar period are collected in part 2.

42 This problem is discussed in Stephen Gundle, "The Communist Party and the Politics of Cultural Change in Postwar Italy," in *The Culture of Reconstruction: European Literature, Thought, and Film, 1945–50,* ed. Nicholas Hewitt (London: Macmillan, 1989).

43 Togliatti's ill-tempered article marking this event, "Vittorini se n'è ghiuto, e soli ci ha lasciato," is contained in *I corsivi di Roderigo.*

44 See, for example, Luigi Arbizzani, Saveria Bologna, Lidia Testoni, eds., *Storie di Case del Popolo: saggi, documenti e immagini d'Emilia Romagna* (Bologna: Grafis, 1982). One specific example is offered in Orlando Pezzoli, *È storia: Casa del popolo Nerio Nannetti–Santa Viola, Bologna* (Bologna: PCI zona Santa Viola, 1981).

45 Palmiro Togliatti, "I compiti del partito nella situazione attuale," in *La politica di Salerno,* 35. The minutes of the meetings of the directorate contained in the Archive of the Partito comunista italiano, Istituto Gramsci, Rome (hereafter cited as PCI Archive) and now deposited in the Fondazione Istituto Gramsci reveal that this lesson was taken seriously. At the meeting of 2 September 1944 Scoccimarro revealed that theatrical and sporting activities had already been organized in Rome. However, some hard-liners found such things distasteful. On 19 June 1945, at another meeting of the directorate, Sereni complained that the Youth Front seemed

to concentrate all its energies on dances and concerts. This was a dangerous state of affairs, he said; instead, "it should also concern itself with the problems of young workers."

46 During the war dancing had been officially banned by government order.

47 Cited in Eugenio Scalfari, *L'Autunno della Repubblica* (Milan: Etas Kompass, 1969), 13.

48 Pietro Cavallo, "America sognata, America desiderata: mito e immagini Usa in Italia dallo sbarco alla fine della guerra," *Storia contemporanea* 4 (1985): 756–58.

49 Gian Piero Brunetta, "Il giardino delle delizie e il deserto: trasformazioni della visione e dei modelli narrativi nel cinema italiano del dopoguerra," in *Schermi e ombre: gli italiani e il cinema nel dopoguerra,* ed. Marino Livolsi (Florence: La Nuova Italia, 1988), 44–56.

50 Lorenzo Quaglietti, *Storia economico-politica del cinema italiano, 1945–1980* (Rome: Editori Riuniti, 1980), 252.

51 UNESCO, *The Film Industry in Six European Countries* (Paris: UNESCO, 1950), 111.

52 The future film director Luigi Comencini, who spent time in Switzerland during this period and therefore could make the comparison, noted that the American films that arrived in Italy seemed to have been selected to stress optimism and democratic sentiments ("Politica sbagliata," *Tempo,* 24 January 1946, 12).

53 Angelo Ventrone, "Tra propaganda e passione: *Grand Hôtel* e l'Italia degli anni Cinquanta," *Rivista di storia contemporanea* 17.4 (1988): 604, 608–9.

54 The history of these publications is sketched in Maria Teresa Anelli et al., *Fotoromanzo: fascino e pregiudizio — storia, documenti e immagini di un grande fenomeno popolare (1946–1978)* (Rome: Savelli, 1979).

55 Leonardo Becciù, *Il fumetto in Italia* (Florence: Sansoni, 1971), 138.

56 Franco Minganti, "Quale Hollywood per il fumetto?" in *Hollywood in Europa, 1945–1960,* ed. D. W. Ellwood and Gian Piero Brunetta (Florence: Ponte alle Grazie, 1991), 160.

57 On the rituals surrounding the Resistance see Stephen Gundle, "La 'religione civile' della resistenza: cultura di massa e identità politica nell'Italia del dopoguerra," in *L'immagine della resistenza in Europa, 1945–60,* ed. Luisa Cigognetti, Lorenza Servetti, and Pierre Sorlin (Bologna: Il Nove, 1996).

58 Vittorini, "Lettera a Togliatti," 2.

59 *Il Politecnico* 1.4 (1945): 1.

60 "Rispondiamo ai lettori," *Il Politecnico* 1.8 (1945): 1.

61 See the testimony to this effect of the painter Pino Guarino in *Storie comuniste: passato e presente di una sezione del PCI a Milano,* ed. Giorgio Colorni (Milan: Feltrinelli, 1979), 143–44.

62 *Il Politecnico* 2.28 (1946): 1.

63 Giulio Trevisani, "La cultura popolare," *Rinascita,* 9.12 (1952): 684–87.

64 Lucio Lombardo Radice, "Cosa leggono i lavoratori," *Vie Nuove,* 17 November 1946, 8. See also Radice, "Perchè si legge all'americana," *Vie Nuove,* 6 October 1946, 8.

65 Radice, "Cosa leggono i lavoratori."

66 Ibid.

67 Giulio Preti, "Cultura popolare in che senso," *Il Politecnico* 3.37 (1947): 6.

68 Leon Trotskij, "Il giornale e i suoi lettori" (1923), in *Rivoluzione e vita quotidiana* (Rome: Savelli, 1976), 47.

69 Directorate meeting, 7 January 1945, PCI Archive; Eugenio Reale complained that 50 percent of *Noi Donne*'s print run was going unsold. The magazine needed to be transformed and relaunched, "as a type to lean toward, think of the magazine *Mary Claire* [sic]," he said, referring to a commercial product published in France. At the meeting of the northern directorate in Milan on 18 September 1945, Giancarlo Pajetta urged the party to establish a sports paper; his brother Giuliano talked of a sports and humor magazine. This idea fizzled out after it was pointed out that it might stoke regional rivalries.

70 Luciano Gruppi, "Note sulla politica culturale del partito nel dopoguerra," *Critica marxista,* no. 5 (1972): 131.

71 Lucio Lombardo Radice, "Invito al 'mea culpa,' " *Vie Nuove,* 1 December 1946, 8; emphasis in the original text.

2. Bread, Love, and Political Strife:
Cold War Communism and the Development of Cultural Policy

1 In the following two works relatively positive judgments on the PCI's cultural policy in the 1950s can be found: Alberto Asor Rosa, "Lo Stato democratico e i partiti politici," in *Letteratura italiana,* vol. 1, *Il Letterato e le istituzioni,* ed. Alberto Asor Rosa (Turin: Einaudi, 1982), 598–615; and Giulio Bollati, *L'italiano: il carattere nazionale come storia e come invenzione* (Turin: Einaudi, 1983), 195–98. Similar views have been expressed by Edoardo Sanguineti in "Perchè quel modello si è esaurito," *Rinascita,* 20 June 1987, 16.

2 Asor Rosa, "Lo Stato democratico e i partiti politici," 607–11.

3 Lorenzo Quaglietti, *Storia economico-politica del cinema italiano, 1945–1980* (Rome: Editori Riuniti, 1980), tables A, B.

4 This point of view is stated, for example, in Mark Koenigil, *Movies in Society (Sex, Crime, and Censorship)* (New York: Speller, 1962), 139.

5 An overview of the political conflicts is provided in Stephen Gundle,

"From Neorealism to *Luci rosse*: Cinema, Politics, and Society, 1945–85," in *Culture and Conflict in Postwar Italy,* ed. Zygmunt Baranski and Robert Lumley (London: Macmillan, 1990).

6 Charles S. Aaronson, ed., *1953 Motion Picture and Television Almanac* (New York: Quigley, 1954), 788.

7 Enrico Giannelli, *Cinema Europeo* (Rome: Edizioni dell'Ateneo, 1953), 88 and table 2.

8 Quaglietti, *Storia economico-politica del cinema italiano,* 252.

9 Gian Piero Brunetta, *Storia del cinema italiano dal 1945 agli anni Ottanta* (Rome: Editori Riuniti, 1982), 54.

10 Compare Ernesto Galli della Loggia, "Ideologie, classi, costume," in *Italia contemporanea, 1945–75,* ed. Valerio Castronovo (Turin: Einaudi, 1976).

11 Lino Miccichè, "Per una verifica del neorealismo," in *Il Neorealismo cinematografico italiano,* ed. Lino Miccichè (Venice: Marsilio, 1975), 23.

12 Nello Ajello, *Lezioni di giornalismo: com'è cambiata in 30 anni la stampa italiana* (Milan: Garzanti, 1985), 89.

13 Simonetta Piccone Stella and Annabella Rossi, *La fatica di leggere* (Rome: Editori Riuniti, 1964), 11.

14 De Gasperi and Linda Christian appeared together on the cover of *Oggi,* 3 February 1949.

15 Luigi Longo, "Per il rafforzamento del partito," report to the central committee, 23–25 September 1948, PCI Archive.

16 Appropriately, it was Sereni who wrote Zhdanov's obituary in September 1948. See "Andrea Zhdanov: modello di combattente per il trionfo del comunismo," *Rinascita* 5.9–10 (1948): 333–34.

17 Pietro Secchia, "Il partito comunista e gli intellettuali," *L'Unità,* 5 February 1948, 3.

18 Emilio Sereni, "Per la cultura italiana" (1948), in *Scienza, marxismo, cultura* (Milan: Edizioni Sociali, 1949), 220.

19 These issues are discussed in Romano Luperini, *Il novecento: apparati ideologici, ceto intellettuale, sistemi formali nella letteratura italiana contemporanea* (Turin: Loescher, 1981), 395–96.

20 See the chapter titled "La battaglia delle idee: il fronte della sinistra," in Brunetta, *Storia del cinema italiano.*

21 For a selection of these writings see Palmiro Togliatti, *I corsivi di Roderigo: interventi politico-culturali dal 1944 al 1964,* ed. Ottavio Cecchi, Giovanni Leone, and Giuseppe Vacca (Bari: De Donato, 1976).

22 The volumes were published by Einaudi in the following order: *Lettere dal carcere* (1947), *Il materialismo storico e la filosofia di Benedetto Croce* (1948), *Gli intellettuali e l'organizzazione della cultura* (1949), *Il Risorgimento* (1949), *Note sul Macchiavelli, sulla politica e sullo Stato moderno* (1949), *Letteratura e vita nazionale* (1950), *Passato e presente* (1951).

23 Benedetto Croce, "Antonio Gramsci, Lettere dal carcere," *Quaderni della "Critica"* 8 (1947): 86–88.

24 Togliatti's major articles and speeches on Gramsci are collected in the volume *Gramsci,* ed. Ernesto Ragionieri (Rome: Editori Riuniti, 1972). Some general observations on Togliatti's highly particular interpretation of the notebooks are made in Stephen Gundle, "The Legacy of the Prison Notebooks: Gramsci, the PCI, and Italian Culture in the Cold War Era," in *Italy in the Cold War: Politics, Culture, and Society, 1948–1958* ed. Christopher Duggan and Christopher Wagstaff (Oxford: Berg, 1995).

25 Sereni relinquished his cultural post to devote all his energies to the campaign for peace. It was no coincidence that his removal followed Togliatti's return to Italy after a period of several months in the Soviet Union during which Togliatti had been pressured by Stalin to abandon his post as secretary of the PCI in order to assume the leadership of the Cominform. On his return Togliatti did not seek to punish those members of the directorate who had backed Stalin's request, although he cannot have been pleased to learn that only Umberto Terracini spoke out against it. He did, however, take immediate steps to regain control of cultural policy. See Albertina Vittoria, *Togliatti e gli intellettuali: storia dell'Istituto Gramsci negli anni cinquanta e sessanta* (Rome: Editori Riuniti, 1992), 32.

26 Salinari's presentation to the cultural commission on 3 April 1952 is conserved among the papers of the cultural commission in the PCI archive along with a record of the other interventions at the meeting. See also Palmiro Togliatti, *La politica culturale,* ed. Luciano Gruppi (Rome: Editori Riuniti, 1974), 195–202.

27 Asor Rosa, "Lo Stato democratico e i partiti politici," 601.

28 This shift, which is explored in Vittoria, *Togliatti e gli intellettuali,* 136–38, was important and Lazar (in *Maisons rouges: les Partis communistes français et italien de la Libération à nos jours* [Paris: Aubier, 1992], 71) and Flores and Gallerano (in *Sul PCI: un'interpretazione storica* [Bologna: Il Mulino, 1992], 198) are quite wrong to downplay it. However, as Marino rightly observes, Gramsci was employed almost exclusively in the PCI's relations with intellectuals. At the grassroots level, Communist political culture consisted first and foremost of Stalin's writings. See Giuseppe Carlo Marino, *Autoritratto del PCI staliniano, 1946–1953* (Rome: Editori Riuniti, 1991). This point is also made by Giovanni Ferrara in *Ferrara con furore,* ed. Giampiero Mughini (Milan: Leonardo, 1990), 92–94.

29 "The cultural sphere," Togliatti had noted in July 1949, "offers us better opportunities today than other fields" (minutes of the meeting of the directorate, 11 July 1949, PCI Archive). The success of the PCI's activities can be gauged by Salinari's proclamation to the cultural commission in 1952 that the Communists had achieved a hegemonic position in the fields of cinema, literature, art, and historiography (papers of the cultural com-

mission, minutes of the meeting, 3 April 1952, PCI Archive). That this conclusion was somewhat exaggerated is shown by Salinari's own dissatisfaction with the fact that the PCI's intellectual influence did not translate into cultural power at a mass level.

30 David Forgacs, "The Making and Unmaking of Neorealism," in *The Culture of Reconstruction: Literature, Film, and Thought in France, Germany, and Italy, 1945–50,* ed. Nicholas Hewitt (London: Macmillan, 1989).

31 See, for example, the condescending attitude adopted toward *Il Calendario del Popolo* in "Il 'Calendario' e la cultura," *Rinascita* 7.2 (1955). The original note was unsigned, but it was later included in Togliatti, *La politica culturale.*

32 These questions are discussed in Gian Carlo Ferretti, *Il mercato delle lettere: industria culturale e lavoro critico in Italia dagli anni Cinquanta a oggi* (Turin: Einaudi, 1979), 5–23; and Pio Baldelli, *Politica culturale e comunicazioni di massa* (Pisa: Nistri-Lischi, 1968).

33 "Contro l'oscurantismo imperialista e clericale," resolution of the cultural commission of the PCI, August 1949, PCI Archive.

34 Two excellent contributions that merit far wider attention than they appear to have received are Saveria Bologna, "Associazionismo culturale e mutamento sociale: le Case del Popolo nella provincia di Bologna" (Dott. Lett. thesis, Università degli Studi di Bologna, 1979–80); and Catia Mazzeri, "Comunisti emiliani e cultura popolare (1945–56)" (Dott. Lett. thesis, Università degli Studi di Bologna, 1979–80). See also Catia Mazzeri, "Comunisti e cultura a Modena negli anni della ricostruzione (1945–54)," *Rassegna di Storia dell'Istituto Storico della Resistenza in Modena e provincia* 1.1, n.s. (1981): 89–104.

35 Giacomo Calandrone, *Un comunista in Sicilia, 1946–1951* (Rome: Editori Riuniti, 1972), 60.

36 Luciano Casali and Dianella Gagliani, "Movimento operaio e organizzazioni di massa: il PCI in Emilia-Romagna (1945–1954)," in *La ricostruzione in Emilia-Romagna,* ed. Pier Paolo D'Attorre, Istituto Gramsci (sezione dell'Emilia Romagna) (Parma: Pratiche, 1980), 272.

37 Mazzeri, "Comunisti e cultura," 96–98; and "Comunisti emiliani," 508–22.

38 Ferretti, *Il mercato delle lettere,* 19–20.

39 Mazzeri, "Comunisti e cultura," 98.

40 An account of the movement by one of its protagonists is Luciano Leonesi, *Il romanzo del Teatro di Massa* (Bologna: Cappelli, 1989).

41 Mazzeri, "Comunisti e cultura," 99.

42 Enzo Muzii, "Il convegno nazionale del Teatro di Massa," *Emilia* 1.1 (1952): 8–10.

43 Vittorio Capecchi, "Classe operaia e cultura borghese: ipotesi di ricerca in Emilia-Romagna," in *Famiglia operaia, mutamento culturale, 150 ore,* ed. Vittorio Capecchi et al. (Bologna: Il Mulino, 1982).

44 Anonymous, "Lo spettacolo del Teatro di Massa allo stadio comunale," *La Verità,* 9 September 1950, 8.

45 Ernesto De Martino, "Il mondo popolare nel teatro di massa," *Emilia* 1.3 (1952): 91–93.

46 Ernesto De Martino, "Il folklore progressivo emiliano," *Emilia,* September 1951, 251–54.

47 Ernesto De Martino, "Intorno a una storia del mondo popolare subalterno," *Società* 3 (1949): 411–35. This essay, along with other contributions to the debate on the culture of the popular classes, is reproduced in *Dibattito sulla cultura delle classi subalterne (1949–50),* ed. Pietro Angelini (Rome: Savelli, 1977). A further, wider selection of materials is contained in *Cultura popolare e marxismo,* ed. Raffaele Rauty (Rome: Editori Riuniti, 1976). See also Ernesto De Martino, "Il folklore progressivo," *L'Unità,* 26 June 1951, 3.

48 Cesare Luporini, "Intorno alla storia del mondo popolare subalterno" (1951), reprinted in Angelini, *Dibattito sulla cultura delle classi subalterne.*

49 Tiziano Tamignini, "Merita maggiore attenzione l'attività del teatro popolare," *La Verità,* 11 October 1952, 8.

50 For some reflections on the experience of Mass Theater see Baldelli, *Politica culturale;* and Gianni Bosio, *L'intellettuale rovesciato* (Milan: Edizioni del Gallo, 1967), 112–14.

51 Carlo Lizzani, "Per una difesa attiva del cinema popolare," *Rinascita* 5.2 (1948): 91.

52 Franca Faldini and Goffredo Fofi, eds., *L'avventurosa storia del cinema italiano – raccontato dai suoi protagonisti, 1935–59* (Milan: Feltrinelli, 1979), 218. De Santis raised this point publicly at the conference "Problems of Realism in Italy" held at the Gramsci Institute in Rome in January 1959. See *Il Contemporaneo* 11 (1959): 36.

53 Massimo Mida, "Perchè sono morte le cooperative," *Cinema nuovo* 6.104 (1957); reprinted in *Sciolti dal giuramento: il dibattito critico-ideologico sul cinema negli anni Cinquanta,* ed. Guido Aristarco (Bari: Dedalo, 1981).

54 Lizzani, director of three party-financed documentaries, described their aims and their realization in "Tre documentari democratici," *Quaderno dell'attivista,* 1 June 1950, 16–17. For an overall view of the documentaries made by the PCI since 1945 see Archivio storico audiovisivo del movimento operaio, "L'immagine audiovisiva di un partito politico: il PCI" (Rome, 1982), mimeo.

55 Carlo Lizzani, "I film per il 'partito nuovo,' " in *Il 1948 in Italia: la storia e i film,* ed. Nicola Tranfaglia (Florence: La Nuova Italia, 1991), 100.

56 Pietro Ingrao, *Le cose impossibili: un'autobiografia raccontata e discussa con Nicola Tranfaglia* (Rome: Editori Riuniti, 1990), 70.

57 Minutes of the directorate meeting, 6 December 1950, PCI Archive.

58 "I compiti fondamentali della stampa comunista," resolution of the PCI directorate, 6 December 1950, PCI Archive.

59 The best insights into the world of Communist journalism in this period are to be found in Fidia Gambetti, *Comunista perchè come* (Rome: Vecchiarelli, 1992); and Marcello Venturi, *Sdraiati sulla linea* (Milan: Mondadori, 1991).

60 Minutes of the directorate meeting, 6 December 1950, 8, PCI Archive.

61 Felice Fabrizio, *Storia dello sport in Italia: dalle società ginnastiche all'associazionismo di massa* (Florence-Rimini: Guaraldi, 1977), 56–61.

62 Ibid., 152–58; and Mazzeri, "Comunisti emiliani," 314–39.

63 On the origins of the festivals of the Communist press, subsequently *feste dell'Unità,* see Eva Paola Amendola and Marcella Ferrara, *È la festa: quarant'anni con l'Unità* (Rome: Editori Riuniti, 1984); and Claudio Bernieri, *L'Albero in piazza: storia, cronaca e leggenda delle Feste dell'Unità* (Milan: Mazzotta, 1977).

64 See Marino, *Autoritratto del PCI staliniano,* 33.

65 Pietro Ingrao, "Le feste dell' '*Unità,* ' " *Rinascita* 5.9–10 (1948): 372.

66 Carlo Felice Casula, "I comunisti e la comunicazione," in Tranfaglia, *Il 1948 in Italia,* 134.

67 Alessandro Curzi and Pietro Pieralli, "Problemi dell'organizzazione e dell'attività tra i giovani," *Rinascita,* 12.11 (1955): 724.

68 Giuseppe Turroni, "Alla scoperta del pubblico," *Rassegna del film* 2 (1954): 28–29.

69 See, in particular, Antonello Trombadori, "*Riso amaro* di De Santis e il problema della realtà nell'arte," *Vie Nuove,* 25 September 1949, 14–15, and the polemic thus provoked. Among the contributions to the debate were Carlo Muscetta, "L'arte e la critica," *Vie Nuove,* 9 October 1949, 15; Umberto Barbaro, "L'arte di tendenza," *Vie Nuove,* 16 October 1949, 15; Antonello Trombadori, "Alla ricerca della pianta uomo," *Vie Nuove,* 6 November 1949, 15; Trombadori, "La polemica su *Riso Amaro,*" *L'Unità* (Rome), 19 October 1949, 3. With a letter to *Vie Nuove,* Togliatti himself intervened to reprove Trombadori for being too heavy-handed in his criticism of a film that was in any event better than any bourgeois product (13 November 1949, 15).

70 De Santis gave vent to his anger at a meeting of the cultural commission in 1956, during which he attacked the sectarian theories of neorealism that had flourished in the early 1950s and deplored the abrasive style of Alicata (papers of the cultural commission, minutes of the meeting, November 1956, PCI Archive).

71 Minutes of the meeting of the directorate, 13 June 1950, PCI Archive; Associazione Amici dell'*Unità,* "Grande concorso per l'elezione della 'stellina dell'*Unità.*' "

72 Cited in *Vie Nuove,* 2 July 1950, 17.

73 PCI, *VIII Congresso del Partito comunista italiano: atti e risoluzioni*

(Rome: Editori Riuniti, 1957), 142–43. It is worth reproducing in full the relevant passage from Marchesi's speech: "We must combat the widespread idea that everything in the Communist world is gloomy, heavy, and long-faced. It is not our job to cultivate buffoonish frivolity but — do not laugh comrades — to cultivate smiles, yes. Smiling means openness, understanding, intelligence, pleasantness. Furrows in the brow, when they are the product of the passing of time, are welcome, but when they spring from the bottom of the soul they obscure and impede human coexistence. It is good to banish those lines whenever possible and divert Man's eye and thoughts toward the many beautiful things of the world. We see some illustrated magazines produced in the socialist world where joyous, carefree thoughts seem to have disappeared. In the fields and in the factories, in the midst of machinery, only calls for harder work seem to find a place. You would think that the harder men work the happier they are. Even the portrayal of leisure and feast days has an air of seriousness and tedium. This is not the way to lift the spirits of tired men. Comrade Longo knows a thing or two about this, for he has opened the columns of *Vie Nuove* to beautiful girls. Mere frivolity? So what if it is. This is the sort of propaganda that opens all doors. It attracts an audience among all eyes and ears, of rich and poor alike, and it is applauded in all quarters." For a fuller treatment of the coverage of Hollywood in the Communist press see Stephen Gundle, "Il PCI e la campagna contro Hollywood (1948–1958)," in *Hollywood in Europa, 1945–1960,* ed. D. W. Ellwood and Gian Piero Brunetta (Florence: Ponte alle Grazie, 1991).

74 *Vie Nuove,* 2 January 1949, 2. Pellicani wrote *Zeta Zeta* because he did not wish to write "Coca-Cola," a beverage against which the Italian Communists, like their comrades in France, were conducting a strenuous campaign.

75 The first figure was published in *Vie Nuove,* 3 February 1952, 23; the second, 12 September 1954, 3.

76 Despite the effort to make the magazine more popular, the one issue that outsold all others was the special edition produced in March 1953 to mark the death of Stalin. Much to the chagrin of the staff of *Vie Nuove,* the considerable profits that it generated were not ploughed back into the magazine. Instead, they were used to subsidize a range of other Communist publications.

3. What's Good for Fiat Is Good for Italy:
Television, Consumerism, and Party Identity in the 1950s

1 Cited in Franca Faldini and Goffredo Fofi, eds., *L'avventurosa storia del cinema italiano — raccontato dai suoi protagonisti, 1960–1969* (Milan: Feltrinelli, 1981), 1.

2 On the question of Americanization in the 1950s see Stephen Gundle,

"L'americanizzazione del quotidiano: televisione e consumismo nell'Italia degli anni Cinquanta," *Quaderni storici* 21.62/2 (1986): 561–94.

3 Giorgio Galli, *Il bipartitismo imperfetto: comunisti e democristiani in Italia* (Bologna: Il Mulino, 1966), 9–14.

4 Vittorio Castronovo, *La storia economica,* in *Storia d'Italia,* vol. 4, tome 1 (Turin: Einaudi, 1975), 436.

5 Tullio De Mauro, *Storia linguistica dell'Italia unita* (Bari: Laterza, 1986), 106–7, 111–16.

6 Umberto Eco, "Verso una civiltà dell'immagine," *Pirelli,* 14.1–3 (1961): 32–42. This essay includes "Fenomenologia di Mike Bongiorno" (37–38). On the paradigmatic nature of the quiz see Alberto Abruzzese and Francesco Pinto, "La radiotelevisione," in *Letteratura italiana,* vol. 2, *Produzione e consumo,* ed. Alberto Asor Rosa (Turin: Einaudi, 1983), 845n.

7 Mauro Calamandrei, "La città in campagna," *L'Espresso,* 25 January 1959, 12–13.

8 Lidia De Rita, *I contadini e la televisione* (Bologna: Il Mulino, 1964), 225.

9 Omar Calabrese, *Carosello o dell'educazione serale* (Florence: Cleuf, 1975), 18. See also Laura Ballio and Adriano Zanacchi, *Carosello story* (Turin: ERI, 1987).

10 Paul Ginsborg, *A History of Contemporary Italy: Society and Politics, 1943–1988* (Harmondsworth: Penguin, 1989), 220.

11 Giulio Mazzocchi, "Come si viveva prima, durante e dopo," *I problemi di Ulisse* 83–87 (1979): 74.

12 Antonio Bellucci, "Trent'anni fa l'Italia si ritrovò per strada," *La Repubblica,* 12 January 1985, 17.

13 See Arnold M. Rose, *Indagine sull'integrazione sociale in due quartieri di Roma* (Rome: Università di Roma–Istituto di statistica, studi e inchieste, 1959).

14 Alessandro Pizzorno, *Comunità e razionalizzazione* (Turin: Einaudi, 1960), 184.

15 Moravia was cited in Cesare Mannucci, *Lo spettatore senza libertà* (Bari: Laterza, 1962), 46. For Bocca's comment see *Miracolo all'italiana,* 2d ed. (Milan: Feltrinelli, 1980), 5.

16 Episode described in Piero Bairati, *Vittorio Valletta* (Turin: UTET, 1987), 254–55. The model was illustrated in some detail in the left-wing press. See, for example, *Vie Nuove,* 4 May 1952, 20.

17 Paolo Spriano, *Le passioni di un decennio, 1946–1956* (Milan: Garzanti, 1986), 195. Khrushchev's speech was published by the *New York Times* on 4 June 1956.

18 Davide Lajolo, *I Rossi* (Milan: Rizzoli, 1974), 14. See also Leonardo Sciascia, "La morte di Stalin," in *Gli zii di Sicilia* (Turin: Einaudi, 1958).

19 Andrea Colasio, "L'organizzazione del PCI e la crisi del 1956," in *La*

sinistra e il '56 in Italia e in Francia, ed. B. Groppo and G. Ricamboni (Padua: Liviana, 1987), 92–93.

20 The most detailed account of the relationship between intellectuals and the party in 1956 is provided by Nello Ajello in chapters 11–13 of *Intellettuali e PCI, 1944–1958* (Bari: Laterza, 1979). See also Albertina Vittoria, *Togliatti e gli intellettuali: storia dell'Istituto Gramsci negli anni cinquanta e sessenta* (Rome: Editori Riuniti, 1992), chaps. 8–10; and Spriano, *Le passioni di un decennio.*

21 See, in particular, Luciano Barca, "Economia in primo piano"; and Alessandra Pizzorno, "Avere coraggio," both reprinted in the anthology *Gli intellettuali di sinistra e la crisi del 1956,* ed. Giuseppe Vacca (Rome: *Rinascita*-Editori Riuniti, 1978).

22 Papers of the cultural commission, meeting of 23–24 July 1956, speech of Italo Calvino, PCI Archive.

23 Vacca, *Gli intellettuali di sinistra e la crisi del 1956.*

24 Pizzorno, "Avere coraggio," 122.

25 The contributions to the *Cinema Nuovo* debate are now collected in *Sciolti dal giuramento; il dibattito critico-ideologica sul cinema negli anni cinquanta,* ed. Guido Aristarco (Bari: Dedalo, 1981). Paolo Gobetti's article, "Confessioni di un critico comunista," appears on pp. 83–109. The debate is set in the context of the left's campaigns on cinema in Gian Piero Brunetta, *Storia del cinema italiano dal 1945 agli anni Ottanta* (Rome: Editori Riuniti, 1982), in the chapter titled "La battaglia delle idee: il fronte della sinistra."

26 The causes of the critics' failure to persuade ordinary filmgoers to abandon comedies and melodramas for more artistically valid films in the late 1940s and early 1950s was the subject of a debate, initiated by Ugo Casiraghi, in *L'Unità* in 1955.

27 Mario Alicata, "Troppo poco gramsciani" (1956), in *Intellettuali e azione politica,* ed. R. Martinelli and R. Maini (Rome: Editori Riuniti, 1975), 248–56.

28 See Ajello, *Intellettuali e PCI,* 403–6; Spriano, *Le passioni di un decennio,* 210–20; Vittoria, *Togliatti e gli intellettuali,* chap. 10.

29 In *Togliatti e gli intellettuali,* Vittoria quotes Sergio Bertelli to this effect (123). Dissident intellectuals were called in individually, often repeatedly, and berated by party officials who demanded that they recant.

30 Compare Gian Carlo Ferretti, *"Officina": cultura, letteratura e politica negli anni Cinquanta* (Turin: Einaudi, 1975).

31 Alberto Asor Rosa, "Lo Stato democratico e i partiti politici," in *Letteratura italiana,* vol. 1, *Il Letterato e le istituzioni,* ed. Alberto Asor Rosa (Turin: Einaudi, 1982), 615.

32 See "Relazione sull'attivita dei Gruppi parlamentari e delle Commissioni centrali," *VII Congresso del Partito comunista italiano: documenti per i delegati* (Rome: PCI, 1951), 128–30.

33 Mario Alicata, "Degradazione della cultura italiana in regime democristiano e clericale," *Rinascita* 2 (1958): 117.

34 Francesco Pinto, *Intellettuali e tv negli anni '50* (Rome: Savelli, 1977), 62–69.

35 Arturo Gismondi, "Passatempo dopolavoristico o strumento di cultura?" *Televisione* 1 (1964): 10.

36 Giorgio Amendola, "La seconda assemblea dei comunisti della fabbriche" (1960), in *Classe operaia e programmazione democratica* (Rome: Editori Riuniti, 1966).

37 Contained in "Più voti ai comunisti perchè la Costituzione divenga realtà," 1958 election pamphlet.

38 Giorgio Amendola, "Lotte di massa e nuova maggioranza" (1960), in *Classe operaia e programmazione democratica,* 34.

39 Amendola, "La seconda assemblea dei comunisti delle fabbriche," 71.

40 Enrico Berlinguer, "Lo stato del partito in rapporto alle modificazioni della società italiana," *Critica marxista* 1, nos. 5–6 (1963): 211–12.

41 Ibid., 207.

42 Giorgio Amendola, "Riscossa operaia," speech to the second conference of factory Communists (1961), in *Classe operaia e programmazione democratica,* 119. He spoke as workers began once more to flex their muscles prior to the renewal in 1962 of the metalworkers' national contract.

43 Liliano Faenza, *Comunismo e cattolicesimo in una parrocchia di campagna: vent'anni dopo (1959–1979)* (Bologna: Cappelli, 1979), 192.

44 See Alessandro Portelli, *Biografia di una città: storia e racconto — Terni, 1830–1985* (Turin: Einaudi, 1985), 328–29.

45 Francesco Alberoni et al., *L'attivista di partito* (Bologna: Il Mulino, 1967), 270–76.

46 Giuseppe Carlo Marino, *Autoritratto di un PCI staliniano, 1946–1953* (Rome: Editori Riuniti, 1991), 55.

47 Ludovico Geymonat, "Per un intervento al covegno di studi gramsciani," in *Studi gramsciani — Atti del convegno tenuto a Roma nei giorni 11–13 gennaio 1958* (Rome: Editori Riuniti, 1958).

48 Luigi Arbizzani, Saveria Bologna, and Lidia Testoni, eds., *Storie di Case del Popolo: saggi, documenti e immagini d'Emilia Romagna* (Bologna: Gratis, 1982), 226–29.

49 In Bologna the PCI federation advised Case del popolo not to purchase television sets, advice that was for the most part ignored. See ARCI-Bologna, "La Casa del Popolo 'Corazza,' " 24, undated mimeo.

50 Paul Ginsborg, "Family, Culture, and Politics in Contemporary Italy," in *Culture and Conflict in Postwar Italy* by Zygmunt Baranski and Robert Lumley (London: Macmillan, 1990), 34. For a satirical treatment of the rivalry that the advent of television unleashed between Communists and Catholics see "La macchina sovietica," in *Lo spumarino pallido,* by Giovanni Guareschi (Milan: Rizzoli, 1981).

51 Carlo Galluzzi, *Garibaldi fu ferito* (Milan: Sperling and Kupfer, 1985), 162. For an account of the use of slide shows in propaganda in Treviso see Ivo Dalla Costa, *Pietro Dal Pozzo: un testimone del nostro tempo* (Treviso: ACPTV, 1987), 254–56.

52 "Processo alla TV: il controfagotto come la classica arma a doppio taglio," *Vie Nuove,* 26 February 1956, 8.

53 Saverio Tutino, "Il vizio segreto della televisione," *Vie Nuove,* 26 February 1956, 8.

54 Galluzzi, *Garibaldi fu ferito,* 163.

55 See *Vie Nuove,* 21 February 1954, 20.

56 As Edda Campagnoli, a dark-haired girl who won the title of Miss *Vie Nuove* Milan, she took part in the 1952 final of the competition. By the time she appeared on television her appearance had completely changed. "With silk dresses, pearl necklaces, and her hair styled in the Hollywood fashion, she seemed more like a star than a simple assistant. She and Mike made a perfect couple," writes Laura Delli Colli in *Dadaumpa: storie, immagini, curiosità e personaggi di trent'anni di televisione in Italia* (Rome: Gremese, 1984), 27.

57 PCI, "Rapporto di attività del comitato centrale e progetto di tesi per il IX congresso del PCI" (Rome: PCI, 1959), 77.

58 Although some critics deplored the large payments that popular singers received for their appearances at party festivals, Claudio Villa, who made no secret of his support for the PCI, denied any financial gain. "I never spared myself for the Communists, often going free of charge (something almost no one did) to *feste dell'Unità* and other events even in the most inaccessible places of the peninsula," he wrote in his autobiography, *Una vita stupenda* (Milan: Mondadori, 1987), 160.

59 Gambetti was dismissed without warning or explanation by Gian Carlo Pajetta, the head of press and propaganda. He records the episode with anger in *Comunista perchè come* (Rome: Vecchiarelli, 1992), 52. Although Macciocchi dispensed with many of the intellectual and literary collaborators attracted to *Vie Nuove* by Gambetti, she did recruit some of her own, notably Curzio Malaparte and Pier Paolo Pasolini.

60 Maria Antonietta Macciocchi, "Alcune note sull'attività e sui problemi di *Vie Nuove,*" 20 September 1959, 2, papers relating to *Vie Nuove,* PCI Archive (Via delle Botteghe Oscure).

61 Ibid., 6.

62 Davide Lajolo to Alessandro Natta of the PCI secretariat, 4 May 1970, papers relating to *Vie Nuove,* PCI Archive (Via delle Botteghe Oscure). In this letter Lajolo (editor of *Vie Nuove* 1969–78) lamented the fact that the magazine was "known only as a Communist paper whose advertising profile qualifies it (albeit a little unjustly) as an exclusively male weekly." On Macciocchi's attempts to render *Vie Nuove* more feminine (which included suppressing the highly successful beauty contests) see her contri-

bution to the special insert on the weekly's history in *Giorni–Vie Nuove,* 13 October 1976, 64.

63 Stephen Gundle, "Cultura di massa e modernizzazione: *Vie Nuove* e *Famiglia Cristiana* dalla guerra fredda alla società dei consumi," in *Nemici per la pelle: sogno americano e mito sovietico nell'Italia contemporanea,* ed. Pier Paolo D'Attorre (Milan: Franco Angeli, 1991), 253–56.

64 Marino, *Autoritratto di un PCI staliniano,* 38.

65 Documents on the "Concorso per il mese della stampa comunista 1950," papers relating to *l'Unità,* PCI Archive (Via delle Botteghe Oscure).

66 See, for example, Nilde Jotti, "La questione dei fumetti," *Rinascita* 8.12 (1951): 583–85.

67 Giuliana Saladino, "I fumetti e la nostra propaganda," *Quaderno dell'attivista,* 20 February 1956, 12–14.

68 "Rapporto di attività del comitato centrale e progetto di tesi per il IX congresso del PCI," 77.

69 *L'Unità* reached its maximum print run of 488,000 per day in 1949, a figure that steadily declined to 367,000 in 1956, before picking up again in 1959. On the development and functioning of the paper see Giovanni Bechelloni and Milly Buonanno, "Il quotidiano del partito: *L'Unità,*" in *Il Partito comunista italiano,* ed. Massimo Ilardi and Aris Accornero (Milan: Feltrinelli, 1982).

70 "Nota sull'*Unità* (febbraio–giugno 1960) per la segreteria," papers relating to *l'Unità,* PCI Archive.

71 Bechelloni and Buonanno, "Il quotidiano del partito," 872.

72 Galli, *Il bipartitismo imperfetto,* 273–75.

73 Marcella Filippa, "Operai a Torino negli anni Cinquanta: cultura, tempo libero, immaginario, miti," in *Solidarietà e classe operaia: contributi per una storia sociale,* ed. Marcella Filippa et al. (Rome: Ediesse, 1988).

74 Giorgio Triani, "Riflessioni e problemi d'oggi," in Arbizzani, Bologna, and Testoni, *Storie di Case del Popolo,* 317–21.

75 Gianni Rondolino has suggested that the article was in fact written by Antonello Trombadori. See *Luchino Visconti* (Turin: UTET, 1981), 402. In September 1986 I asked Trombadori if this was true. He chose neither to confirm nor to deny the allegation.

76 Luchino Visconti, "Oltre il fato dei Malavoglia," *Vie Nuove,* 22 October 1960, 26–27.

77 See Roberto Barbagallo and Franco Cazzola, "Le organizzazioni di massa," in Ilardi and Accornero, *Il Partito comunista italiano;* and Agopik Manoukian, *La presenza sociale del PCI e della DC* (Bologna: Il Mulino, 1968), 275–92. Also relevant is Milly Buonanno, "La politica culturale delle associazioni: il caso dell'ARCI," in *Politica culturale? studi, materiali, ipotesi,* ed. Giovanni Bechelloni (Bologna: Guaraldi, 1970).

78 See, for example, Gianni Toti, *Il tempo libero* (Rome: Editori Riuniti, 1961).

79 *Le ore libere* 5.12–13 (1961) contains the proceedings of ARCI's national cultural convention.

80 ARCI, *Tesi per il terzo congresso nazionale* (Rome: ARCI, 1962), 7.

81 Ibid., 2.

82 ARCI, *Struttura organizzativa e attività sociale svolta dall'ARCI nel quadrennio 1960–1963* (Rome: ARCI, 1964), 4.

83 Compare Barbagallo and Cazzola, "Le organizzazioni di massa," 876.

84 For more on the intervention of Macaluso see PCI, *V Conferenza nazionale d'organizzazione: atti e risoluzioni* (Rome: Editori Riuniti, 1964), 53.

4. From Elvis Presley to Ho Chi Minh: Youth Culture and Cultural Conflict between the Center Left and the Hot Autumn

1 Lidia De Rita, *I contadini e la televisione* (Bologna: Il Mulino, 1964), 61.

2 Guido Vicario, "Nati dopo il diluvio: la parola ai ventenni," *Vie Nuove,* 11 June 1964, 40.

3 See Franco Rositi, "La cultura giovanile," in *Informazione e complessità sociale: critica delle politiche culturali in Italia* (Bari: De Donato, 1978), 80–83. Rositi argues that the conflicts between youth culture and the prevailing adult culture in the 1960s were precisely about resistances to the installation of the cultural models of mass society.

4 Mario De Luigi, *L'industria discografica in Italia* (Rome: Lato Side, 1982), chaps. 2, 3.

5 Compare P. G. Grasso, *Gioventù di metà secolo* (Rome: A.V.E., 1954) and Guido Baglioni, *I giovani nella società industriale* (Milan: Vita e Pensiero, 1962).

6 Ian David Mellor, *Italy through a Looking Glass, 1943–64* (Lugano: private publication, 1964), 137.

7 Ugoberto Alfassio Grimaldi and Italo Bertoni, *I giovani degli anni sessanta* (Bari: Laterza, 1964).

8 Baglioni, *I giovani nella società industriale,* 264.

9 "Lettera di un giovane," *Rinascita,* n.s., 21 July 1962, 2. The letter's anonymous author, Franco Gatti, joined the party after his unexpected dialogue with Togliatti. After taking part in the protests of 1968 he moved to Potere Operaio, only to drop out of political activity in the 1970s. He died in September 1989. His story is briefly recounted in Renzo Foa, "Togliatti e noi magliette a strisce," *L'Unità,* 20 September 1989, 2.

10 Gianni Toti, "Autobiografie dell'avvenire," *Vie Nuove,* 9 January 1964, 22.

11 *Nuova Generazione,* n.s., 12, 16–23 March 1958, 10.

12 ". . . vieni sacro fantasma," *Nuova Generazione,* n.s., 12, 16–23 March 1958, 10.

13 Ibid.

14 Maria Maffei, "Rivolta a 45 giri," *Noi Donne,* 27 March 1965, 9.

15 See, for example, Rino Dal Sasso, "I giovani e i sociologhi," *Il Contemporaneo,* 24 April 1960, 73–76.

16 Pietro Ingrao, "Un primo dibattito sul pluralismo politico" (1964), in *Masse e potere* (Rome: Editori Riuniti, 1990), 194–95.

17 Luca Pavolini, "I giovani non sono 'una difficoltà,'" *Rinascita,* 3 March 1967, 8.

18 See Morandi's testimony in Corrado Incerti, "Da compagni a soci," *Panorama,* 10 July 1988, 58–60. Compare also Gianni Morandi, "La lunga estate del cantagiro," in *Il sogno degli anni '60,* ed. Walter Veltroni (Rome: Savelli, 1981), 151.

19 See the debate reported by Lina Angliel in "L'azione unitaria del PCI per transformare l'Italia," *L'Unità,* 16 April 1967, 1–2.

20 A brief summary of the history of API is offered in Bologna, "Associazionismo culturale e mutamento sociale," 151–55.

21 Adult organizers of the Pioneers were frequently denounced on the instigation of Church authorities for corrupting minors. No one was ever convicted, however. One famous case is discussed in Andrea Colasio, "Il processo ai Pioneri di Pozzonovo: forme di conflitto politico nel Veneto degli anni '50," *Venetica* 2 (1984): 40–62.

22 Orlando Pezzoli, *È storia: Casa del popolo Nerio Nannetti–Santa Viola, Bologna* (Bologna: PCI zona Santa Viola, 1981), 112.

23 Bologna, *Associazionismo e mutamento sociale,* 211n.

24 Rino Serri, "L'organizzazione giovanile 1945–68," in *Il Partito comunista italiano,* ed. Massimo Ilardi and Aris Accornero (Milan: Feltrinelli, 1982), 774–77.

25 Minutes of the directorate meeting, 13 July 1956, PCI Archive. During a debate on the state of the FGCI, Enrico Berlinguer reported that "up to 1953 many young people came to us hoping for a radical change in the situation. Today the tendency to seek our individual solutions or to explore Catholic reformism or social democracy has increased." "Up to the age of twenty-five," he said, "young people are not very attracted by the party. Lots of FGCI members do not join the party after doing their military service" (2–3). At a meeting of the cultural commission later the same year, a certain Fasano of the FGCI suggested, with remarkable perspicacity, that perhaps the arrival in Italy of a sort of "American spirit" of ambitious individualism was not entirely a bad thing, because "it upsets to some degree the passivity, timidity, and narrowness of outlook that are easily absorbed in certain sectors of our society." The American spirit therefore should not be rejected; rather, he argued that it should be integrated with the collective outlook and solidarity of the party and the working-class movement. See papers of the cultural commission, meeting of November 1956, 4, PCI Archive.

26 Achille Occhetto, *A dieci anni del '68,* ed. Walter Veltroni (Rome: Editori Riuniti, 1978), 42.

27 See Alessandro Curzi, "Sessanta, Sesso, Sinistra," in Veltroni, *Il sogno degli anni '60.*

28 Compare, for example, P.S., "Il solito volto bestiale dell'America di Kennedy," *Nuova Generazione* 18, 19 May 1963, 16.

29 Giuseppe Vacca, "Politica e teoria nel marxismo italiano negli anni sessanta," in *Il marxismo italiano degli anni sessanta: la formazione teorico-politica delle nuove generazioni,* Istituto Gramsci (Rome: Editori Riuniti–Istituto Gramsci, 1972), 72.

30 See Istituto Gramsci, *Tendenze del capitalismo italiano: atti del convegno di Roma 23–25 marzo 1962,* vol. 1, *Le relazioni e il dibattito* (Rome: Editori Riuniti, 1962).

31 Alberto Asor Rosa, "Il punto di vista operaio e la cultura socialista," *Quaderni rossi* 2 (1962): 117–30.

32 Pier Paolo Pasolini, "Cultura dopo l' 'impegno,' " *Vie Nuove,* September 1965, 30.

33 Alberto Asor Rosa, "Lo Stato democratico e i partiti politici," in *Letteratura italiana,* vol. 1, *Il Letterato e le istituzioni,* ed. Alberto Asor Rosa (Turin: Einaudi, 1982), 629–32.

34 Gian Carlo Ferretti, *Il mercato delle lettere: industria culturale e lavoro critico in Italia dagli anni Cinquanta a oggi* (Turin: Einaudi, 1979), 130–33.

35 Rossana Rossanda, "Sulla politica culturale e gli intellettuali" (interview by Carla Pasquinelli), *Problemi del socialismo,* n.s., 6 (1985): 167.

36 On these and related changes see Albertina Vittoria, *Togliatti e gli intellettuali: storia dell'Istituto Gramsci negli anni cinquanta e sessanta* (Rome: Editori Riuniti, 1992), chap. 15.

37 Palmiro Togliatti, *Memoriale di Yalta* (Rome: Editori Riuniti, 1970), 10.

38 For Rossanda's own reflections on her experience see "Sulla politica culturale e gli intellettuali." See also Luciano Gruppi, "Note sulla politica culturale del partito nel dopoguerra," *Critica marxista,* no. 5 (1972): 162–65.

39 See Magri's contribution in Istituto Gramsci, *Tendenze del capitalismo italiano,* 1:323–35.

40 "Saluto ai lettori," *Il Contemporaneo* 79, December 1964, 3–4.

41 Rossana Rossanda, "Unità politica e scelte culturali," *Rinascita,* 28 August 1965, 19–23. For some considered reflections on the issues raised in this article see Luciano Gruppi, "Palmiro Togliatti: cultura e metodo," *Rinascita,* 18 September 1965, 23–24.

42 Significantly, the ideological section of the PCI, which had been a subunit of the organizational section, was closed at this time. More modestly, it became the department of the cultural section concerned with party schools (Rossanda, "Sulla politica culturale e gli intellettuali," 170).

43 Renato Guttuso, "Una azione culturale comunista," *Rinascita,* 22 January 1964, 35–37.

44 Cited in Gian Franco Venè, "Per chi suona il piffero," *L'Europeo,* 12 September 1965, 13.

45 Ibid.

46 It may be argued that the attack was also the product of hostility to Rossanda as a woman. Although there is no concrete evidence to this effect, anecdotal evidence suggests that it may have been a factor. Women intellectuals were rare, and Rossanda was the first woman since the 1940s to hold high office in the PCI.

47 Compare the contribution of Arcangelo Leone de Castris in Istituto Gramsci, *Il marxismo italiano degli anni sessanta,* 291–300.

48 The proposal is outlined in Rossana Rossanda, "Un programma politico per la cultura," *Rinascita* 4, 22 January 1966, 37–38. See also her other articles: "Gli intellettuali e il partito," *Rinascita,* 14 March 1964; and "Un rapporto nuovo col mondo della cultura," *Rinascita,* 26 June 1965.

49 See, for example, Rossanda's lengthy reply to a young Communist who asked why the party did not actively resist mass culture ("A colloquio con i lettori," *L'Unità,* 1 May 1965, 4). Meanwhile, the problem of light entertainers performing at the *feste dell'Unità* continued to be the cause of bitter arguments. "Is it really possible that our party must be thought of as one of the pillars of the light music industry? Is it possible that the attention of the masses cannot be drawn to the great themes of our struggles except by the rhythms of the twist or the bossa nova?" the critic Sergio Liberovici wrote in an angry letter to *Rinascita* (16 February 1963, 31).

50 Luciano Gruppi, " 'Cultura di massa' o unità culturale?" *Rinascita,* 24 December 1966, 20.

51 Compare the testimony of director Francesco Maselli in *L'avventurosa storia del cinema italiano – raccontato dai suoi protagonisti, 1960–1969,* ed. Franca Faldini and Goffredo Fofi (Milan: Feltrinelli, 1981), 428–30.

52 Mino Argentieri, "Dove va il cinema italiano?" *Rinascita,* 25 August 1967, 14.

53 Mino Argentieri, "Cinema e cultura di massa," *Il Contemporaneo* 69 (1964): 61–77. A similar attack was launched on De Santis by Pio Baldelli at ARCI's February 1961 cultural convention. See *Le ore libere* 5.12–13 (November–December 1961): 67–68.

54 Vittorio Spinazzola was one of the first to make this point. See "Sciolti dal giuramento," *Cinema nuovo,* 1 March 1958, 150–52.

55 Compare the articles published in the special number of the *Il Contemporaneo* supplement in *Rinascita,* 25 August 1967, esp. Libero Bizzarri, "Subordinati a queste ragnatele: i metodi e le cifre dell'invadenza americana," 22–24.

56 On the difficulties of Italian cinema in the 1960s see the responses of Elio

Petri and others to the questionnaire, "Quattro domande agli uomini di cinema," *Rinascita,* 25 August 1967, 25–27.

57 Elio Petri recalled how, after making a series of advertisements for Shell, he accepted an offer from a manufacturer of mass-produced furniture. "Making those *Caroselli* I felt like a thief toward those who would have assimilated the advertising message through the TV," he said (Faldini and Fofi, *L'avventurosa storia del cinema italiano 1960–1969,* 215). Among the other artists identified with the left who made television commercials were Dario Fo and the Taviani brothers.

58 See Paul Ginsborg, *A History of Contemporary Italy: Society and Politics, 1943–1988* (Harmondsworth: Penguin, 1989), chap. 9; Robert Lumley, *States of Emergency: Cultures of Revolt in Italy from 1968 to 1978* (London: Verso, 1990); and Sidney Tarrow, *Democracy and Disorder, Protest and Politics in Italy, 1965–75* (Oxford: Oxford University Press, 1989).

59 See Alberto Giasanti, *La controriforma universitaria: da Gonella a Malfatti* (Milan: Mazzotta, 1977), 38–41.

60 Goffredo Fofi, *Il cinema italiano: servi e padroni* (Milan: Feltrinelli, 1971), 19.

61 Milly Buonanno, "La politica culturale delle associazioni: il caso dell'ARCI," in *Politica culturale? studi, materiali, ipotesi,* ed. Giovanni Bechelloni (Bologna: Guaraldi, 1970), 228.

62 ARCI-Bologna, *La Casa del Popolo "Corazza"* (Bologna: ARCI, undated).

63 Bologna, "Associazionismo culturale e mutamento sociale," 158.

64 Ibid., 159.

65 See Filippo M. De Sanctis, *Pubblico e associazionismo culturale* (Rome: Bulzoni, 1976), 157–75.

66 Buonanno, "La politica culturale delle associazioni," 231.

67 Bologna, "Associazionismo culturale e mutamento sociale," 167. See also Lumley, *States of Emergency,* 124–29.

68 Chiara Valentini, "Con chi vuole discutere Dario Fo?" *Rinascita,* 13 November 1970, 20.

69 Eduardo Fadini, *La storia di Dario Fo* (Milan: Feltrinelli, 1977), 14–15.

70 Adriano Seroni, "A proposito di un 'giornale murale,' " *Rinascita,* 8 October 1966, 27.

71 Franco Scottoni, "Perchè 'tempo libero tempo di rivoluzione,' " *Rinascita,* 28 November 1969, 27; Adriano Seroni, "Cultura di massa: partiamo del reale," *Rinascita,* 23 January 1970, 4. The "wall newspaper" was defended by the vice-president of ARCI, Arrigo Morandi, in "L'ARCI e la ricerca di una linea autonoma," *Rinascita,* 30 January 1970, 19–20. In this article Morandi referred openly to the need for a genuinely antagonistic left culture.

72 Morandi, "L'ARCI e la ricerca di una linea autonoma," 19.

73 See Giovanni Bechelloni, "Appunti sull'organizzazione della cultura in Italia," in Bechelloni, *Politica culturale?*

74 Giuseppe Chiarante, *La rivolta degli studenti* (Rome: Editori Riuniti, 1968), 61.

75 Luigi Longo, "Il movimento studentesco nella lotta anticapitalista," *Rinascita,* 3 May 1968, 16.

76 Tarrow, *Democracy and Disorder,* 179–81.

77 Lumley, *States of Emergency,* 244–46.

78 Giorgio Amendola, *La classe operaia italiana* (Rome: Editori Riuniti, 1968), 169.

79 Gerardo Chiaromonte, *Le scelte della solidarietà democratica: cronache ricordi e riflessioni sul triennio 1976–1979* (Rome: Editori Riuniti, 1986), 18.

80 Ibid., 20.

5. Crisis, Austerity, Solidarity: The Question of Hegemony in the 1970s

1 See Stephen Hellman, *Italian Communism in Transition: The Historic Compromise in Turin, 1975–80* (New York: Oxford University Press, 1988); and Leonardo Paggi and Massimo D'Angelillo, *I comunisti italiani e il riformismo* (Turin: Einaudi, 1986), chap. 3. Other significant contributions to the debate on the Historic Compromise include Giuseppe Vacca, *Tra compromesso e solidarietà: La politica del PCI negli anni '70* (Rome: Editori Riuniti, 1987); Gerardo Chiaromonte, *Le scelte della solidarietà democratica: cronache ricordi e riflessioni sul triennio, 1976–1979* (Rome: Editori Riuniti, 1986); Aldo Schiavone, *Per il nuovo PCI* (Bari: Laterza, 1985); and the essays in *Laboratorio politico* 2.3 (1982). See also Tobias Abse, "Judging the PCI," *New Left Review* 153 (1985): 5–40; Stephen Gundle, "The PCI and the Historic Compromise" and Tobias Abse, "Reply to Gundle," both in *New Left Review* 163 (1987): 27–39; and Stephen Hellman's comments on this debate in "Italian Communism in Crisis," in *The Socialist Register, 1988,* ed. Ralph Miliband, Leo Panitch, and John Saville (London: Merlin Press, 1988), 244–88. A number of points of general value are made in Patrick McCarthy, "Era possibile gestire il compromesso storico?" *Polis* 4.2 (1990): 361–70. Finally, see Donald Sassoon, *One Hundred Years of Socialism: The West European Left in the Twentieth Century* (London: I. B. Tauris, 1996), chap. 20.

2 Marco Revelli, *Lavorare a Fiat* (Milan: Garzanti, 1990), 35.

3 Hellman, *Italian Communism in Transition,* 58–60.

4 Robert Lumley, *States of Emergency: Cultures of Revolt in Italy from 1968 to 1978* (London: Verso, 1990), 133.

5 By the mid-1970s ARCI and UISP counted over one million members.

They embraced 2,750 recreational circles, 7,000 sports clubs, and some 500 cultural circles. They also owned numerous case del popolo and sports grounds. See Pasquale Chessa, "Con 'Prolekulter' è sempre domenica," *L'Espresso,* 1 August 1976, 12–13.

6 Ibid.

7 These responses are discussed in Giampaolo Borghello, *Linea rossa: intellettuali, letteratura e lotta di classe, 1965–1975* (Venice: Marsilio, 1982), 237–40. See also Romano Luperini, *Marxismo e gli intellettuali* (Venice: Marsilio, 1974), pt. 3.

8 Istituto Gramsci, *Il marxismo italiano degli anni sessanta: la formazione teorico-politica delle nuove generazioni* (Rome: Editori Riuniti–Istituto Gramsci, 1972).

9 Giovanni Berlinguer, *Dieci anni dopo: cronache culturali, 1968–1978* (Bari: De Donato, 1978), 9. This book collects the articles and speeches of one of the protagonists of Communist cultural policy in the 1970s.

10 The intervention of Salinari, chief cultural spokesman between 1951 and 1955, was particularly harsh. See "L'arte, la realtà e il partito," *Rinascita,* 20 April 1973, 25–26. Amendola intervened with "Ma sono tre le culture?" *Rinascita,* 4 August 1978, 7–8.

11 Giorgio Napolitano, "Sul problema della direzione culturale," *Rinascita,* 9 November 1973, 19–20. Fabio Mussi, a young cadre with responsibilities in this field, offered a first response to Salinari in "Dopo il realismo e dopo gli anni '60," *Rinascita,* 11 May 1973, 19–20.

12 Berlinguer, *Dieci anni dopo,* 17.

13 As Arcangelo Leone de Castris observed, "The intellectuals are not the Gramscian mediators of consensus; rather, the intellectual masses are the destined recipients of a production of consensus exercised by the cultural apparatus of industrial capitalism" (in *Ideologia letteraria e scuola di massa: per un' analisi sociale dell'organizzazione didattica,* ed. Arcangelo Leone de Castris [Bari: De Donato, 1975], 20).

14 See Claudio Bernieri, *L'Albero in piazza: storia, cronaca e leggenda delle Feste dell'Unità* (Milan: Mazzotta, 1977), chap 3.

15 Ibid.

16 Arrigo Morandi, "Nuovi ruoli e linee d'azione del movimento associativo," in *Cultura di massa e istituzioni,* Arrigo Morandi et al. (Bari: De Donato, 1976), 13–41. See also ARCI-UISP, *Progetto politico-culturale* (Rome: ARCI-UISP, 1974).

17 Morandi was careful to avoid setting up an opposition between individual freedom and collective responsibility or urge the repression of consumption and restriction of choice. See "Nuovi ruoli e linee d'azione del movimento associativo," 24.

18 ARCI, *Il Contributo dell'associazionismo per superare la crisi con lo sviluppo culturale e civile del paese: atti del Congresso nazionale ARCI-UISP,* Naples, 1–3 November 1976, 32.

19 "Relazione di Giorgio Napolitano," in PCI, *Battaglia delle idee e rinnovamento culturale: atti del Comitato centrale e della Commissione centraledi controllo del PCI, Roma 13–15 gennaio 1975* (Rome: Editori Riuniti, 1975), 24.

20 "Gli intellettuali nella società" (1975), in Berlinguer, *Dieci anni dopo*, 202–3.

21 "Introduzione," in Berlinguer, *Dieci anni dopo*, 15.

22 Giorgio Napolitano, "Crisi della scuola e trasformazione rivoluzionaria della società italiana," *Critica marxista* 9.1 (1971): 20.

23 "Relazione di Giorgio Napolitano," 26.

24 On these themes see Alberto Asor Rosa, *Intellettuali e classe operaia* (Florence: La Nuova Italia, 1973).

25 "Relazione di Giorgio Napolitano," 28–29.

26 Adriana Seroni, "La donna è cambiata e vuole cambiare la società," (1975), in *La questione femminile in Italia, 1976–77* (Rome: Editori Riuniti, 1977), 150.

27 Gloria Zuffa, "Le doppie militanze: donna comunista, donna femminista," *Memoria* 19–20 (1987): 41.

28 Luigi Manconi, *Solidarietà, egoismo: buone azioni, movimenti incerti, nuovi conflitti* (Bologna: Il Mulino, 1990), 88–89.

29 Zuffa, "Le doppie militanze," 42.

30 Paolo Sylos Labini, *Saggio sulle classi sociali in Italia* (Bari: Laterza, 1974). The book provoked a polemic between Sylos Labini and Giuliano Procacci in *L'Unità*, 29 November 1974. An extended debate, revealing stern resistance to the idea of the decline of the working class, took place in *Rinascita* between December 1974 and May 1975. See Giuseppe Bedeschi, *La parabola del marxismo in Italia* (Bari: Laterza, 1983), 127n.

31 Giorgio Triani, "Riflessioni e problemi d'oggi," in *Storie di Case del Popolo: saggi, documenti e immagini d'Emilia Romagna,* ed. Luigi Arbizzani, Saveria Bologna, and Lidia Testoni (Bologna: Grafis, 1982), 330–31.

32 Ibid., 331.

33 Communists were surprised to discover in 1979 that political involvement was not a source of special satisfaction for workers belonging to the party and that salary questions were accorded central importance. See R. Mannheimer, M. Rodriguez, and C. Sebastiani, *Gli operai comunisti* (Rome: Editori Riuniti, 1979). The importance of home ownership and family-oriented leisure emerges clearly in Maura Franchi and Vittorio Reiser, *Esperienza e cultura dei delegati* (Reggio Emilia: Bonhoeffer, 1984), chap. 4.

34 See Franco Chiarenza, *Il cavallo morente: trent'anni di radiotelevisione italiana* (Milan: Bompiani, 1978).

35 This continued well after 1976. Marino Livolsi highlighted the almost structural incompatibility between Enrico Berlinguer's idea of austerity

and the consumerism and false optimism of the mass media ("Mass media e cultura dell'austerità," *Rinascita,* 11 March 1977).

36 See Chiarenza, *Il cavallo morente.*

37 See Fabio Giovannini, "Intellettuali e mass media negli anni sessanta," *Democrazia e diritto* 31.1–2 (1991): 153–77.

38 Enzo Forcella, "Riforma e monopolio: quale 'filosofia'?" *La Repubblica,* 7 September 1976. Cited in ibid.

39 Leonardo Paggi, "Scacco alla strategia dell'anticomunismo," *Rinascita,* 7 March 1978, 23–24.

40 Colletti's detachment from Marxism is examined in Bedeschi, *La parabola del marxismo in Italia,* 129–34, along with other aspects of Marxism's crisis.

41 Bedeschi, *La parabola del marxismo in Italia,* 146. The debates of the mid-1970s are reconstructed in Guido Liguori, "Apogeo e crisi della cultura gramsciana in Italia," *Democrazia e diritto* 31.1–2 (1991): 117–41.

42 *Re Nudo* 65 (May 1978): 25–27.

43 Vivid descriptions of events at the 1976 Parco Lambro festival are offered in Marisa Rusconi, "Com'è difficile essere giovani," *L'Espresso,* 11 July 1976, 6–8; and Umberto Eco, "Ma la città del sole non si fabbrica così," *L'Espresso,* 11 July 1976, 8–12.

44 Alessandro Carrera, *Musica e pubblico giovanile* (Milan: Feltrinelli, 1980), 170.

45 Gianni Borgna, *Il tempo della musica: i giovani da Elvis Presley a Sophie Marceau* (Bari: Laterza, 1983), 135–36.

46 Toni Negri, *Dall'operaio massa all'operaio sociale* (Milan: Feltrinelli, 1979).

47 The historian Giuliano Procacci wrote in 1975 of the way in which the critique of American models seemed to coincide with their appropriation. The diffusion of ideas of ecology and zero growth, he said, was tantamount to an "American anti-americanism." Much to be preferred to this "internal and subaltern criticism" was the "more authentic and more productive" criticism based on the European Enlightenment tradition of which Marxism was an extension ("Appropriazione e critica dell'americanismo," *Rinascita,* 21 March 1975, 11–12). A debate was initiated in *La Rinascita* on the state of youth culture in autumn 1976 by Fabio Mussi. The contributions to it are collected in Mussi et al., *I giovani e la crisi della società* (Rome: Editori Riuniti, 1977).

48 See Giorgio Amendola, "La lotta, i sacrifici, la felicità individuale," in Mussi et al., *I giovani e la crisi della società;* and Amendola, "Ai giovani l'ultima intervista," *L'Unità,* 6 June 1980, 4. In the mid-1970s, even young Communists remained convinced that their own culture was strong enough to "correct" and overcome ideas and behavioral norms of an American derivation. See Fabio Mussi, "I giovani e la politica: ide-

ologia e collocazione dei movimenti giovanili," in *PCI, classe operaia e movimento studentesco,* ed. Gregorio Paolini and Walter Vitali (Rimini-Florence: Guaraldi, 1977), 165. However, grave doubts crept in by the end of the decade. This is evident in an *Il Contemporaneo* supplement to *Rinascita* dedicated to "Il radicalismo degli anni settanta," published in the issue of 20 July 1979. On these problems see also Gad Lerner, Luigi Marconi, and Mario Sinibaldi, *Uno strano movimento di strani studenti* (Milan: Feltrinelli, 1978).

49 Michele Salvati, "Col senno di poi (Politica ed economia tra l'unità nazionale e il nuovo centro sinistra)," *Quaderni piacentini,* n.s., 6 (1982): 3–23; Paul Ginsborg, *A History of Contemporary Italy: Society and Politics, 1943–1988* (Harmondsworth: Penguin, 1989), 387–95.

50 See Enrico Berlinguer, "Una politica di austerità ispirata a giustizia sociale per trasformare e rinnovare il paese: la relazione e le conclusioni di E. B. al Comitato centrale del PCI del 18–20 Ottobre 1976," pamphlet for internal distribution (1976); and Enrico Berlinguer, *Austerità: occasione per trasformare l'Italia* (Rome: Editori Riuniti, 1977).

51 Napoleone Colajanni, *Comunisti al bivio: cambiare fino in fondo o rassegnarsi al declino* (Milan: Mondadori, 1987), 128–29.

52 These and other reactions are discussed in Gabriele Giannantoni, "Politica e cultura negli anni Settanta II," *Critica marxista* 16.2 (1978): 60–61.

53 Bobbio expressed his view in an interview published in *Il Corriere della sera,* 22 January 1977.

54 Berlinguer, *Dieci anni dopo,* 22; Aris Accornero, "Tre impatti difficili: DC, potere, specialismi," *Laboratorio politico* 2.3 (1982): 180.

55 PCI, *Proposta di progetto a medio termine* (Rome: Editori Riuniti, 1977).

56 Lerner, Marconi, and Sinibaldi, *Uno strano movimento di strani studenti,* 53. Alberto Asor Rosa was one of the first Communists to grasp the implications of the emergence of what he called a "second society." See Alberto Asor Rosa, "Le due società" (20 February 1977), in *Le due società: ipotesi sulla crisi italiana* (Turin: Einaudi, 1977).

57 Malfatti's proposals are set in context by Alberto Giasanti, in *La controriforma universitaria: da Gonella a Malfatti* (Milan: Mazzotta, 1977), 81–82, 86.

58 Gianni Borgna, "I giovani," in *Dal '68 a oggi: come siamo e come eravamo,* ed. Antonio Gambino et al. (Bari: Laterza, 1979), 400–402; see also Aldo Tortorella, "Cultura e crisi: le ragioni di una battaglia," in Paolini and Vitali, *PCI, classe operaia e movimento studentesco,* 214–17.

59 See Simon Parker, "Local Government and Social Movements in Bologna since 1945" (Ph.D. thesis, Cambridge University, 1992) for the most detailed reconstruction of the events of March 1977 in Bologna. See also Lumley, *States of Emergency,* chap. 20; and, for a view from inside the movement, various authors, *Bologna marzo 1977 . . . fatti nostri* (Verona: Bertani, 1977); Franco Berardi offers some considered reflections in

Dell'innocenza: interpretazione del '77 (Bologna: Agales, 1989). For the Communist response see PCI, *I comunisti e la questione giovanile: atti della sessione del Comitato centrale del PCI — Roma 14–16 marzo 1977* (Rome: Editori Riuniti, 1977); "Appendice" to Paolini and Vitali, *PCI, classe operaia e movimento studentesco;* and interview with Fabio Mussi, in Renato Zangheri, *Bologna '77* (Rome: Editori Riuniti, 1978). Although some Communists felt it was possible to intervene to orient the movement in a more positive direction, the prevailing view was that events showed that the violent wing had seized control. In consequence, no dialogue was possible. It is worth noting that, despite this extreme polarization, the posters of ARCI's Leopardi circle were not ripped from the walls of the university zone (Bologna, "Associazionismo culturale e mutamento sociale," 302).

60 Isabella Peretti and Claudio Vedovati, "PCI, modernizzazione e movimenti," *Democrazia e diritto* 26.1 (1986): 221.

61 Gerardo Chiaromonte, *Col senno di poi* (Rome: Editori Riuniti, 1990), 95.

62 See, for example, the proceedings of the Gramsci Institute conference held in October 1977: Istituto Gramsci, *La crisi della società italiana e gli orientamenti delle nuove generazioni,* ed. Franco Ferri (Rome: Editori Riuniti, 1978).

63 See interview with Emmanuele Rocco, in *Un ministro ombra si confessa,* by Fernando Di Giulio (Milan: Rizzoli, 1979).

6. Welcome to Prosperity:
Economic Growth and the Erosion of Left-Wing Culture

1 Giuseppe Turani, *1985–1995: Il secondo miracolo economico italiano* (Milan: Sperling and Kupfer, 1986).

2 Gad Lerner, *Operai* (Milan: Feltrinelli, 1988), 76.

3 Ronald Inglehart, *The Silent Revolution: Changing Values and Political Style among Western Publics* (Princeton: Princeton University Press, 1977). See also his *Culture Shift in Advanced Industrial Society* (Princeton: Princeton University Press, 1990). In addition, see Scott Flanagan, "Value Change in Industrial Society," *American Political Science Review* 81 (1987): 1303–19. These models are compared by Dalton in *Electoral Change in Advanced Industrial Societies: Realignment or Dealignment?* ed. Russell Dalton, Scott Flanagan, and Paul A. Beck (Princeton, N.J.: Princeton University Press, 1984), 20.

4 Pierluigi Battista, "Intellettuali e politica," *Pagina* 8 (1983): 12–21; David Forgacs, *Italian Culture in the Industrial Era, 1880–1980* (Manchester: Manchester University Press, 1990), 149–51.

5 Forgacs, *Italian Culture in the Industrial Era,* 44.

6 Alberto Asor Rosa, "Il capitale da lezione ai partiti di sinistra," *La Repub-*

blica, 13 August 1988, 1, 6; Paul Ginsborg, *A History of Contemporary Italy: Society and Politics, 1943–1988* (Harmondsworth: Penguin, 1989), 424–25.

7 Alessandro Cavalli and Antonio De Lillo, *Giovani anni 80* (Bologna: Il Mulino, 1986), 162.

8 Aldo Tortorella's address to the central committee, Enrico Berlinguer's intervention, and the debate were published in *L'Unità,* 3–6 December 1981.

9 See Renzo di Rienzi, "Lasciamoci cosi," *L'Espresso,* 6 June 1982, 18–22.

10 See Sudhir Hazareesingh, *Intellectuals and the French Communist Party: Disillusion and Decline* (Oxford: Clarendon Press, 1991).

11 Fabrizio Coisson, "Ritratto di partiti con esterni," *L'Espresso,* 13 December 1981, 6–10.

12 Gino Liguori, "Apogeo e crisi della cultura gramsciana in Italia," *Democrazia e diritto* 31.1–2 (1991): 141.

13 Gianfranco Pasquino, "La cultura politica dei comunisti tra opposizione e governo," *Democrazia e diritto* 26, no. 1 (1986): 10.

14 Massimo Cacciari, *Krisis* (Milan: Feltrinelli, 1976); Gianni Vattimo and Pier Aldo Rovatti, *Il pensiero debole* (Milan: Feltrinelli, 1983), especially the essay by Vattimo, "Dialettica, differenza, pensiero debole." See also Gianni Vattimo, *La fine della modernità* (Milan: Garzanti, 1985).

15 Volume 2, issue 203 (1982) of *Laboratorio politico* was dedicated to the Historic Compromise (Luigi Graziano, "Il compromesso storico e i dilemmi dell'eurocomunismo," *Democrazia e diritto* 1 [1983]: 98–109).

16 Eric Hobsbawm, "Il marxismo oggi: un bilancio aperto," in *Storia del marxismo* (Turin: Einaudi, 1982), 4:5–52; Louis Althusser, "The Crisis of Marxism," in *Power and Opposition in Post-Revolutionary Societies,* by Rossana Rossanda et al. (London: Ink Links, 1979); Cesare Luporini, "Commemorazione del centenario della morte di Carlo Marx," summary of speech held at the sixteenth PCI congress, in "L'uomo, il politico, lo scienziato," supplement to *L'Unità,* 6 March 1983. Nicos Poulantzas also moved beyond Marxism in his final work, *State, Power, Socialism* (London: New Left Books, 1980), which sought to appropriate Foucault's post-Marxist theories of power.

17 Enrico Berlinguer, "Rinnovamento della politica e rinnovamento del PCI," *Rinascita,* 4 December 1981, 13.

18 Ignazi highlights the confusion in the text by Gruppi cited above in chapter 5, note 107. In relation to representative democracy, "really existing socialism," the revolutionary tradition, and Marxist-Leninism, the party held positions that were contradictory, the fruit more of its practical evolution than an attempt to achieve consistency (*Dal PCI al PDS* [Bologna: Il Mulino, 1992], 42–44).

19 Barbagli and Corbetta found that 79 percent of PCI members thought there was socialism in the USSR, 17 percent that there was not, and 4 percent

did not know. In all respects except the field of civil liberties, the Soviet Union was seen to be a superior society in Italy. Faith in the Soviet model was somewhat less, but still very marked, among the recruits of the 1970s (Marzio Barbagli and Pier Giorgio Corbetta, "Una tattica e due strategie: inchiesta sulla base del PCI," in *Dentro il PCI,* by Marzio Barbagli et al. [Bologna: Il Mulino, 1979], 19–29).

20 Giovanna Guidorossi, *Gli italiani e la politica: valori, opinioni, atteggiamenti dal dopoguerra a oggi* (Milan: Franco Angeli, 1984), 193.

21 Cavalli and De Lillo, *Giovani anni 80.*

22 Renato Mannheimer, "Vecchi e nuovi caratteri del voto comunista," in *Vent'anni di elezioni in Italia, 1968–87,* ed. Mario Caciagli and Alberto Spreafico (Padua: Liviana, 1990), 57, table 4.

23 Loredana Sciolla and Luca Ricolfi, *Vent'anni dopo: saggio su una generazione senza ricordi* (Bologna: Il Mulino, 1989), 106–13. See also Aldo Garzia, "Arcipelago giovani: una ferita antica," *Democrazia e diritto* 26.1 (1986): 139–53.

24 Giorgio Grossi, *Rappresentanza e rappresentazione: percorsi di analisi dell'interazione fra mass media e sistema politico in Italia* (Milan: Franco Angeli, 1985), 141.

25 The changes in political communication are mapped out and discussed in Jader Jacobelli, ed., *La comunicazione politica in Italia* (Bari: Laterza, 1989). See also Antonio Pilati, "Spettacolorizzazione dei mass media e modificazioni del sistema politico italiano," in *Comunicazioni di massa e sistema politico,* by R. Biancheri et al. (Milan: Franco Angeli, 1982).

26 See William E. Porter, "The Mass Media in the Italian Elections of 1979," in *Italy at the Polls, 1979,* ed. Howard R. Penniman (Washington, D.C.: AEI, 1979); and Porter, "The Mass Media in the Italian Elections of 1983," in *Italy at the Polls, 1983,* ed. Howard R. Penniman (Durham, N.C.: AEI/Duke University Press, 1987).

27 On the poor usage of mass communications by the parties see Gabriele Calvi and Giuseppe Minoia, *Gli scomunicanti* (Milan: Lupetti and Co., 1990); and Gianfranco Pasquino, "Alto sgradimento: la comunicazione politica dei partiti," *Problemi dell'informazione* 3.4 (1988): 477–97. See also Paolo Mancini, "Tra di noi: sulla funzione negoziale della comunicazione politica," *Il Mulino* 39.328 (1990): 267–87.

28 Grossi, *Rappresentanza e rappresentazione,* 148–49.

29 Paolo Franchi, "Sistema informativo e dibattito precongressuale," *Problemi del socialismo,* n.s., 6 (1985): 189–201, 193–94; Giuseppe Caldarola, "Giornali comunisti e 'zone franche,'" *Rinascita,* 7 February 1987, 12.

30 See Gianfranco Pasquino, "I mass media e la comunicazione politica," in *La complessità della politica* (Bari: Laterza, 1985), 96–99.

31 Adriano Aprà, "I club-cinema da dove? Verso dove?" in Giovanni Grassi, *L'altro schermo* (Florence: La Nuova Italia, 1983), 23–24.

32 The role of Goffredo Fofi was crucial here. See his *Totò: l'uomo e la maschera* (Rome: Samonà e Savelli, 1972).

33 Silvano Belligni, "Gli amministratori comunisti: un profilo provvisorio e alcune ipotesi," in *Il Partito comunista italiano,* ed. Massimo Ilardi and Aris Accornero (Milan: Feltrinelli, 1982), 505. Both Borgna and Veltroni were councilors in Rome.

34 The Roman model of the *assessorato alla cultura* was widely copied such that all cities administered by the left had one by 1982 (Franco Bianchini, "Cultural Policy and Changes in Urban Political Culture: The 'Post-Modern Response' of the Left in Rome [1976–85] and London [1981–86]," 24, European Consortium for Political Research Politics and Culture Workshop, Amsterdam, April 1987, mimeo).

35 Renato Nicolini, "Se nove anni vi sembrano pochi. . . . La rossa stagione delle giunte" in *Roma perchè: la giunta di sinistra analisi di un' esperienza,* by Giovanni Berlinguer et al. (Rome: Napoleone, 1986), 125.

36 Renato Nicolini, in ARCI, *Il Contributo dell'associazionismo per superare la crisi con lo sviluppo culturale e civile del paese: atti del Congresso nazionale dell'Arci-UISP, Naples 1–3 November 1976,* 25–27.

37 Bianchini, "Cultural Policy and Changes in Urban Political Culture," 26. See also Renato Nicolini, *Estate romana* (Rome: Edizioni Sisifo, 1992). Some wondered how it was that a party as centralized and hierarchical as the PCI conceded Nicolini so much freedom. The answer lies in the breakdown of conventional command structures that accompanied the sudden transfer of officials from the party to the commune. "I waited for the whole of 1976 for some comrade from the secretariat to call me to present the lines along which I should have moved," Nicolini wrote, "before I finally grasped a novelty that demanded creativity and personal initiative. More than a lot of theoretical discussions on democratic centralism, the experience immediately after 1976 was decisive in liquidating residues of leaderism, mythologies, and the temptations of a party that itself controls all the articulations of civil society" (in "Se nove anni vi sembrano pochi," 123).

38 Rita Tripodi, "Nicolini di tutta Italia, unitevi!" *L'Espresso,* 18 November 1970, 119–30; Stephen Gundle, "Urban Dreams and Metropolitan Nightmares: Models and Crises of Communist Local Government in Italy," in *Marxist Local Governments in Western Europe and Japan,* ed. Bogdan Szajkowski (London: Pinter, 1986), 88. See also F. M. Petrone, "Tutta la città ne parla," *Rinascita,* 27 July 1979, 16–17.

39 Interview published in *La Repubblica* (Roman edition), 19 July 1979 (page unnumbered). Some of the points listed here are mentioned in Giovanni Bechelloni, *L'immaginario quotidiano: televisione e cultura di massa in Italia* (Turin: ERI, 1984), 55–56.

40 Mauro Felicori, "Feste d'estate: indagine sulla politica culturale dei com-

uni italiani," in *Luoghi e misure della politica,* ed. Arturo Parisi (Bologna: Il Mulino, 1984), 151–52.

41 The most celebrated attack was launched by Claudio Magris and Tito Perlini in "La cultura ridotta a spettacolo," published in *Il Corriere della sera* in two parts on 6 October 1981 and 7 October 1981, reproduced in *Il PCI e la cultura di massa,* ed. Oreste Massari (Rome: Savelli, 1982), 129–40. There was wide press debate, especially in 1979 and 1981. Felicori in fact shows that large sums of public money were not involved. The spending on culture in Rome was one-third of that spent in Bologna and Turin, whereas center and center-right local administrations consistently spent more than their left-wing counterparts (Felicori, "Feste d'estate," 171, 181).

42 Alberto Abruzzese, "L'effimero non lascia edifici, ma modelli," *Rinascita,* 7 December 1979, 29; Gianni Borgna, "Dagli all'effimero," *Rinascita,* 31 August 1985, 15–16.

43 Alberto Abruzzese, "Il funzionamento simultaneo degli apparati di informazione," *La Società* 25–26 (1979): 83.

44 Gianni Borgna, *La grande evasione* (Rome: Savelli, 1980); and Borgna, "Apologia del Festival di San Remo," *L'Unità,* 13 February 1986, 1, 16; Walter Veltroni, ed., *Il calcio è una scienza da amare* (Rome: Savelli, 1982); and Veltroni, *Il sogno degli anni '60* (Rome: Savelli, 1981); Ferdinando Adornato, ed., *Eroi del nostro tempo* (Bari: Laterza, 1986). See also Stephen Gundle, "From *apocalittici* to *integrati*: The PCI and the Culture Industry in the 1970s and 1980s," *Newsletter of the Association for the Study of Modern Italy* 11 (1987): 15–17. While Borgna and Veltroni rose to key positions in the PCI apparatus, Adornato became head of the cultural department of *L'Espresso* and eventually left the party.

45 Alberto Abruzzese, *Il fantasma fracassone: PCI e politica della cultura* (Rome: Lerici, 1982); Stefania Rossini, "Lo strappino," *L'Espresso,* 14 November 1982, 131–39. Despite his claim that the PCI was unreceptive to his views, Abruzzese wrote regularly for *La Rinascita* and was approached by the party to join the management committee of Rome's *Teatro stabile.* He resigned from this post in 1982.

46 The proceedings of the assembly's June 1981 meeting are collected in Massari, *Il PCI e la cultura di massa.*

47 Forgacs, *Italian Culture in the Industrial Era,* 170. It is impossible to list here all the documents and materials through which new positions took shape. The following, however, should be noted: Giuseppe Vacca, ed., *Comunicazioni di massa e democrazia* (Rome: Editori Riuniti, 1980); Commissione culturale del PCI, *Pubblico e privato nella cultura, nella scuola e nella ricerca,* papers from the national conference held on 12–13 January 1987; Walter Veltroni, *Io e Berlusconi* (Rome: Editori Riuniti, 1990). Vacca's role was also important; see, for example, his essay, "La

cultura dei media nella sinistra italiana," in *Il video negli anni '80,* ed. Giuseppe Richeri (Bari: De Donato, 1981).

48 See Grossi, *Rappresentanza e rappresentazione,* 128–37.

49 Alberto Leiss, "La difficile scommessa dell'*Unità*: il quotidiano del PCI tra crisi e riforma," *Problemi dell'informazione* 11.1 (1986): 25–46. The paper's debts rose from 9.7 billion lire in 1980 to 16.6 billion in 1982. See also Giovanni Bechelloni and Milly Buonanno, "Il quotidiano del partito: *'l'Unità,'*" in Ilardi and Accornero, *Il Partito comunista italiano.*

50 Giorgio Fabre, "Prima che la festa cominci," *Rinascita,* 21 February 1987, 11. By comparison, the Socialists' *Avantì* festivals attracted four million visitors and the DC's *feste dell amicizia,* six million. On the organization of the *L'Unità* festivals see Cooperativa Soci de *l'Unità, Il dì di festa* (Rome: Editrice il meto, 1987).

51 Compare Francesco Neri, "Non sono un'industria," *Rinascita,* 28 March 1987, 13. After the mid-1980s the PCI could simply not organize or afford to risk holding national festivals in such places as Naples or Venice. They were always located in Bologna, Modena, or other cities with a strong party presence.

52 Beppe Attene, "Relazione introduttiva," *Atti della seconda conferenze nazionale di organizzazione dell'arci, Turin, June 1979* (Rome: Edizioni Arci, 1979), 12–23; ARCI, *VIII Congresso nazionale 26–29 June 1986 Abano: materiali per la discussione* (Rome: Edizioni Arci, 1986), 6–11.

53 Rino Serri, "Arci: perchè la scelta confederale," *Rinascita,* 19 December 1987, 14.

7. The Last Tango: The Collapse of Communism and the Dissolution of the PCI

1 *L'Unità,* 28 June 1987, 13; 29 June 1987, 9.

2 Gavino Angius, *L'Unità,* 28 June 1987, 9.

3 Giorgio Napolitano, *L'Unità,* 27 June 1987, 10; Gavino Angius, *L'Unità,* 26 June 1987, 13.

4 Armando Cossutta, *L'Unità,* 27 June 1987, 12.

5 There were some isolated voices, mostly on the right of the party, who argued that the new course consisted more of headline grabbing than substance. See Napoleone Colajanni, *La resistibile ascesa di Achille Occhetto* (Florence: Ponte alle Grazie, 1989), 11, 54–58.

6 Piero Ignazi, *Dal PCI al PDS* (Bologna: Il Mulino, 1992).

7 See Adolfo Chiesa, *La satira politica in Italia* (Bari: Laterza, 1990), 284. The whole of chapter 12 is dedicated to *Tango.*

8 Only three or four of the forty contributors to *Tango* were actually members of the PCI. Staino recounted the origins of the supplement in an interview in *Oggi*: "I compagni se la ridono," 17 September 1986, 74–76.

9   *Tango,* 7 April 1986, 2.

10 Mino Fucillo, "Trieste," *La Repubblica,* 18 June 1988, 6.

11 Ibid., 56.

12 Ibid.

13 Fortebraccio's writings, already collected in numerous volumes published by Editori Riuniti, were reprinted in *Cuore.*

14 See Serra's high praise for the concept of austerity in "Dopo la sconfitta," published in *L'Unità* in June 1987 and reproduced in Serra, *Ridateci la Potëmkin* (Milan: Mondadori, 1988).

15 As Gerardo Chiaromonte later wrote, "all of us in the directorate — and members of the secretariat too — learned the news from the press on Monday morning" (*Col senno di poi* [Rome: Editori Riuniti, 1990], 217).

16 See Umberto Eco, "A Guide to the Neo-Television of the 1980s," in *Culture and Conflict in Postwar Italy,* ed. Zygmunt Baranski and Robert Lumley (London: Macmillan, 1990).

17 David Kertzer, "The Nineteenth Congress of the PCI: The Role of Symbolism in the Communist Crisis," in *Italian Politics: A Review,* vol. 6, ed. Robert Leonardi and Fausto Anderlini (London: Pinter, 1992), 87.

18 See "Antonio Gramsci dopo la caduta di tutti i muri," supplement to *L'Unità,* 15 January 1991.

19 See Ritanna Armenni and Vicki De Marchi, eds., *"Chiamateci compagni": cronache della Rifondazione comunista* (Rome: Edizioni Associate, 1991).

20 Ignazi, *Dal PCI al PDS,* 152–53.

Conclusion

1   John Dunn, *The Politics of Socialism: An Essay in Political Theory* (Cambridge: Cambridge University Press, 1984), 3.

2   On these points see Donald Sassoon, *One Hundred Years of Socialism: The West European Left in the Twentieth Century* (London: I. B. Tauris, 1996), chap. 1.

3   Leonardo Paggi, *Americanismo e riformismo: la socialdemocrazia europea nell'economia mondiale aperta* (Turin: Einaudi, 1989), 127.

4   Michael Mann, "Ruling Class Strategies and Citizenship," in *States, War, Capitalism* (Oxford: Basil Blackwell, 1989), 206.

5   D. W. Ellwood, *Rebuilding Europe: Western Europe, America, and Postwar Reconstruction, 1945–1955* (London: Longman, 1992), chap. 12.

6   See Ronald Inglehart, *The Silent Revolution: Changing Values and Political Style among Western Publics* (Princeton: Princeton University Press, 1977) and *Culture Shift in Advanced Industrial Society* (Princeton: Princeton University Press, 1990).

Bibliography

Archival Sources

Archive of the Partito comunista italiano, Istituto Gramsci, Rome
    Minutes of the meetings of the directorate, 1944–58
    Minutes of the meetings of the cultural commission, 1948–58
    Papers concerning *L'Unità* and *Vie Nuove*
    Papers of the Tuscan Federation of the PCI
Published documents and conference proceedings of the PCI and ARCI

Journals, Magazines, and Newspapers

Calendario del Popolo, Il, labor movement weekly
Cinema Nuovo, left-wing film periodical
Contemporaneo, Il, left-wing cultural journal
Critica marxista, Communist theoretical and policy journal
Cronache del cinema e della televisione, Catholic media journal
Democrazia e diritto, Communist-area journal of law and society
Emilia, left cultural journal
Epoca, news weekly
Espresso, L', news weekly
Famiglia Cristiana, Catholic illustrated weekly
Muzak, pop music and New Left politics
Noi Donne, magazine of the left-wing women's association (UDI)
Nuova Generazione, Communist youth journal
Nuovi Argomenti, left cultural journal
Oggi, illustrated weekly
Ombre rosse, New Left politics and culture
Ore libere, Le, magazine of ARCI
Pagina, Socialist-area discussion journal
Panorama, news weekly
Politecnico, Il, left-wing cultural periodical
Quaderni piacentini, New Left theoretical journal

Quaderno dell'attivista, Il, periodical for communist activists
Rassegna del film, film news and reviews
Re Nudo, underground magazine
Rinascita, Communist monthly, later weekly
Società, La, local Communist periodical, Bologna
Studi storici, Communist-area history journal
Unità, L', Communist daily
Verità, La, local Communist weekly, Modena
Vie Nuove, Communist illustrated weekly

Selected Books and Articles

Abruzzese, Alberto. *Il fantasma fracassone: PCI e politica della cultura.* Rome: Lerici, 1982.

Abruzzese, Alberto, and Francesco Pinto. "La radiotelevisione." In *Letteratura italiana.* Vol. 2, *Produzione e consumo,* edited by Alberto Asor Rosa. Turin: Einaudi, 1983.

Abse, Tobias. "Judging the PCI." *New Left Review* 153 (1985): 5–40.

———. "Reply to Gundle." *New Left Review* 163 (1987): 27–39.

Accornero, Aris, Renato Mannheimer, and Chiara Sebastiani, eds. *L'identità comunista.* Rome: Editori Riuniti, 1983.

Adornato, Ferdinando, ed. *Eroi del nostro tempo.* Bari: Laterza, 1986.

Ajello, Nello. *Intellettuali e PCI, 1944–1958.* Bari: Laterza, 1979.

Alberoni, Francesco, et al. *L'attivista di partito.* Bologna: Il Mulino, 1967.

Amendola, Eva Paola, and Marcella Ferrara. *É la festa: quarant'anni con l'Unità.* Rome: Editori Riuniti, 1984.

Amendola, Giorgio. *Classe operaia e programmazione democratica.* Rome: Editori Riuniti, 1966.

———. *La classe operaia italiana.* Rome: Editori Riuniti, 1968.

Amyot, Grant. *The Italian Communist Party: The Crisis of the Popular Front Strategy.* London: Croom Helm, 1981.

Anderson, Perry. *Considerations on Western Marxism.* London: New Left Books, 1976.

Anelli, Maria Teresa, et al. *Fotoromanzo: fascino e pregiudizio – storia, documenti e immagini di un grande fenomeno popolare (1946–1978).* Rome: Savelli, 1979.

Angelini, Pietro, ed. *Dibattito sulla cultura delle classi subalterne (1949–50).* Rome: Savelli, 1977.

Arbizzani, Luigi, Saveria Bologna, and Lidia Testoni, eds. *Storie di Case del Popolo: saggi, documenti e immagini d'Emilia Romagna.* Bologna: Grafis, 1982.

Aristarco, Guido, ed. *Sciolti dal giuramento; il dibattito critico-ideologico sul cinema negli anni cinquanta.* Bari: Dedalo, 1981.

Asor Rosa, Alberto. *Le due società: ipotesi sulla crisi italiana.* Turin: Einaudi, 1977.

Baccetti, Carlo, and Mario Caciagli. "Dopo il PCI e dopo l'Urss: una subcultura rossa rivisitata." *Polis* 6.3 (1992): 537–68.

Baglioni, Guido. *I giovani nella società industriale.* Milan: Vita e Pensiero, 1962.

Bairati, Piero. *Vittorio Valletta.* Turin: UTET, 1987.

Balbo, Laura. *Lettere da vicino: per una possibile reinvenzione della sinistra.* Turin: Einaudi, 1986.

Baldelli, Pio. *Politica culturale e comunicazioni di massa.* Pisa: Nistri-Lischi, 1968.

Ballio, Laura, and Adriano Zanacchi. *Carosello story.* Turin: ERI, 1987.

Baranski, Zygmunt, and Robert Lumley, eds. *Culture and Conflict in Postwar Italy.* London: Macmillan, 1990.

Barbagli, Marzio, et al. *Dentro il PCI.* Bologna: Il Mulino, 1979.

Bassi, Paolo, and Pilati, Antonio. *I giovani e la crisi degli anni settanta.* Rome: Editori Riuniti, 1978.

Becciù, Leonardo. *Il fumetto in Italia.* Florence: Sansoni, 1971.

Bechelloni, Giovanni. *L'immaginario quotidiano: televisione e cultura di massa in Italia.* Turin: ERI, 1984.

———, ed. *Politica culturale? studi, materiali, ipotesi.* Bologna: Guaraldi, 1970.

Bedeschi, Giuseppe. *La parabola del marxismo in Italia.* Bari: Laterza, 1983.

Berlinguer, Enrico. "Lo stato del partito in rapporto alle modificazioni della società italiana." *Critica marxista* 1.5–6 (1963): 194–216.

———. *La proposta comunista.* Turin: Einaudi, 1975.

———. *Austerità: un'occasione per trasformare l'Italia.* Rome: Editori Riuniti, 1977.

Berlinguer, Enrico, et al. *Il ruolo dei giovani comunisti.* Florence: Guaraldi, 1976.

Berlinguer, Giovanni. *Dieci anni dopo: cronache culturali, 1968–1978.* Bari: De Donato, 1978.

Berlinguer, Giovanni, et al. *Roma perchè: la giunta di sinistra analisi di un'esperienza.* Rome: Napoleone, 1986.

Bernieri, Claudio. *L'Albero in piazza: storia, cronaca e leggenda delle Feste dell'Unità.* Milan: Mazzotta, 1977.

Bertelli, Sergio. *Il gruppo: la formazione del gruppo dirigente del PCI, 1936–1948.* Milan: Rizzoli, 1980.

Biancheri, R., et al. *Comunicazioni di massa e sistema politico.* Milan: Franco Angeli, 1982.

Blackmer, Donald, and Sidney Tarrow, eds. *Il comunismo in Italia e in Francia.* Milan: Etas Libri, 1976.

Bocca, Giorgio. *Miracolo all'italiana,* 2d ed. Milan: Feltrinelli, 1980.

Bologna, Saveria. "Associazionismo culturale e mutamento sociale: le Case del Popolo nella provincia di Bologna." Dott. Lett. thesis, Università degli Studi di Bologna, 1979–80.

Borghello, Giampaolo. *Linea rossa: intellettuali, letteratura e lotta di classe, 1965–1975.* Venice: Marsilio, 1982.

Borgna, Gianni. *La grande evasione.* Rome: Savelli, 1980.

———. *Il tempo della musica: i giovani da Elvis Presley a Sophie Marceau.* Bari: Laterza, 1983.

Bosio, Gianni. *L'intellettuale rovesciato.* Milan: Edizioni del Gallo, 1967.

Brunetta, Gian Piero. *Storia del cinema italiano dal 1945 agli anni Ottanta.* Rome: Editori Riuniti, 1982.

Bufalini, Paolo. *Il divorzio in Italia.* Rome: Editori Riuniti, 1974.

Caciagli, Mario, and Alberto Spreafico, eds. *Vent'anni di elezioni in Italia, 1968–87.* Padua: Liviana, 1990.

Calabrese, Omar. *Carosello o dell'educazione serale.* Florence: cleuf, 1975.

Calandrone, Giacomo. *Un comunista in Sicilia, 1946–1951.* Rome: Editori Riuniti, 1972.

Calvi, Gabriele, and Giuseppe Minoia. *Gli scomunicanti.* Milan: Lupetti and Co., 1990.

Capecchi, Vittorio. "Classe operaia e cultura borghese: ipotesi di ricerca in Emilia-Romagna." In *Famiglia operaia, mutamento culturale, 150 ore,* edited by Vittorio Capecchi et al. Bologna: Il Mulino, 1982.

Carrera, Alessandro. *Musica e pubblico giovanile.* Milan: Feltrinelli, 1980.

Casali, Luciano, and Dianella Gagliani. "Movimento operaio e organizzazioni di massa: il PCI in Emilia-Romagna (1945–54)." In *La ricostruzione in Emilia-Romagna,* edited by Pier Paolo D'Attorre, Istituto Gramsci–Emilia-Romagna. Parma: Pratiche, 1980.

Castronovo, Valerio. *La storia economica.* In *Storia d'Italia.* Vol. 4, tome 1. Turin: Einaudi, 1975.

Cavalli, Alessandro, and Antonio De Lillo. *Giovani anni '80.* Bologna: Il Mulino, 1986.

Cavallo, Pietro. "America sognata, America desiderata: mito e immagini Usa in Italia dall sbarco alla fine della guerra." *Storia contemporanea* 4 (1985): 751–85.

Chiarante, Giuseppe. *La rivolta degli studenti.* Rome: Editori Riuniti, 1968.

Chiarenza, Franco. *Il cavallo morente: trent'anni di radiotelevisione italiana.* Milan: Bompiani, 1978.

———. *Le scelte della solidarietà democratica: cronache ricordi e riflessioni sul triennio, 1976–1979.* Rome: Editori Riuniti, 1986.

———. *Col senno di poi.* Rome: Editori Riuniti, 1990.

Chiesa, Adolfo. *La satira politica in Italia.* Bari: Laterza, 1990.

Colasio, Andrea. "Il processo ai Pionieri di Pozzonovo: forme di conflitto politico nel Veneto degli anni '50." *Venetica* 2 (1984): 40–62.

———. "L'organizzazione del PCI e la crisi del 1956." In *La sinistra e il '56 in Italia e in Francia,* edited by B. Groppo and G. Riccamboni. Padua: Liviana, 1987.

Colorni, Giorgio, ed. *Storie comuniste: passato e presente di una sezione del PCI a Milano.* Milan: Feltrinelli, 1979.

Dalla Costa, Ivo. *Pietro Dal Pozzo: un testimone del nostro tempo.* Treviso: ACPTV, 1987.

Dalton, Russell, Scott Flanagan, and Paul A. Beck, eds. *Electoral Change in Advanced Industrial Societies: Realignment or Dealignment?* Princeton, N.J.: Princeton University Press, 1984.

D'Apice, Carmela. *L'arcipelago dei consumi.* Bari: De Donato, 1981.

D'Attorre, Pier Paolo, ed. *Nemici per la pelle: sogno americano e mito sovietico nell'Italia contemporanea.* Milan: Franco Angeli, 1991.

De Castris, Arcangelo Leone, ed. *Ideologia letteraria e scuola di massa: per un'analisi sociale dell'organizzazione didattica.* Bari: De Donato, 1975.

De Grazia, Victoria. *The Culture of Consent: Mass Organisation of Leisure in Fascist Italy.* Cambridge: Cambridge University Press, 1981.

Delli Colli, Laura. *Dadaumpa: storie, immagini, curiosita e personaggi di trent'anni di televisione in Italia.* Rome: Gremese, 1984.

De Luigi, Mario. *L'industria discografica in Italia.* Rome: Lato Side, 1982.

De Mauro, Tullio. *Storia linguistica dell'Italia unita.* Bari: Laterza, 1986.

De Rita, Lidia. *I contadini e la televisione.* Bologna: Il Mulino, 1964.

De Sanctis, Filippo M. *Pubblico e associazionismo culturale.* Rome: Bulzoni, 1976.

Di Loreto, Pietro. *Togliatti e la "doppiezza".* Bologna: Il Mulino, 1991.

Di Nolfo, Ennio. *Le paure e le speranze degli italiani (1943–1953).* Milan: Mondadori, 1986.

Dunn, John. *The Politics of Socialism: An Essay in Political Theory.* Cambridge: Cambridge University Press, 1984.

Eco, Umberto. *Apocalittici e integrati.* Milan: Bompiani, 1964.

Ellwood, D. W. *Italy, 1943–45.* Leicester: Leicester University Press, 1985.

———. *Rebuilding Europe: Western Europe, America, and Postwar Reconstruction, 1945–1955.* London: Longman, 1992.

Ellwood, D. W., and Gian Piero Brunetta, eds. *Hollywood in Europa, 1945–1960.* Florence: Ponte alle Grazie, 1991.

Fabrizio, Felice. *Storia dello sport in Italia: dalle società ginnastiche all'associazionismo di massa.* Florence-Rimini: Guaraldi, 1977.

Fadini, Eduardo, *La storia di Dario Fo.* Milan: Feltrinelli, 1977.

Faenza, Liliano. *Comunismo e cattolicesimo in una parrocchia di campagna: vent'anni dopo (1959–1979).* Bologna: Cappelli, 1979.

Faldini, Franca, and Goffredo Fofi, eds. *L'avventurosa storia del cinema italiano — raccontato dai suoi protagonisti, 1935–59.* Milan: Feltrinelli, 1979.

———. *L'avventurosa storia del cinema italiano — raccontato dai suoi protagonisti, 1960–1969.* Milan: Feltrinelli, 1981.

Farassino, Alberto. *Giuseppe De Santis.* Milan: Moizzi, 1978.

Ferrara, Giovanni. *Ferrara con furore.* Edited by Giampiero Mughini. Milan: Leonardo, 1990.

Ferretti, Gian Carlo. *"Officina": cultura, letteratura, e politica negli anni Cinquanta.* Turin: Einaudi, 1975.

———. *Il mercato delle lettere: industria culturale e lavoro critico in Italia dagli anni Cinquanta a oggi.* Turin: Einaudi, 1979.

Filippa, Marcella, et al. *Solidarietà e classe operaia: contributi per una storia sociale.* Rome: Ediesse, 1988.

Fiori, Giuseppe. *Antonio Gramsci: Life of a Revolutionary.* New York: Schocken, 1970.

———. *Vita di Enrico Berlinguer.* Bari: Laterza, 1989.

Flores, Marcello, and Nicola Gallerano. *Sul PCI: un'interpretazione storica.* Bologna: Il Mulino, 1992.

Fofi, Goffredo. *Il cinema italiano: servi e padroni.* Milan: Feltrinelli, 1971.

———, ed. *Totò: l'uomo e la maschera.* Rome: Samona e Savelli, 1972.

Forgacs, David. *Italian Culture in the Industrial Era, 1880–1980.* Manchester: Manchester University Press, 1990.

Fortini, Franco. *Dieci inverni.* Bari: Dedalo, 1957.

Franchi, Maura, and Vittorio Reiser. *Esperienza e cultura dei delegati.* Reggio Emilia: Bonhoeffer, 1984.

Galli, Giorgio. *Il bipartitismo imperfetto: comunisti e democristiani in Italia.* Bologna: Il Mulino, 1966.

Galli della Loggia, Ernesto. "Ideologie, classi, costume." In *Italia contemporanea, 1945–75,* edited by Valerio Castronovo. Turin: Einaudi, 1976.

Galli della Loggia, Ernesto, et al. *Il trionfo del privato.* Bari: Laterza, 1980.

Galluzzi, Carlo. *Garibaldi fu ferito.* Milan: Sperling and Kupfer, 1985.

———. *Togliatti Longo Berlinguer.* Milan: Sperling and Kupfer, 1989.

Gambetti, Fidia. *Comunista perchè come.* Rome: Vecchiarelli, 1992.

———. *Dietro la vetrina a Botteghe Oscure.* Soveria Mannelli: Rubbettino, 1989.

Gambino, Antonio, et al., ed. *Dal '68 a oggi: come siamo e come eravamo.* Bari: Laterza, 1979.

Giasanti, Alberto. *La controriforma universitaria: da Gonella a Malfatti.* Milan: Mazzotta, 1977.

Ginsborg, Paul. *A History of Contemporary Italy: Society and Politics, 1943–1988.* Harmondsworth: Penguin, 1990.

Gori, Giovanni, and Stefano Pivato. *Gli anni del cinema di parrocchia.* Rimini: Bianco e Nero, undated.

Gorresio, Vittorio. *I carissimi nemici.* 1949. Reprint, Milan: Bompiani, 1977.

Gramsci, Antonio. *Lettere dal carcere.* Turin: Einaudi, 1947.

———. *Il materialismo storico e la filosofia di Benedetto Croce.* Turin: Einaudi, 1948.

———. *Gli intellettuali e l'organizzazione della cultura.* Turin: Einaudi, 1949.

――. *Il Risorgimento.* Turin: Einaudi, 1949.

――. *Note su Machiavelli, sulla politica e sullo Stato moderno.* Turin: Einaudi, 1949.

――. *Letteratura e vita nazionale.* Turin: Einaudi, 1950.

――. *Passato e presente.* Turin: Einaudi, 1951.

――. *Quaderni del carcere.* Vols. 1–4, edited by Valentino Gerratana. Turin: Einaudi, 1975.

Grimaldi, Ugoberto Alfassio, and Italo Bertoni. *I giovani degli anni sessanta.* Bari: Laterza, 1964.

Grossi, Giorgio. *Rappresentanza e rappresentazione: percorsi di analisi dell'interazione fra mass media e sistema politica in Italia.* Milan: Franco Angeli, 1985.

Guizzardi, Gustavo. "Potere, ideologia, organizazioni e classi sociali." In *La DC dal fascismo al 18 aprile,* edited by Mario Isenghi and Silvio Lanaro. Venice: Marsilio, 1978.

Gundle, Stephen. "Urban Dreams and Metropolitan Nightmares: Models and Crises of Communist Local Government in Italy." In *Marxist Local Governments in Western Europe and Japan,* edited by Bogdan Sjaikowski. London: Pinter, 1986.

――. "L'americanizzazione del quotidiano: televisione e consumismo nell'Italia degli anni Cinquanta." *Quaderni storici* 21.62/2 (1986): 561–94.

――. "From *apocalittici* to *integrati*: The PCI and the Culture Industry in the 1970s and 1980s." *Newsletter of the Association for the Study of Modern Italy* 11 (1987): 15–17.

――. "The PCI and the Historic Compromise." *New Left Review* 163 (1987): 27–39.

――. "From Neorealism to *Luci rosse*: Cinema, Politics, and Society, 1945–85." In *Culture and Conflict in Postwar Italy,* edited by Zygmunt Baranski and Robert Lumley. London: Macmillan, 1990.

――. "Cultura di massa e modernizzazione: *Vie Nuove* e *Famiglia Cristiana* dalla guerra fredda alla società dei consumi." In D'Attorre, *Nemici per la pelle.*

――. "Il PCI e la campagna contro Hollywood (1948–1958)." In Ellwood and Brunetta, *Hollywood in Europa.*

――. "The Legacy of the Prison Notebooks: Gramsci, the PCI, and Italian Culture in the Cold War Era." In *Italy in the Cold War: Politics, Culture, and Society, 1948–1958,* edited by Christopher Duggan and Christopher Wagstaff. Oxford: Berg, 1995.

――. "La 'religione civile' della resistenza: cultura di massa e identità politica nell'Italia del dopoguerra." In *L'immagine della resistenza in Europa, 1945–60,* edited by Luisa Cigognetti, Lorenza Servetti, and Pierre Sorlin. Bologna: Il Nove, 1996.

Hellman, Judith Adler. *Journeys among Women.* Cambridge: Polity Press, 1987.

Hellman, Stephen. *Italian Communism in Transition: The Rise and Fall of the Historic Compromise in Turin, 1975–80.* New York: Oxford University Press, 1988.

Hewitt, Nicholas, ed. *The Culture of Reconstruction: Literature, Film, and Thought in France, Germany, and Italy, 1945–50.* London: Macmillan, 1989.

Ignazi, Piero, ed. *Dal PCI al PDS.* Bologna: Il Mulino, 1992.

Ilardi, Massimo, and Aris Accornero, eds. *Il Partito comunista italiano: struttura e storia dell'organizzazione 1921–1979.* Milan: Feltrinelli, 1982.

Ingrao, Pietro. *Masse e potere.* Rome: Editori Riuniti, 1972.

——. *Tradizione e progetto.* Bari: De Donato, 1982.

——. *Le cose impossibili: un'autobiografia raccontata e discussa con Nicola Tranfaglia.* Rome: Editori Riuniti, 1990.

Istituto Gramsci. *Studi gramsciani – atti del convegno tenuto a Roma nei giorni 11–13 gennaio 1958.* Rome: Editori Riuniti, 1958.

——. *Tendenze del capitalismo italiano: atti del covegno di Roma 23–25 marzo 1962.* Rome: Editori Riuniti, 1962.

——. *Il marxismo italiano degli anni sessanta: la formazione teorico-politica delle nuove generazioni.* Rome: Editori Riuniti, 1972.

——. *La crisi della società italiana e gli orientamenti delle nuove generazioni.* Rome: Editori Riuniti, 1978.

Jacobelli, Jader, ed. *La comunicazione politica in Italia.* Bari: Laterza, 1989.

Jocteau, Gian Carlo. *Leggere Gramsci.* Milan: Feltrinelli, 1975.

Lajolo, Davide. *I rossi.* Milan: Rizzoli, 1974.

——. *Ventiquattro anni.* Milan: Rizzoli, 1981.

Lanaro, Silvio. *Storia dell'Italia repubblicana.* Venice: Marsilio, 1992.

Lazar, Marc. "PCF e PCI: alla ricerca dei popoli perduti." *Passato e presente* 27 (1991): 69–104.

——. *Maisons rouges: les Partis communistes français et italien de la Libération à nos jours.* Paris: Aubier, 1992.

Leiss, Alberto. "La difficile scommessa dell'*Unità*: il quotidiano del PCI tra crisi e riforma." *Problemi dell'informazione* 11.1 (1986): 25–46.

Leonesi, Luciano. *Il romanzo del Teatro di Massa.* Bologna: Cappelli, 1989.

Lerner, Gad. *Operai.* Milan: Feltrinelli, 1988.

Lerner, Gad, Luigi Marconi, and Mario Sinibaldi. *Uno strano movimento di strani studenti.* Milan: Feltrinelli, 1978.

Lumley, Robert. *States of Emergency: Cultures of Revolt in Italy from 1968 to 1978.* London: Verso, 1990.

Luperini, Romano. *Marxismo e gli intellettuali.* Venice: Marsilio, 1974.

Manoukian, Agopik, ed. *La presenza sociale del PCI e della DC.* Bologna: Il Mulino, 1968.

Marino, Giuseppe Carlo. *Autoritratto del PCI staliniano, 1946–1953.* Rome: Editori Riuniti, 1991.

Massari, Oreste, ed. *Il PCI e la cultura di massa.* Rome: Savelli, 1982.

Mazzeri, Catia. "Comunisti emiliani e cultura popolare (1945–56)." Dott. Lett. thesis, Università degli Studi di Bologna, 1979–80.

———. "Comunisti e cultura a Modena negli anni della ricostruzione (1945–54)." *Rassegna di Storia dell'Istituto Storico della Resistenza in Modena e provincia* 1.1, n.s. (1981): 89–104.

McCarthy, Patrick. "Era possibile gestire il compromesso storico?" *Polis* 4.2 (1990): 361–70.

Mellor, Ian David. *Italy through a Looking Glass, 1943–64.* Lugano: private publication, 1964.

Miccichè, Lino, ed. *Il Neorealismo cinematografico italiano.* Venice: Marsilio, 1975.

Misler, Nicoletta. *La via italiana al realismo: la politica culturale artistica del PCI dal 1944 al 1956.* Milan: Mazzotta, 1973.

Morandi, Arrigo, et al. *Cultura di massa e istituzioni.* Bari: De Donato, 1976.

Mussi, Fabio, et al. *I giovani e la crisi della società.* Rome: Editori Riuniti, 1977.

Napolitano, Giorgio, et al. *Confronto su un programma a medio termine.* Rome: Editori Riuniti, 1976.

Negri, Toni. *Dall'operaio massa all'operaio sociale.* Milan: Feltrinelli, 1979.

Nicolini, Renato. *Estate romana.* Rome: Edizioni Sisifo, 1992.

Ortoleva, Peppino. *Saggio sui movimenti del 1968 in Europa e in America.* Rome: Editori Riuniti, 1988.

Paggi, Leonardo. *Americanismo e riformismo: la socialdemocrazia europea nell'economia mondiale aperta.* Turin: Einaudi, 1989.

Paggi, Leonardo, and Massimo D'Angelillo. *I comunisti italiani e il riformismo.* Turin: Einaudi, 1986.

Parisi, Arturo, ed. *Luoghi e misure della politica.* Bologna: Il Mulino, 1984.

Pasquino, Gianfranco. *La complessità della politica.* Bari: Laterza, 1985.

———, ed. *Mass media e sistema politico.* Milan: Franco Angeli, 1986.

Passerini, Luisa. *Autoritratto di gruppo.* Florence: Giunti, 1988.

Pezzoli, Orlando. *È storia: Casa del popolo Nerio Nannetti–Santa Viola, Bologna.* Bologna: PCI zona Santa Viola, 1981.

Piccone Stella, Simonetta. "All'origine della cultura giovanile negli anni sessanta: trasgressività, esibizionismo, nuovi consumi." *Problemi del socialismo* 13 (1991): 124–49.

Piccone Stella, Simonetta, and Annabella Rossi. *La fatica di leggere.* Rome: Editori Riuniti, 1964.

Pinto, Francesco, ed. *Intellettuali e tv negli anni '50.* Rome: Savelli, 1977.

Pizzorno, Alessandro. *Comunità e razionalizzazione.* Turin: Einaudi, 1960.

Pronay, Nicholas, and Keith Wilson, eds. *The Political Re-education of Germany and Her Allies.* London: Croom Helm, 1985.

Quaglietti, Lorenzo. *Storia economico-politica del cinema italiano, 1945–1980.* Rome: Editori Riuniti, 1980.

Rauty, Raffaele, ed. *Cultura popolare e marxismo*. Rome: Editori Riuniti, 1976.

Richeri, Giuseppe, ed. *Il video negli anni '80*. Bari: De Donato, 1981.

Rositi, Franco. *Informazione e complessità sociale: critica delle politiche culturali in Italia*. Bari: De Donato, 1978.

Rossanda, Rossana. "Sulla politica culturale e gli intellettuali." *Problemi del socialismo*, n.s., 6 (1985): 159–77.

Salinari, Carlo. *La questione del realismo*. Florence: Parenti, 1960.

Sassoon, Donald. *The Strategy of the Italian Communist Party*. London: Pinter, 1981.

———. *One Hundred Years of Socialism: The West European Left in the Twentieth Century*. London: I. B. Tauris, 1996.

Sciolla, Loredana, and Luca Ricolfi. *Vent'anni dopo: saggio su una generazione senza ricordi*. Bologna: Il Mulino, 1989.

Sereni, Emilio. *Scienza, marxismo, cultura*. Milan: Edizioni sociali, 1949.

Seroni, Adriana. *La questione femminile in Italia, 1976–77*. Rome: Editori Riuniti, 1977.

Serra, Michele. *Ridateci la Potëmkin*. Milan: Mondadori, 1988.

Spinazzola, Vittorio. *Cinema e pubblico*. Milan: Bompiani, 1974.

Spriano, Paolo. *Storia del partito comunista italiano*. Vol. 5, *La Resistenza, Togliatti e il partito nuovo*. Turin: Einaudi, 1975.

Tarrow, Sidney. *Democracy and Disorder: Protest and Politics in Italy, 1965–75*. Oxford: Oxford University Press, 1989.

Tinacci Mannelli, Gilberto. *L'immagine del potere*. Milan: Franco Angeli, 1986.

Togliatti, Palmiro. *Opere*. 6 vols. Rome: Editori Riuniti, 1972–84.

———. *Gramsci*. Edited by Ernesto Ragionieri. Rome: Editori Riuniti, 1967.

———. *Memoriale di Yalta*. Rome: Editori Riuniti, 1970.

———. *La politica culturale*. Edited by Luciano Gruppi. Rome: Editori Riuniti, 1974.

———. *I corsivi di Roderigo: interventi politico-culturali dal 1944 al 1964*. Edited by Ottavio Cecchi, Giovanni Leone, and Giuseppe Vacca. Bari: De Donato, 1976.

Toti, Gianni. *Il tempo libero*. Rome: Editori Riuniti, 1961.

Tranfaglia, Nicola, ed. *Il 1948 in Italia: la storia e i film*. Florence: La Nuova Italia, 1991.

Turani, Giuseppe. *1985–1995: il secondo miracolo economico italiano*. Milan: Sperling and Kupfer, 1986.

Urban, Joan Barth. *Moscow and the Italian Communist Party*. London: I. B. Tauris, 1986.

Vacca, Giuseppe. *PCI, Mezzogiorno e intellettuali*. Bari: De Donato, 1973.

———. *Osservatorio meridionale: temi di politica culturale tra gli anni '60 e '70*. Bari: De Donato, 1977.

———. *Tra compromesso e solidarietà: La politica del PCI negli anni '70.* Rome: Editori Riuniti, 1987.

———, ed. *Comunicazioni di massa e democrazia.* Rome: Editori Riuniti, 1980.

Valcarenghi, Andrea. *Underground: a pugno chiuso.* Rome: Arcana, 1973.

Valentini, Chiara. *Berlinguer il segretario.* Milan: Mondadori, 1987.

Veltroni, Walter. *Io e Berlusconi.* Rome: Editori Riuniti, 1990.

———, ed. *Il sogno degli anni '60.* Rome: Savelli, 1981.

Ventrone, Angelo. "Tra propaganda e passione: *Grand Hôtel* e l'Italia degli anni Cinquanta." *Rivista di storia contemporanea* 17.4 (1988): 603–31.

Venturi, Marcello. *Sdraiati sulla linea.* Milan: Mondadori, 1991.

Villa, Claudio. *Una vita stupenda.* Milan: Mondadori, 1987.

Vittoria, Albertina. *Togliatti e gli intellettuali: storia dell'Istituto Gramsci negli anni cinquanta e sessanta.* Rome: Editori Riuniti, 1992.

Zangheri, Renato. *Bologna '77.* Rome: Editori Riuniti, 1978.

Zolla, Elemire. *Eclisse dell'intellettuale.* Milan: Bompiani, 1959.

Index

Stephen Gundle is Senior Lecturer and Head of the Department of Italian at Royal Holloway, University of London. He is the editor (with Simon Parker) of *The New Italian Republic: From the Fall of the Berlin Wall to Berlusconi* (1995).

Library of Congress Cataloging-in-Publication Data

Gundle, Stephen

Between Hollywood and Moscow : the Italian communists and the challenge of mass culture, 1943–1991 / Stephen Gundle.

p. cm. — (American encounters/global interactions)

Includes bibliographical references.

ISBN 0-8223-2530-6 (cloth) — ISBN 0-8223-2563-2 (pbk.)

1. Partito comunista italiano. 2. Communism and culture — Italy.

3. Popular culture — Italy. I. Title. II. Series.

JN5657.C63 G86 2000

324.245′075′09045 — dc21   00-026025